Queering the Hmong Diaspora

Design by Ani Rucki

Composed in Minion Pro, typeface designed by Robert Slimbach

UNIVERSITY OF WASHINGTON PRESS   uwapress.uw.edu

LIBRARY OF CONGRESS CATALOGING-IN-PUBLICATION DATA

Names: Pha, Kong Pheng author

Title: Queering the Hmong diaspora :
racial subjectivity and the myth of hyperheterosexuality / Kong Pheng Pha.

Description: Seattle : University of Washington Press, 2025. |
Includes bibliographical references and index.

Identifiers: LCCN 2025027016 (print) | LCCN 2025027017 (ebook) |
ISBN 9780295754055 hardcover | ISBN 9780295754062 paperback
| ISBN 9780295754079 ebook

Subjects: LCSH: Refugees—United States | Hmong Americans | Sex—United States

Classification: LCC HV640.4.U54 P48 2025 (print) | LCC HV640.4.U54 (ebook)

LC record available at https://lccn.loc.gov/2025027016

LC ebook record available at https://lccn.loc.gov/2025027017

♾ This paper meets the requirements of ANSI/NISO Z39.48-1992
(Permanence of Paper).

Queering the Hmong Diaspora

RACIAL SUBJECTIVITY AND THE MYTH

OF HYPERHETEROSEXUALITY

KONG PHENG PHA

University of Washington Press   Seattle

For my parents,
Blia Chang and Xaitsav Pha,
and siblings,
Lao Chen, Xeng Ying, Kaochi,
Meria Khaosue, and Chenku

Contents

Acknowledgments

Although this work was over a decade in the making, I have spent a much longer time thinking about the problems and questions addressed in this book. Many people kindly entertained, fostered, and engaged my ideas throughout the years. A few traveled with me from beginning to end. While I take full responsibility for any lingering flaws in this work, I am more than happy to give credit to everyone else who contributed to the good parts of this book. I cannot do justice to the generosity that many have offered me on this long journey. I can only hope these words of gratitude will suffice for the time being.

This book would not exist without the courageous queer Hmong Americans who shared their life stories, perspectives, and ideas with me throughout the research process. Their knowledge and narratives have shaped and anchored this book in such profound ways, and I hope that the final product is something they are proud of. This book also benefited enormously from individuals who generously gifted me their time and knowledge about the marriage bills in Minnesota. Thank you to Representative Andrew J. Dawkins, Senator Mee Moua, Representative Cy Thao, and the attorney Blong Yang for teaching me so much during our interviews. I thank Schoua Na (s u n a h) Yang for sharing their vision of the *No Word for Queer* project with me as part of the epilogue, and I am grateful for their meaningful work that has brought our community together. Various librarians and archivists assisted me during my archival research. Many thanks go out to Mark Pfeifer at the Hmong Resource Center Library; Marlin Heise at the Hmong Archives; Lisa Vecoli of the Jean-Nickolaus Tretter Collection in Gay, Lesbian, Bisexual, and Transgender Studies at the University of Minnesota; and the many rotating reference librarians and archivists at the Minnesota Legislative Reference Library, the Saint Paul Public Library, and the Minnesota Historical Society's Gale Family Library.

The earliest seeds of this book were planted when I was an undergraduate student at the University of Minnesota. In graduate school, my advisers Erika Lee and Jigna Desai carefully guided this project and pushed my thinking beyond what I thought was possible. Their feedback on the earliest iterations of this book helped the project grow into its final form. I am thankful for all the doors they opened for me as a first-generation refugee student. Lisa Sun-Hee Park, Mai Na Lee, Kale Fajardo, and Ma Vang also provided critical commentary on this book in the early stages. Additional faculty at the University of Minnesota from my undergraduate and graduate years offered much-needed encouragement, mentorship, and advice about this project. Thank you to Rose Brewer, Bianet Castellanos, Vichet Chhuon, Roderick Ferguson, Karen Ho, Josephine Lee, Kevin Murphy, Jennifer Pierce, and Elliott Powell.

I was privileged to have forged strong friendships, alliances, and solidarities with a community of scholars across the University of Minnesota, which reinforced to me the significance and urgency of this work. Friends and comrades in the Department of American Studies; the Department of Gender, Women, and Sexuality Studies; the Interdisciplinary Center for the Study of Global Change; and the Critical Race and Ethnic Studies Graduate Writing Group collectively nurtured this work through writing sessions, providing feedback, sharing food and laughter, and checking in with one another during times of crises. For that, I thank Amber Annis, Sarah Atwood-Hoffman, Chip Chang, Anindita Chatterjee, René Esparza, Jess Farrell, Tia-Simone Gardner, Caitlin Gunn, Elena Hristova, Juliana Hu Pegues, Mingwei Huang, Anthony Jimenez, Ezekiel Joubert, Simi Kang, Kidiocus King-Carroll, Michelle Lee, Lars Mackenzie, Rahsaan Mahadeo, Aaron Mallory, Alex Manning, Hana Maruyama, Emily Mitamura, Ahmad Qais Munhazim, Joanna Núñez, Mario Obando, Soham Patel, Naimah Pétigny, Sami Poindexter, Nithya Rajan, José Manuel Santillana Blanco, Ana Cláudia dos Santos São Bernardo, Thomas Sarmiento, Robert Smith III, Stephen Suh, Farrah Tek, Janeke Thumbran, Colin Wingate, and Shana Ye. Thank you to Kari Smalkoski for creating some of my favorite collaborations and fostering some of my deepest thinking on this project. I am proud to have her as a close friend. The late Jesús Estrada-Pérez introduced me to the work of Gloria Anzaldúa and José Esteban Muñoz (rest in power to all three) and was the first person to show me the true potential of queer of color critique. He is truly missed by so many people.

Close colleagues and friends from across the country sustained me with their love and support during the long and hard years of researching, writing, and revising. Mai See Thao is my most loyal writing partner, and I am so proud and lucky to call her one of my greatest friends. Ma Vang has provided inspiration in so many ways, and I continue to be amazed by her brilliance. Aline Lo is one of my greatest advocates, and I will always cherish her words of wisdom. Chong Moua has always been there, and I absolutely cannot live without her humor. Many other colleagues and friends continue to inspire and uplift me, and this book is much better because of their groundbreaking scholarship. I thank Chundou Her, Pao Houa Her, Doua Kha, Mao Lee, Yang Lor, Kaozong Mouavangsou, Chia Youyee Vang, Mai Neng Vang, Choua Xiong, May Kao Xiong, May Yang, and Magnolia Yang Sao Yia.

Many other people offered mentorship, fleshed out ideas, and read drafts of the manuscript throughout the years. Thank you to Mariam Lam, Louisa Schein, Cathy Schlund-Vials, and Dylan Rodriguez for sharing so much knowledge early on about this project. Myrl Beam provided crucial feedback that tremendously improved chapter 4. For a brief while, I was fortunate to chair the Southeast Asian section of the Association for Asian American Studies, whose virtual work sessions provided a dedicated space for collective writing. For witnessing this book's long and unwinding journey and for their unwavering friendship over the years, I thank Paul Michael Leonardo Atienza, Lina Chhun, Karen Buenavista Hanna, Trung PQ Nguyen, Jewel Pereyra, Justin Phan, and Pahole Sookkasikon.

Audiences at the Association for Asian American Studies conferences in San Francisco, Evanston (Illinois), Miami, Portland (Oregon), Madison, Denver, and Seattle; the American Studies Association conferences in Toronto, Atlanta, Honolulu, and Montreal; and the National Women's Studies Association conferences in Milwaukee, Baltimore, and Minneapolis deserve special recognition for their critical engagements with parts of this work. I am also thankful for the opportunities to present my ideas to and receive feedback from audiences at the University of Wisconsin–Oshkosh, Winona State University, and the University of California, Merced.

I was fortunate to begin my academic career in the Universities of Wisconsin system. At the University of Wisconsin–Eau Claire, my colleagues saw the significance of this work and gently urged me to focus on writing even as I struggled to juggle multiple responsibilities across the university. My deepest gratitude goes out to the faculty in the Department of Race, Ethnicity, Gender, and Sexuality Studies and the faculty affiliates in Critical Hmong Studies. Thank you to Rose-Marie Avin, Sandibel Borges, Josephine Kipgen, and Rae Langes. Rose-Marie Avin, in particular, fought hard for me to obtain the financial resources and time needed to write this book. For that, I am truly blessed to call her one of my greatest champions. Additional thanks to my deeply principled and supportive colleagues Ari Anand, Kati Barahona-Lopez, Dorothy Chan, Sarita Mizin, Heather Ann Moody, Kao Nou Moua, Asha Sen, David Shih, Kaia Simon, and Anjela Wong. Thank you also to my undergraduate student researcher Paji Lily Yang for helping me complete the last stretch of research for this book. Conversations with my brilliant students at Eau Claire inspired many ideas in this book and helped me reframe what I thought I knew about Hmong American experiences. Thank you to Yuna Kha, Tou Ger Billy Lor, Susan Vang, and Yer Yang.

I completed this project at the University of Wisconsin–Madison. Colleagues in the Department of Gender and Women's Studies and the Asian American Studies Program provided a welcoming environment so that I could finish writing this book. I am truly thankful for the dynamic group of scholars in Gender and Women's Studies who greeted me and this work with care and compassion: Anna Campbell, Jill Casid, Sara Chadwick, Nina Valeo Cooke, Finn Enke, Christine Garlough, Ruth Goldstein, Jamie Priti Gratrix, Judith Houck, Pernille Ipsen, Rachel Kuo, Maria Lepowsky, Keisha Lindsay, Annie Menzel, Benjamin Mier-Cruz, Katherine Phelps, Kai Pyle, Stephanie Rytilahti, Aurora Santiago Ortiz, Sami Schalk, Leigh Senderowicz, Jess Waggoner, Kate Walsh, and Kelly Ward. I must acknowledge Kelly Ward and Jess Waggoner specifically for immediately looping me into faculty writing groups so that I could have a space to make that final push. Colleagues in Asian American Studies saw the potential of this work, and their excitement for it was what inspired me to keep going. Thank you to Leslie Bow, Cindy I-Fen Cheng, Lisa Ho, Jessica Montez, Victor Jew, Rachel Kuo, Stacey Lee, Lori Kido Lopez, Mai See Thao, Paul Tran, Morris Young, and Timothy Yu. Special recognition goes to Leslie Bow, who read and provided feedback on the entire manuscript. Thank you also to my faculty mentors Lori Kido Lopez and Sami Schalk for constantly checking in on me as I transitioned to Madison. Additional colleagues across the University of Wisconsin–Madison offered ideas, advice, companionship, enthusiasm, and food when I needed it most. Thank you to Ian Baird, Kasey Keeler, Nam Kim, Bailey Smolarek, Sasha Suarez, Nhu Truong, Zoua Vang, and Matthew Wolfgram.

Many great books have never been written because their authors did not have institutional funding and support. I am thankful that I can publish this book with the support of grants and fellowships from the various institutions with which I have been affiliated. At the University of Minnesota, a Diversity of Views and Experience Fellowship and a Summer Pre-Dissertation Research Fellowship from the Office for Diversity in Graduate Education, an ICGC Scholar Fellowship from the Interdisciplinary Center for the Study of Global Change, and a Beverly and Richard Fink Summer Research Fellowship from the College of Liberal Arts allowed me to conduct early research for this book. At the University of Wisconsin–Eau Claire, grants from Summer Research Experiences for Undergraduates, University Research and Creative Activity, and the Vicki Lord Larson and James Larson Tenure-Track Time Reassignment Collaborative Research Program and funding from the Chancellor's Office for Critical Hmong Studies provided financial resources and reassigned time for me to complete additional research and writing. At the University of Wisconsin–Madison, a Nellie McKay Fellowship from the Provost's Office enabled me to complete the manuscript.

I am very proud to publish this book with the University of Washington Press, a press that has produced some of the greatest books in the field of Asian American studies. I thank my talented editor Mike Baccam, who believed in this project early on and steered it smoothly through the review process. I could not have survived this process without his guidance and encouragement. Many thanks also to the rest of the University of Washington Press team for helping with the book production and marketing process. Thank you to Jane Lichty for her superb copyediting and Chris Dodge for his professional indexing. Two anonymous reviewers provided insightful feedback that tremendously enhanced the focus of this book. I truly thank them for their time attending to this work. I give my utmost gratitude to artist extraordinaire Koua Mai Yang (Dej Txiaj Ntsim) for her striking artwork on the book's cover. Parts of chapter 4 were published in a special issue on Asian American and Pacific Islander activism in *Amerasia Journal*. Thank you to Arnold Pan, Diane Fujino, and Robyn Rodriguez for that early feedback, which ultimately enhanced the chapter and the book as a whole.

Friends and loved ones sustained me while I wrote this book. Linda Her, Lue Her, Fue Khang, Terry Lee, Chong Vang, and Mindy Yang were all there when we were fighting for our freedom. Billy Moua steadfastly stood by me through the most tumultuous moments over the past decade. It was extremely difficult to survive the pandemic, complete our educations, provide caretaking, overcome health challenges, and move across state lines as we navigated many disruptive personal and professional transitions. I have so much gratitude and respect for your support and patience, more than I can even put into words. You are everything to me.

My family supported me through very challenging times, even when it appeared I could no longer go on doing this work. My parents, Blia Chang and

Xaitsav Pha, instilled in me a need to have a strong passion in life. As young refugee parents struggling to survive in the United States after being forcibly displaced from their homeland, their sacrifices in life provided me with the strength I needed to persist. Thank you both for helping me see my purpose and place in this world. My siblings and in-laws have always been my biggest source of comfort and inspiration: Lao Cher, Panee, Xeng Ying, Kaochi, Steven, Meria Khaosue, and Chenku. My whole world changed when my precious nephews Sunsu and Konyeng were born, right in time to see this book published! This book is for you all.

Queering
the Hmong
Diaspora

Introduction

CONSTRUCTING HYPERHETEROSEXUAL

SUBJECTS

University of Wisconsin–Madison law professor Leonard Kaplan made national headlines when he made extremely derogatory remarks about Hmong Americans during his legal formalism course on February 15, 2007. Law students present in the course approximated Kaplan's statements as "Hmong women are better off now that Hmong men are dying off in this country," "All Hmong men purchase their wives, so if he wants to have sex with his wife and she doesn't consent, you and I call it rape, but the Hmong guy is thinking, 'Man, I paid too much for her,'" "Hmong men have no skills other than killing," and "All second-generation Hmong end up in gangs and other criminal activity."[1] Both Hmong American law students present during Kaplan's lecture and community members were infuriated by the racist portrayals that he illustrated with his sweeping generalizations of Hmong. Many wondered how and why an authority figure such as a tenured law professor at a major research university could confidently make such ill-informed statements about a community of color and in a city where there is a substantial population of that community. Some Hmong Americans understood this controversy as another episode in the enduring anti-Hmong racial violence directed toward their communities in Wisconsin since their arrival in the United States in the mid-1970s. Others saw this ordeal as an opportunity to educate the wider university about Hmong American experiences.[2] Student activists on campus and advocates from the larger community capitalized on this event to demand the hiring of Hmong American studies faculty members and the establishment of a Hmong American studies program at the university to counter Kaplan's harmful generalizations.[3]

Kaplan's remarks exposed the interconnections between minoritized racial, gendered, and sexual formations in the United States. Conjuring violent racialized descriptions of Hmong through imagery of men as gang members sexually assaulting women and husbands purchasing wives, his statements sought to produce a link between men's violence and women's victimization. Kaplan's comment that husbands purchase their wives aligns with a long history of colonial understandings of Hmong gender and sexual politics, particularly through and within structures of marriage as the basis of gendered and sexual violence. Hmong's historical practice of a groom providing a dowry — popularly known as the "bride price" — to a bride's family as a process of initiating and commencing a marriage has been represented in dominant culture and scholarship as "selling" and "buying" women. The assumption, then, is that women are purchased as property and thus can be sexually violated at will by their husbands. Kaplan's statements were easily marked as disparaging Hmong as a racial and ethnic group, but his comments were also provocatively gendered and sexualized in nature.

Kaplan later addressed the controversy during an invitation-only forum at the Rotary Club of Madison in which he complained that "political correctness" had trumped the "truth" of things.[4] During the forum he insinuated that Hmong cultural and social life is inherently violent and that knowledge of these characteristics is simply the "truth." In essence, Kaplan further fueled his racist remarks by intimating that Hmong American students and community members were denying this supposed "truth" about their native culture while infringing on his academic freedom. The Critical Hmong Studies Collective, a group of Hmong studies scholars across the United States, argued in an essay in *Diverse: Issues in Higher Education* that this case should not be reduced to an isolated incident but represents the long-standing invisibility and the racial, gendered, and sexual distortions of Hmong social, cultural, and political life in the United States.[5] Kaplan's remarks exemplify the racial anxieties over gender and sexuality within liberal societies as they pertain to minoritized polities.

Queering the Hmong Diaspora: Racial Subjectivity and the Myth of Hyperheterosexuality studies how racialized renderings of Hmong in the United States are simultaneously laden with imagery of gendered and sexual violence. What Kaplan strings together — racialization, gender and sexual violence, and essentialized conceptualizations of culture—forms what I term *hyperheterosexuality*. That is, Kaplan conjured the racialized, gendered, and sexualized images of Hmong vis-à-vis a legal and epistemological archive that has constructed racialized sexualities in the United States through a framework of criminality. Hyperheterosexuality is a racialized ideological framing of Hmong's gender and sexual politics across a variety of behaviors, practices, and acts that subsequently forms the basis of their ongoing marginalization in the contemporary age of sexual and queer liberalism in the United States. This ideological framing of Hmong's alleged hyperheterosexuality includes representations of "deviant," "criminal," "problematic," or otherwise nonnormative gendered and sexual social relations and intimacies such as the culture seemingly rationalizing sexual violence, wife buying and selling through the dowry / bride price, bride kidnapping, polygamy, cousin marriage, teenage and underage marriage framed as parental sexual coercion, and the forced invisibility of queer sexualities and identities.[6] More specifically, it encompasses Hmong's historical configurations and manifestations of gender and sexuality, mostly within kinship and familial intimacies, that have been construed as violent and oppressive toward women, girls, and queer people through an uncritical deployment of an essentialized native culture. Legal studies as a field of knowledge accentuates Hmong's cultural and racial differences and constructs them as premodern subjects caught in a modern criminal legal system. Thus, nearly all traces of gender and sexuality—and its wider ecosystem of kinship, sex, marriage, sex crimes, gender and sexual identities, and queerness—are laden with assorted "cultural" considerations about Hmong in the dominant consciousness. *Queering the Hmong Diaspora* grapples with all these difficulties in order to magnify current understandings of the intersection of race, gender, and sexuality within minoritized communities and their implications for minoritized belonging.

Thus, this book asks: How do arrangements and practices within Hmong society lend themselves to the racialization of gender and sexuality? What are the connections between "culture" and race, gender, and sexuality in the age of sexual and queer liberalism? Kaplan's statements evidence the American majority's lack of knowledge about Hmong Americans. However, they also reveal that a certain sector of the American mainstream does in fact possess a selective knowledge about Hmong Americans. This is precisely the paradox that *Queering the Hmong Diaspora* addresses. Knowledge about Hmong Americans continues to proliferate within popular, legal, and media discourses because there exists an epistemological archive of supposed "truths" about minoritized and racialized gender and sexuality from which to draw. This selective knowledge is especially crucial when the following questions are considered: How did Kaplan know these "truths" about Hmong society? In what historical, political, and social contexts can these racial, gendered, and sexual constructions be situated and understood? How and why do these ideas about Hmong continue to persist over time, arguably into the present, and across several sociopolitical fields of study? How do these "truths" about Hmong's culture of gender and sexuality become common knowledge, and how are they so easily accessible within various social domains as a means of racial subjection and subjectification? How do Hmong Americans negotiate, deconstruct, and refuse these racialized constructions in their quest for belonging?

It is tempting to document Hmong's gender and sexual politics as cultural truth in the ethnographic sense, as Kaplan did. The most credible scholars of Hmong studies—usually those who have lived among Hmong people for significant amounts of time or who are Hmong themselves—have noted discrepancies, contradictions, and inconsistencies among the meanings, symbolism, and actual practices of gender, sexuality, kinship, and marriage across a variety of social, political, and national contexts. These incongruities challenge interpretations of Hmong's gender and sexual politics and practices as rooted in a bounded cultural system independent of sociopolitical, economic, and historical factors. While hyperheterosexuality is an ideological construction imposed on Hmong as a method of racialization and racial subjugation, it cannot be understood as emblematic of an entire people whose history, social life, and political realities have been shaped by multiple phases of migration, displacement, and resettlement within a variety of national and political contexts. *Queering the Hmong Diaspora* does not seek to establish a truth about who Hmong are or to define the "true" politics and practices of gender and sexuality or culture on the basis of their known marriage or kinship practices. In fact, this book actively works to untangle dominant ideas about Hmong as a people whose existence is bounded by a culture of gender and sexual violence. It explores how Hmong racialized subject formation in the United States intersects with their known and perceived gender and sexual "abnormalities" that, over time, have come to be viewed as violent, criminal, and oppressive toward women and queer people within the contemporary ideological and contradictory contexts of sexual and queer liberalisms.

The ideology of hyperheterosexuality closely reflects what scholars have characterized as hypersexuality—the purported sexual excessiveness of racialized and minoritized communities. Prevailing assumptions about hypersexuality denote people of color displaying and embodying strange, unwarranted, exotic, primitive, uncontrollable, and criminal sexualities. In the United States and beyond, heterosexuality is the norm that shapes much of our social and political worlds. Yet heterosexuality—in my characterization of it as both a sexual orientation *and* a system of power—has several attendant structures attached to it at the intersection of race, class, and gender, among other categories of difference. The feminist scholar Patricia Hill Collins, in her groundbreaking text *Black Feminist Thought: Knowledge, Consciousness, and the Politics of Empowerment*, deployed the expression "hyperheterosexuality" in two instances in describing white heterosexuality as a form of "normalized heterosexuality," which positions Black and African heterosexuality as abnormal and pathological regardless of individual behavior.[7] Hyperheterosexuality denotes the ways Black heterosexuality—specifically manifested in the tropes of the male rapist and the female jezebel—underlies dominant conceptions of Black sexuality as wild, out of control, and excessive. Such racial constructions also have relevance to other communities of color, for example, Latinos, whose masculinities are constructed in popular discourse as criminal or dangerous or who are exoticized as "Latin lovers," and Latinas, whose femininities are hypersexualized as hot-tempered, salacious, fiery, or sassy, but who are also desexualized as motherly domestic workers.[8] Hyperheterosexuality operates as an ideology and discursive invention that informs dominant representations of both normalized (white) and racialized (Black, Latinx, etc.) heterosexuality in the United States as a means of demarcating social and political inclusion and exclusion.[9]

In representations of Asian American women, the film studies scholar Celine Parreñas Shimizu asserts that hypersexuality is "a form of bondage that ties the subjectivity of Asian/American women."[10] Stereotypes of Asian American women as being sexually available have dominated mainstream discourse since at least the late nineteenth century. These racialized and sexualized constructions can be traced back to exclusionary legislation such as the Page Act of 1875, which effectively barred Chinese women suspected of prostitution from entering the United States, to prevent the denigration of white normalized heterosexuality.[11]

Linked to this racist and sexist legislative history is the representation of Asian American women as sexually excessive, cunning, and deceitful in popular culture throughout the twentieth century. This is particularly germane to the trope of the "dragon lady," who is seen as both sexually calculating and dangerous. She deploys her sexuality to achieve her own nefarious agendas. Relatedly, the trope of the Asian American "lotus blossom" is represented as docile and sexually submissive. Her sexuality is always present and is readily consumable. Her docility is exacerbated by her hyperwillingness to serve the sexual interests of white men.[12] In addition to this degrading imagery, this book extends these representations to include the desexualized and hypervictimized refugee woman. Unlike the Asian American women characters in the films analyzed by Shimizu, the Hmong refugee woman does not have the mediated space to reclaim her racialized sexuality. Altogether, the violence materialized through these controlling images can be physical as much as ideological and imaginative.[13] Asian American women's seeming sexual availability discursively frames the domestic abuse and sexual violence they encounter both in larger American culture and in everyday life.[14] Thus, Asian American women's racial subject formation is intertwined with the ideological dimensions of their sexual formation and the symbolic, epistemic, and material violence that accompanies it.

Asian American men, in comparison, have been emasculated or hyposexualized within media representations and everyday life, at least since the mid-twentieth century. Mediated through what the literary scholar David L. Eng identifies as the historical conjunctures of Chinese exclusion, Japanese American internment, Cold War diplomacy, and the emergence of the model minority stereotype, Asian American men's racial castration has prevailed in US society to the point where their hyposexuality is commonsensical in popular and daily discourse.[15] For example, when indicating racial preferences on heterosexual dating apps such as OkCupid and Tinder, women of all ethnicities notoriously exclude Asian American men.[16] On gay dating and hookup apps such as Grindr or Jack'd, phrases like "No Fats, No Femmes, No Asians" or "Gook Free Zone" are commonly found on user profiles to render gay Asian American men as undesirable sexual partners.[17] The systematic expunction of Asian American men's sexuality and the manufacturing of their personhood as "gay" or "queer" regardless of their actual sexualities, in essence, leaves no room for a complex or empowered heterosexual identity. Asian American men are represented as undesirable objects who possess minimal sexuality or sexual desires, binding their desexualized object-status to their racialized subjecthood. Scholars have attempted to reframe Asian American men's feminization as empowering. Most notably, Shimizu and Nguyen Tan Hoang, in their paradigm-shifting work in film studies, argue for embracing "straitjacket masculinities" and a politics of "bottomhood."[18] Cynthia Wu's analysis of Asian American intraracial desires has also allowed for an empowering racialized masculinity rooted in Asian American coalition to emerge.[19] These scholars' provocation of the radical potential of queer Asian American men (and Asian American men in general) as hyposexual is quite generative in rethinking Asian American men's sexual subjecthood as expressed through visual and literary mediums but still leaves unaddressed the discursive representational *oversexualization* of some Asian American men, including Hmong Americans, particularly within legal domains.

The concept "hyperheterosexuality" encapsulates Hmong's gender and sexual politics as situated within larger discourses of racialized sexuality in the United States—mostly as a means of problematizing the gendered and sexual logics that underlie processes of Asian American racialization. Constructions of Hmong sexuality in dominant discourse are racially dehumanizing, like most of the historical and contemporary productions of Black, Latinx, and Asian American sexuality, but they also possess idiosyncratic elements that diverge from the gendered and sexual racializations generated within, by, and about contemporary Asian America. Hmong Americans' construction as hyperheterosexual subjects positions their heterosexualities as deviant and nonnormative, the opposite of white Americans' assumed normalized heterosexuality. Cohering Hmong as hyperheterosexual subjects positions Hmong masculinity as hyperviolent and Hmong femininity as hypervictimized. Contrary to the construction of Asian American men's racially castrated masculinities as gay or queer within popular discourse, Hmong Americans' supposed hyperheterosexuality elides queerness and renders Hmong American heterosexual men as much overdesiring subjects as undesirable objects.

Like Black and Latino American men, Hmong American men are racialized as hypermasculinized "rapists" and "gang members," but unlike in broader representations and dominant perceptions of Asian American men, they are not readily racialized as "gay" or "queer." Hmong American femininity and Hmong American women, in comparison, are rendered as desexualized, victimized objects rather than desiring subjects. Unlike Black, Latina, and Asian American women, Hmong American women are not racialized as sexually cunning "dragon ladies," sexually willing "lotus blossoms," sassy spitfires, or sexually out-of-control "jezebels," but instead are constructed as sexual victims who possess very little sexuality, sexual desire, or sexual agency. These constructions of Hmong hyper-heterosexuality complicate racialized representations and racial formations in the United States, as they reveal alternative mechanisms and structuring logics that underlie larger ideological constructions of racialized gender and sexuality within liberal nation-states.

Additionally, hyperheterosexuality as a structure of power bears accompanying systems of oppression. Concepts such as heterosexism and heteropatriarchy are similar to hyperheterosexuality but are also distinct. Heterosexism is a system of power that privileges one form of sexual expression (heterosexuality) as inherently superior to others. Through this presumed superiority, those whose embodiments and modes of existence are closer in proximity to heterosexuality dominate those whose embodiments and modes of existence are not. Homophobia is one facet of heterosexism that ostracizes and punishes lesbians and gays for existing in a heterosexual world. Relatedly, heteropatriarchy operates as a constellation of meanings, ideas, symbolisms, and practices that position male heterosexuality as inherently superior to any other gendered or sexual existence. In that vein, masculinity and masculine conquerhood, in which men are assumed to have unlimited sexual access to women's bodies and labor and women's happiness is contingent on men's approval, are central to heteropatriarchy as a system of power.[20] Gender inequality is also most polarizing in heterosexual intimacies. As such, the notion of hyperheterosexuality also implies a heightened gender inequality among Hmong. The intersection of power that undergirds the ways heterosexuality and maleness are practiced and imagined sustains the dominant and dominating structures of heterosexism and heteropatriarchy that constitute and mediate the ideology of hyperheterosexuality.

Hyperheterosexuality, as it is understood through all the various known Hmong gender, sexual, and kinship politics and practices, comprises elements of what may be considered heterosexism and heteropatriarchy, but it also overlaps with racialization that positions people of color as exhibiting sexuality and sexual power beyond even recognizable forms of patriarchy. Hyperheterosexuality closely aligns with understandings of hypersexuality as a racialized sexual formation, as witnessed time and again in representations of people of color in dominant media, in which Hmong also come to stand in as deviant within the context of normalized heterosexuality. Hyperheterosexuality is an ideological framing of racialized and minoritized gender and sexuality that contributes to ongoing discussions and debates about racial, gender, and sexual justice in Asian American studies, American studies, critical ethnic studies, feminist studies, and queer studies.

Since their earliest history, Hmong and their modes of life have been represented by dominant groups as violent and resistant to change, paving the way for contemporary racist characterizations of Hmong, as evidenced in the Kaplan episode. The historian Mai Na M. Lee states that "stereotypes of the Hmong as a group who could not be brought into mainstream civilization date back to ancient Chinese records."[21] Referred to by the derogatory name Miao—a category conflating a host of ethnic minorities deemed "barbarians"—Hmong were historically drawn into bloody conflict with Han dynasties from as early as the twenty-third century BCE (2207) to the late nineteenth century (1873).[22] Stereotypes of Hmong as warlike and barbaric accompanied them on their southward migrations in the mid- to late nineteenth century and became the basis of their subjugation under French rule in Indochina. Hmong's resistance to French colonialism fueled new constructions of them as crazy primitives refusing to be civilized by the rational empire.

Messianic leader Pa Chay Vue's resistance against the French in northern Vietnam and Laos from 1918 to 1921 was the singular historical episode that solidified the colonial constructions of Hmong as unreasonable and "insane." Vue amassed adherents through claims of being a messiah sent from the heavens to lead Hmong in a struggle against French colonial oppression. The heavens imbued Vue with literacy and a magical power to transform balls of yarn into explosives to protect his army as it ambushed the French and then instantaneously disappeared afterward. Such spiritual and fantastic elements of war confounded the French.[23] In fact, the French had already begun to undermine Vue's rebellion through ideology, perhaps a much greater weapon than Vue's army. The French called it the Guerre du Fou, or Madman's War or War of the Insane, to depict Vue as a "lunatic" and, by extension, the entire Hmong people as "crazy." While Vue's effective resistance was grounded in anticolonialism, official French historiography remembers it as a "fanaticism of suspicious tribes, superstitious to excess, blindly obedient . . . to leaders who impressed them with practices of the lowest kinds of witchcraft."[24] Hmong's long history of resistance against Qing and French oppression—compounded by their structural exclusion of self-representation in official historiography—crystallized their image as irrational violent warriors in the minds of their oppressors. The refusal to accept colonialism, domination, assimilation, imperialism, and civility throughout their history was met with both physical *and* ideological opposition from the dominant Han and French powers.

These historical ideological representations of Hmong had enduring political consequences that extended to their twentieth-century history as proxy soldiers in the United States' secret war in Laos from 1960 to 1975. Intent on eliminating communism at all costs in the aftermath of World War II and at the height of the Cold War, the United States capitalized on France's defeat and exit from mainland Southeast Asia in 1954 by expanding its own empire into the Asia-Pacific region as it competed with the Soviet Union in a race for world dominance. The Central Intelligence Agency (CIA) conscripted proxy soldiers from among Laos's Indigenous populations to fight communism on behalf of the United States. Under military leader General Vang Pao, nearly thirty thousand Hmong (among other ethnic minorities) fought in "special guerrilla units" in the United States' secret army against the communist Pathet Lao and North Vietnam, intercepting supplies along the Ho Chi Minh Trail and rescuing American pilots downed during bombing missions across Laos. Hmong also became fighter pilots themselves as the war progressed.[25] Indigenous soldiering, as Evyn Lê Espiritu Gandhi terms it, was advantageous to the United States for two reasons.[26] First, the United States was able to skirt the Geneva Conventions, in which it had formally agreed to respect Laos's political neutrality. The United States influenced and intervened in the politics of the region by performing humanitarian activity through the United States Agency for International Development (USAID) while disseminating pro-American, anticommunist propaganda among Laos's ethnic minorities.[27]

Second, Indigenous soldiering meant that the United States could avoid sending its own troops to die on the battlefields. In fact, as testimonies from former proxy soldiers in oral history projects and documentaries suggest, "One Hmong that died in Laos meant one American going home."[28] American soldiers were also wholly inexperienced in the guerrilla warfare occurring in the thick Laotian jungles. The so-called primitives who were essentialized as nature itself presented a favorable alternative. Hmong's conscription as proxy soldiers by the CIA stemmed from the colonial epistemologies of their perceived primitivism and location outside of normative geography and temporality. As the scholar Ma Vang maintains, "U.S. Cold War cartography deployed as an asset colonial tropes about Hmong closeness to nature and the idea of a people inextricably connected to the very landscape they called home."[29] Hmong's statelessness also contributed to their appeal as ideal proxy soldiers at a foreign policy level, as the historian Alfred W. McCoy contends: "Hmong were a tribe, not a nation, [so] their sacrifice incurred no formal obligation from the United States."[30] Hmong's historical representations as fierce and warlike suggested their willingness to serve as proxy soldiers for a larger empire without jeopardizing formal diplomatic relations with any Southeast Asian state.

Additionally, the fact that Hmong lived in remote mountains in northeastern Laos was strategic from a military perspective. North Vietnamese and Pathet Lao forces often engaged in combat in this region, where there was a substantial Hmong population. Hmong's remoteness—as an indicator of their primitivity—relegated combat away from military outposts, including the CIA's secret military base Long Cheng.[31] Ultimately, the racialized construction of Hmong as violent warriors and the remoteness of their combat zones as indicative of their primitivity were heralded as *assets* to the United States in its quest to crush communism across the region. This amalgamation of Hmong's statelessness and their status as a "tribe" reinforced a host of racial colonial ideas about Indigenous people as barbaric and detached from formal geopolitics, yet it also demonstrated their potential to be "civilized" by absorption into the imperial activities of the nation-state. Hmong's racialization as warriors conjoined with the United States' desire to effectively carry out a military campaign through an inexpensive and manageable ethnic minority population bolstered Hmong's attractiveness as proxy soldiers.[32]

Hmong's "primitivity" thus operated as a double-edged sword. On the one hand, their closeness to nature led to their perception as model proxy soldiers who could navigate Laos's harsh jungle terrains during war. Having a secret army that was somehow "naturally" fit for jungle warfare meant the United States could have a real possibility of winning a guerrilla war. Concomitantly, Hmong could be exploited as a cheap labor force for the empire as a so-called archaic tribe. On the other hand, their primitivity was a liability for the United States, as they required heavy training in modern weapons and artillery, such as assault rifles and T-28 Trojan planes. Hence, Hmong's "soldiering through empire"—as the historian Simeon Man calls it—was one method of "civilizing" them into becoming imperial subjects through colonial expansionism and militarism.[33] Indigenous soldiering constituted the process of transporting Hmong from premodernity to modernity so that they could give up their lives for the imperial nation rather than for the autonomy and sovereignty of their people. That is, Hmong were "not-yet-modern subjects" who by soldiering were malleable enough to depart from nature and enter the fold of a Western nation-state.[34] However, unlike the

CHamoru and Māori soldiers who also fought and died for the United States during the Vietnam War, Hmong soldiers occupied a suspended political reality in which their racial status oscillated between primitive allies, alien soldiers, and patriotic Americans-in-becoming.[35]

As a result of the war, 17,000 Hmong soldiers died out of an estimated total Hmong prewar population of 350,000. Thousands more civilians also perished due to starvation or disease in the immediate aftermath of the secret war.[36] After losing the war, the United States abandoned its so-called allies in its secret army and retreated from Southeast Asia in 1975. Only some 2,000 to 3,500 people were airlifted out of the CIA's secret military base Long Cheng in May 1975 as the Pathet Lao overtook the country in the wake of communist victory. Those stranded in Laos hid in the jungles, trekked on foot, and crossed the Mekong River to find safety across international borders. Hmong were transformed into refugees and displaced into various camps established by the United Nations along the Laos-Thailand border, where some languished for over a decade. The United States was obligated to "rescue" its former proxy soldiers, passing the 1980 Refugee Act and resettling over one million combined Hmong, Lao, Cambodian, and Vietnamese refugees throughout the late 1970s and up until 2006.

Starting in 1976, many in the Thai camps were resettled as political refugees in the United States, France, Australia, Canada, French Guiana, and Germany. Some voluntarily repatriated back to Laos, while those who did not want to be or could not be immediately resettled to a third nation were forced to seek refuge at the Thai Buddhist monastery Wat Tham Krabok, until they were finally resettled later under family reunification programs in the United States from 2004 to 2006. Some 47,430 ethnic minorities from Laos were resettled in the United States from 1975 to 1980. In 1980 alone, 27,242 refugees from Laos, of which 90–95 percent were Hmong, entered the United States.[37] Irregular but increasing waves of resettlement meant that the Hmong population in the United States saw steady growth throughout the subsequent decades. By 1990, it had reached 94,439 and, by 2000, had expanded to 186,310, representing a 97 percent increase. The Hmong population continued to flourish as it grew to 260,073 by 2010 and 335,919 by 2020, representing a 29 percent increase in this ten-year period.[38] The states with the largest Hmong populations today are California, Minnesota, Wisconsin, North Carolina, and Michigan. However, 26 percent of the total US Hmong population is located in Minnesota's Twin Cities metropolitan area, with 88,679 Hmong living in the counties of Ramsey, Hennepin, Anoka, and Washington as of 2020. Secondary migration from other states in the 1980s and 1990s, including Pennsylvania, South Dakota, Hawaii, and Indiana, slowly transformed the Twin Cities area into the largest Hmong ethnic enclave in the United States, with some community members and scholars calling the Twin Cities the "Hmong capital of the world."[39]

THE POLITICAL LIFE OF "CULTURE"

Kaplan was able to construct his remarks as "truth" because he understood the gendered and sexual pathologies supposedly found among Hmong to be deterministic of their native "culture." Such understandings of Hmong can be situated in much the way Hmong studies emerged as a field of inquiry—through the writings of anthropologists studying Hmong culture. Thus, an analysis of the culture concept as it traveled from academic anthropology to the public realm (law, public policy, media, activist spaces, and diasporic communities) in the current political phase of liberal multiculturalism is necessary to understanding its ongoing consequences for Hmong's historical and contemporary racialized, gendered, and sexualized subject formations. Indeed, "culture" has been a contentious idea in academic studies for well over a century and remains one of the central concepts of academic anthropology. The problematics of "culture" are attributed to a fragmented world system that categorizes people into their respective unique nation-states, in which distinctive cultures are stagnantly bounded. This system of organization, however, also rests on an asymmetrical geopolitical field that reproduces disproportionate power relations between nation-states (or, more precisely, between Europe and the rest of the Global South) resulting from brutal histories of European colonialism.[40]

Historically for anthropologists in the Global North, studying primitive societies of a "different culture" entailed physical travel to a distant location in the Global South. Anthropology's emergence as an academic and scientific discipline in the nineteenth century inherits and represents early Western political thought delineating the "West" from the "Other" as an unmarked site of universal progress. The imagined duality fundamental to the organization of these competing geographies frames the emergence of colonialist expansion and capitalist exploitation in the spaces deemed to hold the Other. Even as early anthropological definitions of culture may not necessarily essentialize the thought patterns or practices of any particular people, the unequal power relations between the Global North and South that coalesced with colonial expansion, increasing globalization, and capitalism's uneven development alongside the rise of racialized social sciences in the second half of the nineteenth and first half of the twentieth centuries recalibrated the culture concept with racial undertones.

Progressive anthropologists have rightly scrutinized the contradictions of the culture concept and its slippery attachment to racial hierarchies dating back to the early twentieth century. In turn, discussions about the culture concept in anthropology today look radically different from those of even two or three decades ago. Franz Boas, the father of American anthropology, and influential anthropologists such as James Clifford, Renato Rosaldo, Lila Abu-Lughod, Michel-Rolph Trouillot, Kamala Visweswaran, and Lee Baker, among many others, shifted anthropological paradigms by challenging the prevailing prescription of culture as emblematic of civilization or race.[41] Culture, they contended, was not constitutive of race and thus was completely illogical as the basis of racial hierarchies and inequality. Rather than classical anthropology's treatment of ethnographic inquiry as an objective scientific pursuit, these progressive anthropologists privileged subjectivity, contextual sensitivity, and affective compositions that structure human experience. According to Trouillot's analysis of culture's deployment outside anthropology, culture in theory had the potential to underscore the social constructionist and socialized dimensions of human behavior.[42] However, its anti-essentialist potential slipped away as it was co-opted by those in the public sphere (politicians, journalists, corporate elites) who adopted the concept throughout the second half of the twentieth century to reframe human behavior in racist and essentialist ways. Abu-Lughod, Visweswaran, and Baker have demonstrated how those outside anthropology have reified culture as an essentialized concept itself by now using culture rather than race to explain human difference.[43] Delineating human differences through the framework of culture renders culture a construct just as static as race. That is, culture is assumed to be learned and so deeply ingrained that it can effortlessly be reduced to innate behavior. Culture and race are both social constructs but nonetheless continue to be entangled concepts that have implications for the kind of racial, gendered, sexualized, and queer political projects examined in *Queering the Hmong Diaspora*.

The slippery conflation of culture, race, civility, and difference is particularly germane in the case of a stateless people like Hmong, who have long been fascinating objects of study for missionaries and anthropologists.[44] While one of the earliest known works of Hmong history, *Histoire des Miao*, was written and published by French Catholic priest François Marie Savina in 1924, it was not until the 1960s and 1970s that anthropologists began producing more extensive work about Hmong life and culture primarily in the Southeast Asian context.

Some of the first academic accounts of Hmong life, particularly of Hmong's gender and sexual politics and kinship practices, were from ethnohistorical studies conducted by Australian anthropologist William Robert Geddes and British anthropologist Robert G. Cooper. Geddes's research on the Hmong of northern Thailand stemmed from his observation of inevitable economic changes imposed on Hmong highlanders by the Thai government and its quest to eliminate opium production among the highland tribal peoples, along with its continuing contestations over ethnic minorities' management of land. Describing Hmong responses and resistance to economic modernization as a form of "addiction to self-determination" and "stubborn independence," Geddes also took liberty in highlighting the inner worlds of Hmong marriage systems by overemphasizing the bride price and polygamy among highlanders.[45]

Cooper's account of Hmong life described kinship and gender relations in much more unequal terms, explicitly highlighting the supposed hyperheterosexuality of Hmong highland society and particularly of the bride price within wedding and marriage systems.[46] Cooper described marriages in Hmong highland societies as mirroring a "master-servant relationship" and as a form of "institutionalized selling of women by men" that was the "major item of expenditure and investment in a Hmong's life."[47] While Cooper attributed the unequal division of labor between men and women in the highlands to the physical characteristics required to complete different agricultural tasks (such as cutting down trees), he concluded: "What started as a logical division of labour based on a physical marginal distinction has developed in Hmong society into a major psychological distinction between the sexes. . . . It is on the basis of this psychological distinction that man controls woman."[48] The colonial constructions that Cooper imposed on Hmong society in the organization of gender and its attendant implications for the sexual division of labor were attributed to culture and the supposed gendered and sexual inequalities inherent within it. While Geddes and Cooper remained sympathetic to their research participants even as they distorted Hmong's complex societies in the Southeast Asian context, these early anthropological studies crystallized the colonial gaze on Hmong cultural and racial difference that continues to haunt the field of Hmong studies and define scholarly work on Hmong people well into the twenty-first century.

Culture's transformation from a concept anthropologically bounded to make sense of the lives of Hmong highland "primitives" to one that aligns with the preservation of unique differences within a liberal multiculturalist paradigm in the United States shows how the culture concept has transmuted—but nonetheless remains significant—for Hmong across a variety of social and political contexts. Hmong's cultural difference as an indicator of their racial difference is compounded by their statelessness in the diaspora, as their nationalism is not understood in relation to the finitude of a nation-state. It is accurate that Hmong Americans, and Hmong across the diaspora, historically have no bounded nation-state in which to stake a territorialized homeland. Because of their Indigenous soldiering in the United States' secret war in Laos, Hmong were transformed into globally displaced refugees in the aftermath of 1975. The schematic depiction of refugees with nothing but the clothes on their backs re-creating a community in their respective diasporic locations meant that their subsequent community-building efforts must revolve around immaterial concepts such as identity and "culture." As the anthropologist Gary Yia Lee observes, "Hmong do not have any enduring icons or monuments destroyed by the war which have to be physically rebuilt. At most, they have *cultural items* or *traditions* which became lost or forgotten during the war and after relocation to the West, such as ethnic costumes, embroideries and musical instruments."[49]

As the concepts "cultural items," "tradition," and "culture" traveled across the diaspora, their reformulation in the context of forced displacement and refugee resettlement became more salient as Hmong began to rebuild their lives in their resettlement locations. Hmong communities across the globe have labored to survive and reconstruct their communities through the maintenance and preservation of language and culture even as they are a people more fragmented today than ever before in their history.[50] Anthropologists who have carefully studied Hmong, including Nicholas Tapp, Gary Yia Lee, Prasit Leepreecha, and Sangmi Lee, explain that this fracturing that displaced Hmong to various parts of the world has concurrently manufactured innumerable versions of culture with respect to the contexts of their resettlement nations.[51] While the laws and politics of the various nation-states in which Hmong refugees have resettled since the mid-1970s have come to influence their social and political lives, Hmong communities have nonetheless strived to maintain parts of their unique culture to ensure some accessible global diasporic connection.[52] In short, "culture" or related concepts such as "tradition" may have become even more pronounced as Hmong across the diaspora have taken measures to re-create and maintain their unique sense of cultural identity, for example, by developing culture preservation courses and disseminating nostalgic ethnic media.[53] Ironically, the culture concept is strengthened amid displacement and dispersal even as Hmong become increasingly heterogeneous as a contemporary transnational people.

In the United States, culture is deployed in racialization and othering to differentiate "uncultured" modern subjects like white Americans from "cultured" subjects like immigrants and people of color within liberal multiculturalism. Immigrants in the United States are understood in relation to their homelands and bring with them the cultures of their original nation-states. As immigrants traverse borders to establish lives in new lands, so too do their religious beliefs, foodways, languages, art and music, and conceptions of family and community. This sense of cultural diversity and cultural pluralism is central to the politics of race and ethnicity in the United States following the culture concept's morphing into a political construct outside academic anthropology. Liberal multiculturalism situates differentially unique cultures and racial and ethnic groups within a singular liberal nation-state whereby such subjects can thrive and coexist, albeit often in tension. Space can be prescribed as distant or localized, but nonetheless groups are still compartmentalized into their own subcultural spaces within the liberal nation-state in ways that have devastating social and political consequences. This problem of localized space is muddied by the simultaneous visibility of culture for certain peoples and invisibility for others. As the literary scholar Jodi Melamed has demonstrated, even as "diversity" across American social life was being embraced as a result of the race-based social movements of the 1960s to the 1980s, the racial project of liberal multiculturalism that was concretized in the 1990s intensified social inequalities by divorcing society's problems from structures of power and projecting them onto certain racialized and minoritized populations.[54] It became possible, then, for previously disenfranchised racially and ethnically minoritized subjects to claim visibility and inclusion as Americans while simultaneously experiencing invisibility and exclusion as a cultural other. Accordingly, culture, space, and race are uncritically linked to position immigrants as out of space and time.[55]

Culture is rendered as static to justify and exacerbate racist and white supremacist ideologies that position certain subjects as "modern" and others as "premodern" or even, as Visweswaran has termed, "unmodern."[56] That is, culture is assigned political meanings and framed as self-evident to delineate the boundaries of social inclusion and exclusion, most notably in debates on Indigenous sovereignty, immigration exclusion, civil rights, and legal citizenship. The culture concept has been both oversimplified and abstracted so that its meanings have become muddied and synonymous with race and civility. As an exemplar of cultural pluralism in the United States, liberal multiculturalism postulates a diversified nation-state of color-blind "equality." The central tenets of liberal multiculturalism since at least the 1970s included the reduction of cultural and racial differences to aesthetics, which was then co-opted by the state to dematerialize antiracism and absorb minoritized populations into structures of capitalism.[57] In the United States, a liberal multiculturalist society, culture is mobilized in ways that appear inclusive but are in fact quite exclusive. The problem with a liberal multiculturalist diagram of cultural pluralism is that it manufactures a racial hierarchy rather than racial equality. Thus, the schema of immigrant assimilation and acculturation into a liberal multicultural society that also paradoxically possesses no culture fails precisely because it produces heightened racial anxieties about those deemed other as distinguished by their supposed cultural excess despite the romances of a post-racial and post-culture society.

The proclamation of culture as the unifier of Hmong across the globe is especially noticeable in the United States because it also functions as the basis for minoritized ethnonational identity formation against the contexts of white supremacy and white nativism. In other words, "culture" or "tradition" serves as the identification marker for Hmong Americans in the absence of a territorial nation-state. As the sociologist Jeremy Hein has noted, a majority of Hmong American refugee leaders have adopted a migrant orientation with regard to belonging by emphasizing the preservation of an authentic culture within internal Hmong American communities as opposed to a minority orientation defined through addressing problems of racial discrimination by dominant society.[58] While Hein's model is not an entirely encapsulating view, it nonetheless is symptomatic of the ways culture features as a prominent element of fostering belonging and nationalism among Hmong in the United States. Culture becomes a contested domain of belonging in part because, as refugees, Hmong Americans are understood as having only their culture as the thing over which they still hold significant power and which they are actively working to maintain against the backdrop of assimilationist ideologies imposed on minoritized polities in the United States.

To take a more comprehensive view beyond Hmong, culture is also a persistent optic in Asian American racialization in the United States and has been since at least the 1940s. The most prominent and enduring racialization of Asian Americans — and specifically East Asian Americans — is their status as model minorities. Asian culture is seen as superior, as it supposedly forms the foundation for Asian economic success in the United States. Asian Americans are popularly depicted as apolitical, upwardly mobile, hardworking, successful, and educated by adhering to the exemplary Confucian ethics of hard work, respect, and the pursuit of knowledge. It is assumed that "Asian cultural values" drive Asian Americans to excel economically and educationally. This essentializing portrait of Asian culture ideologically links race and difference to construct a racialized image of East Asian Americans as even more educationally, economically, and *culturally* superior to white Americans within contemporary liberal multiculturalism. In actuality, the model minority stereotype chiefly operates as a form of racial management and political demonization of Black people and other people of color, demanding social transformation by deeming them culturally inferior.[59] Culture, race, and ethnic identity are distinct spheres but nonetheless come to constitute one another in the United States precisely through their easy and slippery conflation, as "it is often the distinct identity that comes first, and the cultural distinction that is created and maintained because of it."[60] In other words, "Asian" is seen as a conspicuous racial identity, which is further compounded by its "cultural" signifiers.

The positioning of East Asian American cultural superiority through the model minority trope is a stark difference from representations of Hmong refugees in the United States. Hmong American families are popularly portrayed in media and academic studies as dysfunctional in the sense of neglectful parenting due in part to Hmong parents' status as so-called illiterate refugees. Hmong culture is perceived as inhibiting the full potential of—rather than being advantageous to—their children. Depictions of Hmong's perceived hyperheterosexuality, such as bride kidnapping and teenage marriages framed as culture, are popularly understood as examples of Hmong parents' enactment of cultural practices that are detrimental to women and girls.[61] Ironically, Hmong American cultural dysfunction bolsters the hegemonic ideology of the model minority myth, signifying the ways that Hmong Americans can never achieve its ideals in contradistinction to East Asian Americans. The Hmong American family unit stands in as the failure of culture juxtaposed to the "success" of the racialized East Asian American family. The specificity of Hmong culture is inscribed as an outlier to the hegemonic racialized images of East Asian American cultural and economic superiority. The deployment of culture in this way racializes Hmong Americans as dysfunctional Asians rather than successful model minorities.

While the deployment of culture in dominant discourse causes migrant subjectivities to stagnate, in reality the culture concept is a highly unstable notion that, as the cultural studies theorist Stuart Hall once argued, operates to be more a "production of identity" grounded in a "re-telling of the past."[62] I scrutinize "culture" in this book as contingent and relational to, rather than constitutive of, the social and political. This position suggests that social phenomena and practices all have discursive elements that are bound up in meaning. Hmong culture is no different from any other cultural formations in that its animations are wholly discursive and contingent on a host of interpretations across time, space, and localized contexts. Ultimately, my treatment of culture in this book is never as an essentialized concept because of my commitments to dislodge its dominant orthodoxies as stagnant, dysfunctional, and universally bounded, especially as it concerns Hmong's gender and sexual politics and practices. By examining the debates, disagreements, and differences in which Hmong Americans themselves both understand and misunderstand—and use and misuse—culture, I showcase its instability as an overarching framework to understand Hmong's gender and sexual politics and practices specifically and Hmong racial subjectivity and subject formation more broadly. Staking belonging in culture enables Hmong Americans to contest and redefine their social and political goals in accordance with their shifting social and political realities.

THE QUEER UNGOVERNABILITY OF THE "REFUGEE PROBLEM"

That race, gender, sexuality, and an essentialized structure of culture coalesce to form the ideology of hyperheterosexuality that subsequently frames Hmong racial subject formation is no coincidence when considering how Hmong became a "refugee problem" in the 1970s and 1980s.[63] The refugee category itself established an alternative set of ideologies about Hmong and continues to frame Hmong primitivity, backwardness, and incivility through their gender and sexual politics and practices. In fact, Hmong's arrival in the United States in 1975 established the next phase of their racialization: as strange Asian immigrants overtaking the country. Foreign policy failures and clandestine military activities in Southeast Asia contributed to the public's lukewarm reception of Southeast Asian refugees in the post-1975 period, with Hmong emerging as a relatively unknown population seemingly appearing out of nowhere on the shores of the United States. Media depictions of Southeast Asian refugees from the 1970s to the 1990s documented refugee suffering and suggested the need for Americans to welcome the downtrodden. However, these same media representations simultaneously paralleled the alarmist portrayals of immigrants arriving in the United States throughout the twentieth century. That is, the influx of refugees reinforced the national crisis of strange newcomers invading the country, with Southeast Asians being viewed as a "refugee problem" because of their perceived unusual cultural and kinship practices, calculating behavior for taking advantage of social services, and overall seeming incompatibility with modernity.[64]

One of the first major articles about Hmong Americans to appear in the mainstream US media was a 1980 *Washington Post* piece titled "Hmongtana," detailing the early Hmong refugee communities in Montana and across the country. In it, the journalist Margot Hornblower reported that a spokesperson from a local assistance center tried to "persuade Philadelphia Hmong not to shoot city pigeons with their crossbows" and how "one American landlord was stunned to find all the porcelain missing from the bathtub in a Hmong apartment" because "the women were beating their clothes clean with rocks."[65] Thus, Hmong's perceived abnormalities as a primitive people heightened the racial anxieties that white Americans had over refugees, with one 1983 *New York Times* article later describing the situation as "the gap between the culture they left and the technological society they now live in."[66]

The "Hmongtana" article also produced additional anxiety about Hmong refugees, namely, their oversexualized cultures and kinship practices. The article was among the first to describe in detail that General Vang Pao, who led military efforts in the United States' secret war in Laos, had relocated to Missoula, Montana, where he lived with sixteen of his twenty-six children, four of his six wives, and his eighty-eight-year-old mother. These immediate facts sensationalized Hmong's high fertility rates and nonnormative family dynamics. Vang had "divorced" all but one wife before the US government permitted him to enter the country, although four wives ultimately remained in his household. This press coverage suggested that Vang could be and was successfully incorporated into heteronormative logics of marriage in the United States vis-à-vis refugee resettlement, but his continuing polygamy nonetheless reinforced Hmong kinship as "culturally" distinct from legal kinship. Vang's "divorcing" of his wives—or, rather, his "marrying" of one wife—was a technique based on normative legal conventions of marriage and kinship and allowed him to resettle in the United States. Yet Hmong still do not necessarily assimilate into the legal configurations of monogamous marriage upon their resettlement in the United States. While that may be true, the article described Vang as living outside the legal formations of marriage, despite his legal marriage to one wife and "not marrying" his other wives. Such a narrative calls into question the heteronormative logics that underlie his resettlement altogether. Vang's marriages to his remaining three wives were all legitimate within Hmong marriage systems outside the US-based formation of legal marriage but were suddenly reformulated as "polygamous" in US legal nomenclature even though he "did not marry" those wives legally.

It may also be the case that the state contradicts this image of successful heteronormative assimilation by informally and unofficially condoning the continuation of Vang's "marriages" to his other wives. In dominant American culture, monogamous heterosexual marriage is normative, acceptable, celebrated, and legally sanctioned. Nonmonogamy is considered nonnormative, abject, and criminal. The fascination with Vang's polygamous marriages demonstrated that Hmong heterosexual culture is nonnormative against the backdrop of US heteronormative monogamy, as the scholar Cathy J. Cohen has shown, because Hmong's heterosexual kinship practices are oversexualized beyond the boundaries of normalized heterosexuality—and are thus positioned as more distant from heteronormativity.[67] In Foucauldian terms, sexuality is a realm of regulation precisely because it proliferates the life (rather than death) of populations.[68] This logic suggests that refugee resettlement also functioned as a procedure of power that sought to regulate, control, deploy, and discipline refugee bodies for the proper management of sexuality upon resettlement in the United States. Beyond General Vang, documents that recorded refugees' family size, children, and occupation compounded state governmentality of biological life, including sexuality.[69] For Vang, the bestowing of US legal and cultural citizenship in the form of refugee resettlement ironically relied on him perpetuating the illusion of a heteronormative gender and sexual order despite his heightened hyperheterosexuality.

While legal constructions and limitations surrounding acceptable kinships may be deemed necessary in order to uphold state governmentality, Vang's decision to remain in de facto marriages and live with four of his six wives gestures toward a larger politics whereby Hmong preserve their traditional formations of kinship seemingly independent of law, which also raises issues about Hmong refugees' queerness opposite normalized sexuality. In sum, Hmong refugees in the United States have discovered ways to adhere to legal, heteronormative matrimony on paper while continuing to maintain their "deviant" polygamous marriages in practice. Refugee resettlement and immigration structures did not fully stem the "problem" of polygamy, because the state simultaneously disciplined Hmong refugees into heteronormative kinship formations but also failed to stop polygamy entirely. The state may even have been aware of, and tolerated, the existence of plural marriage among Hmong for quite some time prior to their resettlement in the United States. "Hmong marriage" presents an anomaly for the state to control and properly regulate kinship or sexuality. The failure of the state to enact control represents the extended argument in *Queering the Hmong Diaspora*, that Hmong refugees are ungovernable racial subjects possessing non-normative gender and sexual politics and practices who are multiply subjected to and detached from state management and assimilation while persistently imagining, embodying, and enacting their own versions of sexuality and kinship that may be empowering, decolonial, antiracist, feminist, and queer.

Things never fit easily into the picture of heteronormative belonging, and that is certainly the case for General Vang. The state's failure to remake Hmong refugees into heteronormative citizens presents opportunities for it to fabricate racial and sexual discourse about refugees in order to legally and politically contain them in the future. In some ways, there is a willingness on the part of the state to allow Hmong refugee migration to the United States despite the understanding that polygamy cannot be entirely eradicated. The "refugee problem" lies precisely in this contradiction, of the state's complicity in authorizing so-called deviant sexualities and kinship practices among refugees, while also seeking to regulate these, and Hmong Americans' quest for belonging, while not entirely achieving it. If white capitalistic heteronormative citizenship is one goal of refugee resettlement, then the refugee as a troubling political, racial, gendered, sexualized, and ontological figure has great potential to problematize processes of heteronormative governmentality in the current phase of sexual and queer liberalism.

Ultimately, the contradictions of refugee resettlement and its intersections with gender and sexuality—particularly Hmong's insistence on preserving their modes of life outside the tyranny of normalized heterosexuality (or homonormativity, for that matter)—reveal a larger politics of refusal among Hmong. Hmong's nonnormativity confronts the politics of inclusion and racial liberalism through resettlement, but it also antagonizes dominant frameworks of contemporary sexual and queer liberalism that seek to remake subjects into respectable citizens with legal rights. Indigenous studies scholars Glen Coulthard, Audra Simpson, and Jodi Byrd, among others, have provided some of the most poignant critiques against inclusion as a tactic for minoritarian and Indigenous freedom.[70] In fact, inclusion reifies the very structures that excluded the subjugated populations in the first place. The state, as the exclusionary apparatus that performs the injury of differential treatment, seeks to rectify itself through inclusion of difference while simultaneously demanding the subjugated polities assimilate into the dominant structure. In the context of Indigenous peoples in the Americas, Simpson argues that "recognition is the gentler form, perhaps, or the least corporeally violent way of managing Indians and their difference, a multicultural solution to the settlers'

Indian problem."[71] As Hmong Americans are considered problematic refugees who possess premodern gender and sexual cultures, recognition is conjured as the most "gentle" form of racial management under the veneer of conferring belonging and citizenship.

However, the difficulties presented by Vang suggest that Hmong American kinship practices are deemed even *too* problematic to be properly recognized (and regulated). Simpson elaborates on these alleged "problematic" cultures in describing the impossibility of Indigenous recognition by the state, arguing, "This inclusion, or juridical form of recognition, is only performed, however, *if* the problem of cultural difference and alterity does not pose too appalling a challenge to norms of the settler society, norms that are revealed largely through law in the form of decisions over the sturdiness, vitality, and purity of the cultural alterity before it."[72] In this sense, Simpson asserts that even recognition is not possible for certain populations, particularly Indigenous people who are perceived by the settler colonial government as *too* threatening. Hmong Americans as an apparently premodern and problematic racialized refugee population become one of the appalling alterities that Simpson describes. Throughout *Queering the Hmong Diaspora*, Hmong Americans confront various systems of racial management that have concretized through contradictions within liberalism, mostly against rhetorics of women's rights and lesbian and gay rights. Hmong Americans, and queer Hmong Americans in particular, refuse a politics of recognition that constructs their gender and sexual politics and practices through the frame of a premodern culture in order to manage and assimilate them into normalized heterosexuality and homonormativity. The impossible containment of Hmong within heteronormative state logics lies at the heart of this book.

READING THE BOOK

Queering the Hmong Diaspora is structured as two distinct yet interrelated parts that unfold over four chapters. All of the chapters address the construction of Hmong's supposed hyperheterosexuality, but they use diverse interdisciplinary methodologies to analyze its deployment in a variety of domains. The first two chapters examine the intersections of Hmong American racial, gender, and sexual formation in media and law to illuminate how hyperheterosexual understandings of Hmong Americans have come to divest them of access to belonging. Hmong Americans' perceived violent heterosexual culture structures distorted understandings of Hmong Americans/refugees within both dominant knowledge and Hmong epistemologies. The focus on media and law—as two major arenas in which dominant society inaugurates and exerts its ideological powers—establishes the overarching framework of how the racializing logics that undergird Hmong American gender and sexual formation converge with and diverge from normative understandings of Asian American racial, gender, and sexual formations. Chapter 1 maps out the ideology of hyperheterosexuality more pointedly by analyzing two discourses of sexual violence among Hmong— namely, power and gang sexual violence—that were heavily documented in local media in the early 1990s and up to 2015 as central narratives indispensable to the ideology of hyperheterosexuality. Ultimately, the law and media linked sexual crimes to culture in order to racialize and subjugate Hmong Americans. Chapter 2 continues the investigation of law through the legislative domain. It analyzes a series of marriage bills proposed in the Minnesota legislature from the 1990s to 2006 and reveals how hyperheterosexuality as a prevailing racial ideology obstructed Hmong Americans from accessing belonging and cultural citizenship through marriage benefits provided by the state. The chapter examines legislative hearings conducted in the Minnesota Senate and House, augmented by interviews with key legislators and lawyers, and argues that Hmong Americans' cultural differences in their practice of polygamy and "underage marriage" haunt their quest for belonging.

Chapters 3 and 4 shift to analyzing the politics of queerness in Hmong America as a means of refusing the racializing logics of hyperheterosexuality. These chapters demonstrate the way hyperheterosexuality has come to preclude queerness within both US and Hmong ethnonationalist discourses and how queer Hmong American critical imaginations and vernacular activist organizing paradoxically usurp and dislodge culture as a force against hyperheterosexuality and queer liberalism's illusory exceptionalist narratives of progress. Queer Hmong American critical imaginations and vernacular activism operate as a politics of refusal that does not adhere to white supremacist, state-based, or Hmong ethnonationalist formations of social and political belonging, while still embracing a particular element of Hmong gender and sexual difference that may be empowering. Chapter 3 draws from interviews with queer Hmong Americans to examine their experiences of forced erasure within the framework of hyperheterosexuality and to show how queerness is an absent dimension of this particular formation of Hmong American racialization. Queer Hmong Americans have resisted their social positioning within this ideological structure in order to exist otherwise, critically imagining empowering, antiracist, and queer forms of spirituality and cosmology anchored in Hmong epistemologies of birth and rebirth. Chapter 4 analyzes the strategies of the queer Hmong and Southeast Asian American activist collective MidWest Solidarity Movement (MWSM) to defeat a 2012 marriage ballot initiative in Minnesota. In examining a photographic campaign by MWSM, using ethnography and participant observation conducted during the ballot initiative battle from 2011 to 2012, and drawing on interviews, it looks at how queer Hmong Americans disidentified with the fight for legalizing same-sex marriage in the United States to reenvision life-making and community building through a vernacular activism.

The epilogue takes its cue from nonbinary performance artist S U N A H's *No Word for Queer* project, which centralizes queerness as a creative analytic to subvert hyperheterosexuality and imagine newfound lifeworlds of racial, gender, sexual, and queer justice for Hmong Americans. As a queer Hmong American activist, scholar, student, and community member who has worked with Hmong American youth and elders on issues of civic engagement, electoral politics, college student organizing, racial justice, and queer justice over the past decade and a half, and as someone who occupies a privileged positionality in the academy, I am intent on amplifying the experiences of my community to highlight the imaginative labor undertaken and counternarratives crafted by Hmong Americans as they navigate contradictory racialized, gendered, and sexualized scripts. *Queering the Hmong Diaspora* demonstrates that the constructions of Hmong as culturally different at the intersections of race, gender, and sexuality—and the subsequent potential of queerness—have implications for how to reimagine belonging and justice for minoritized communities in the United States.

CHAPTER 1

Stories of Commotion

THE HYPERHETEROSEXUALITY OF SEXUAL VIOLENCE

Throughout the 1990s and the first decade of the twenty-first century, accounts of sexual violence against women and girls in Hmong communities across the United States surfaced as exceptional chronicles that accentuated apprehensions about Hmong culture and its status within the liberal US gender and sexuality system. Stemming from narratives of anxious racialized sexualities, two central representations of sexual violence exist that intensify the discourse of a criminal hyperheterosexual Hmong culture in the United States. As a queer and feminist studies scholar committed to antiracism and social justice, I argue that culture as an ideological concept continues to frame any kind of sex acts—including sexual violence—among Hmong through criminal hyperheterosexuality. I contend that racializing Hmong as hyperheterosexual subjects within dominant legal and media discourse at the expense of women and girls does little to provide justice for survivors in addressing sexual violence, even though such framings are purportedly deployed as a means of delivering justice to them. In fact, legal and media representations of sexual violence against Hmong women and girls reinforce their marginalization through their gendered racialization as perpetual asexual victims. Hmong women's and girls' racialized victimhood binds them to a subjectivity in which they possess no agency over their sexual subjecthood. While Hmong women's and girls' voices and experiences are systematically absent in dominant narratives—a discursive effect that admittedly also bears imprints in this chapter—I aim to provide necessary critiques about the intersections of race, gender, and sexuality of minoritized polities in the United States, and specifically their production of Hmong as hyperheterosexual subjects outcasted from normalized heterosexuality. I hope to not trivialize sexual violence in this chapter. Rather, I examine the effects and representations of sexual violence that implicate Hmong in epistemologies of criminalized sexuality as it intersects with discourses about their cultural and racial irregularities. In doing so, I reframe how to pursue justice for survivors of sexual violence.

I read legal proceedings and media representations of intraethnic sexual violence among Hmong to demonstrate the symbolic and ideological dimensions of the hyperheterosexuality of culture. First, two cases in the early 1990s involved powerful Hmong American men who sexually assaulted unsuspecting refugee Hmong women whom they were supposed to assist in finding employment. All survivors in the cases were painted as unsophisticated women who possessed no formal education and had recently been resettled in the United States as refugees. Thus, the supposed powerful hypermasculinized position of both men as educated professionals and the powerless hyperfeminized position of the women as recently resettled refugees with no education were emphasized in the criminal trials as dimensions of Hmong's excessive (men's) and nonexistent (women's) sexualities. The cases were quarreled in courts sutured with elements of culture embedded in both the prosecution and the defense. Both the two legal proceedings and their subsequent spectacularized media representations highlighted the precarious position of culture in US law as a mechanism of racially marginalizing Hmong from normalized heterosexuality. Second, gang sexual violence in the late 1990s to the 2010s was reported extensively in the media to fabricate a discourse of gang culture rooted in criminalized hyperheterosexuality. In particular, reports of gangs sexually assaulting teenage girls persisted as an archetype of Hmong men's criminal sexualities and Hmong women's and girls' hypervictimized asexuality. In all of the cases, the young ages of the survivors and the gang membership of the perpetrators were spectacularized to produce discursive and ideological effects that reinforced the racial archetypes of Hmong as premodern criminal subjects worthy of surveillance, punishment, and incarceration.

To be sure, the specificity of Hmong as hyperheterosexual subjects is not divorced from how communities of color are interpellated in the long-standing surveillance and criminalization of minoritized gender and sexuality. Intersectionality enables us to see how women of color's vulnerability to experiencing sexual violence in their homes, communities, and society writ large is systematically maintained through the overlapping forms of subordination that uphold structures of power. Their experiences are compounded by the ideological dichotomies that are constructed through law and general attitudes more broadly in which "good" women can claim victimhood while "bad" women cannot. Kimberlé Crenshaw's advocacy of Black women experiencing discrimination at the intersection of racism and sexism shows that Black women are precisely the ones most harmed by the strict regulation of women's sexual conduct.[1] The devaluation of Black women's experiences of sexual violence reflects the continuing surveillance of both women's bodies and sexualities and people of color's sexual crimes as essential to their race and culture. Hyperheterosexuality as an ideological formation is also entrenched in these cultural narratives about women's sexual victimhood, which oftentimes position Hmong women and girls as the prototype of the "good" victim whose gendered and sexual oppression arose through no fault of her own. Race, gender, and sexual scripts on violence can simultaneously position women of color as doubly suspicious and credible in ways that foreclose justice for survivors. The legal and media construction of Hmong women and girls as believable victims through the frame of their subjugation within their native culture informs how Hmong are idiosyncratically interpellated within dominant cultural narratives on racialized sexual violence.

Reporters and Hmong community members alike turn to culture as a means of cohering sexuality more broadly, and sexual violence in particular, when Hmong Americans are implanted in sensational headlines. Thus, I pose this inquiry: Why is it that Hmong and non-Hmong alike continue to rely on culture to explain sexual behavior more generally, and sexual crimes specifically? To what extent should cultural difference be used at all to explain sexual violence, gender subordination, and Hmong's sexuality, sexual politics, sexual acts, and sexual crimes in the United States? How might this framing preclude justice for survivors? Following legal scholars like Leti Volpp who have studied the role of "culture" in law as it pertains to gender and sexuality, I contemplate "when do we call behavior 'cultural'? And when do we not? Why do we distinguish behavior in this way? And what are the consequences of this difference in recognition and naming?"[2] Sensationalized stories take on a life of their own beyond the legal proceedings and representational images. The coded image of racialized sexuality is proliferated within the larger social field, where it accumulates meaning pertinent and fundamental to the disciplining and representations of minoritized subjects. Both law and media produce, transform, and construct the racialized, gendered, and sexualized ideologies that undergird subject formation itself. That is, the diffusion of knowledge produced about Hmong Americans is filtered through the discourse of hyperheterosexuality in law, which in turn is mediated through media. This frame manufactures a formation of racialized subjectivity not as "truth" but as ideology, in which "ideologies therefore work by the transformation of discourses (the disarticulation and re-articulation of ideological elements) and the transformation (the fracturing and recomposition) of subjects-for-action."[3]

I perform close readings of legal and media texts about two idiosyncratic representations of sexual violence among Hmong Americans to extract the framings of culture and their attendant effects on the ways law and media—as two subsidiary tentacles of liberal US society—cohere Hmong American cultural and racial difference. Hmong's entangled racialized subject formation is compounded by their refugee status, presenting a convoluted arrangement of gender and sexuality that enhances the constantly shifting representations of minoritized polities in the United States. Untangling the social dynamics that inform Hmong's racialized gender and sexual statuses, in turn, will hopefully foster a renewed discourse about justice for survivors of sexual violence.

THE SPECTACLES OF POWER RAPE

On March 14, 1990, New Chue Her, a twenty-six-year-old college-educated employment counselor who worked at a refugee resettlement and employment agency, picked up an eighteen-year-old Hmong refugee woman from her apartment under the pretense of taking her to a job interview. Instead, he drove her to the Highway Motel on West Seventh Street in St. Paul, threatened her with a gun, violently threw her against a wooden bed frame, and sexually assaulted her.[4] A trial for Her was conducted in July 1990, and a Ramsey County District Court jury convicted him of first-degree criminal sexual conduct. On January 15, 1991, Ramsey County district judge David Marsden sentenced Her to seven years and two months in prison for the crime. In one of the most well-known criminal sexual assault cases involving a Hmong American defendant in the history of Minnesota, *State v. New Chue Her* is emblematic of the uneasy predicament of culture, gender, and sexual politics in US law. The trial itself was spectacularized by the courts and subsequently filtered through local newspaper articles in the St. Paul *Pioneer Press* and the Minneapolis *Star Tribune*. First, the prosecution and defense deliberated on the sexual and moral norms among Hmong that can account for sexual violence and other sexual acts such as adultery. Second, the case became a racialized spectacle regarding the question of translating terminology about sex and sexual violence from the Hmong language into English. These two dimensions entrenched hegemonic ideas about the gendered and sexual politics of racialized others in the United States.

Questions of Hmong cultural differences regarding sexual violence and women's sexual behavior figured prominently at Her's trial. Both the defense and the prosecution introduced "cultural evidence" in order to prove Her's innocence or guilt. Thus, law's cultural relativist frameworks deployed by both the defense and the prosecution framed Hmong cultural and racial difference against an exceptionalized white supremacist judiciary.[5] The defense claimed that the survivor's allegations were a maneuver to utilize the procedures of Hmong culture to entrap Her into marriage.[6] Considering Hmong people's structures of communal governance in the Southeast Asian context in which families lived together in tight-knit highland villages, marriage was considered a morally just accountability measure in the case of sexual assault, in that the perpetrator was required to care for the survivor and the potential child. In the US context, when a sexual assault did occur among Hmong, particularly in the early years of their resettlement as refugees, the party causing the harming and the party that was harmed were both willing to resolve the injury in this way, but the criminal legal system prohibited them from doing so.[7] Sexual assault among Hmong is arbitrated no longer under these terms but through the criminal legal system, which enacts punishment through incarceration.

Her's defense distorted this contextual history, claiming that Hmong culture imposed compulsory marriage as the consequence of sex between unmarried men and women, to provide credence to the assertion that the survivor was deploying such a strategy to ensnare Her into marriage. In the case of married individuals, argued the defense, the man must pay damages to the woman's husband for purportedly violating his "property" by "having sex" with his wife. Therefore, the defense argued that what had transpired on March 14, 1990, more or less constituted "adultery" rather than sexual assault. In this enormously faulty argument, Hmong cultural norms supposedly dictate that the appropriate route of reconciliation should be for the male paramour to compensate the survivor's husband rather than for the defendant to be penalized by the criminal legal system.

An "uncle" of the survivor was called on to testify during pretrial hearings and stated that in the context of Laos, a sexual assault survivor and the perpetrator himself would *both* be punished by being handcuffed together and left out to burn in the sun.[8] The testimony of the unnamed "uncle," a supposed cultural expert who is authentic in his knowledge of Hmong sexual norms, indicates that sexual transgressions should result in both parties' punishment as a means of exonerating Her as the sole transgressor. This testimony was inadmissible in court, but it demonstrates how the defense relied on "cultural evidence" by using a cultural expert to explain how the quandary of sex would have been handled in a different geographical, temporal, and historical context. In essence, Her's defense claimed that the survivor consented to sexual intercourse, but fearing that her husband might physically abuse her for committing "adultery," she instead feigned rape as a technique to absolve her own sexual promiscuity and project the wrongdoing solely onto Her.

The defense relied on "cultural evidence" and cultural difference to discredit the survivor and to disavow sexual assault as another form of sexual act, namely, adultery. The irony in this argument is that Her's lawyers must denigrate his culture in order to defend him as a Hmong. Framing the survivor as the property of her husband means she is transformed into an object through the institution of marriage, where sexual agency does not exist. Her transmutation as object through marriage and her subsequent transgression of her assigned objecthood mean she is no longer a human who should be vindicated, because she has acquiesced to her culture. The subsequent irony at play is that she is simultaneously a victim entrapped as an object in her culture as much as she is a transgressor for attempting to sexually break free from it.

The prosecution, however, purported that the repressive Hmong culture renders women socially, politically, and sexually powerless, thus denying women any agency to initiate sex with men, let alone male strangers. The prosecution called on another "cultural expert," this time a Hmong American social worker, Tong Vang, to testify that in the Hmong culture, it is improper for women to initiate sex or intimate sexual gestures toward men. Vang's testimony cements the prosecution's argument that because Hmong women are completely sexually powerless in their native culture, then it must have been Her who initiated the sexual contact and the successive sexual violence, not the survivor. During the trial's cross-examination, assistant county attorney Jeanne Schleh questioned Her intently about whether Hmong society would place blame on a rape victim rather than on the man who committed the rape. Not surprising, under intense scrutiny Her responded, "In my culture, there is no such thing as rape."[9] Her's reply presented the perfect opportunity for Schleh to argue in her closing statement that Her should indeed be convicted of sexual assault because "this is not his country, this is our country."[10] Schleh further stated:

> It is not proper in Hmong culture for a woman to initiate sex, even with her husband. It is not proper for a woman to touch a man. It is not proper for a woman to kiss a man, and especially in public. There are cultural taboos you heard, even about being alone with a man not of your own class. Ask yourself if the woman you saw here is the kind of vixen that this defendant describes. The kind of vixen she would have to be so outside her own culture in behavior. Ask yourself whether in the light of all that you have heard about this culture, this woman would persuade a leader of the Hmong community to go against his principles, to go against his culture.[11]

Schleh's racially inflammatory closing statement deploys culture to expound the constraints of women's sexual behavior. The remarks render the survivor as asexual and achieve the symbolic composite of her subjugated sexual personhood. She is not a desiring subject in any context, but only a desirable object in "her own culture."

Schleh's statement defines the contours of proper sexual behavior and delineates the confines that constitute Hmong women's sexual subjectivity. Through this line of reasoning, the Hmong woman is completely at the mercy of her husband as his *wife* in marriage and is further subjugated by male strangers as the *victim* of a sex crime. Furthermore, the Minnesota Court of Appeals admitted that the survivor's "lack of sophistication was a major theme of the prosecution's case."[12] The prosecution "emphasized [the survivor's] unfamiliarity with what a motel was" and further argued that "Her, who had significant power over [the survivor's] life through his threat to cut off her welfare benefits, took advantage of a woman far beneath him in social status."[13] The woman's inability to speak English, lack of sophistication, and overall helplessness are attributes of her refugee status. Ultimately, the woman is subjugated by her threefold status as a Hmong wife, a rape victim, and a refugee, emblematic of Volpp's description of the abject victims found not in US civil society but rather in unfree, uncivil societies.[14] While Her's defense argued that Schleh's closing statement amounted to racism and was an invocation of racial inflammation, the court ruled that it was merely a plea to *law* rather than *culture* and was not a scheme to exacerbate racist stereotypes.[15] Ironically, though, Schleh did indeed anchor her closing statement in conceptions of Hmong's restrictive cultural norms on women's sexual behavior rather than on a presumed universalistic, cultureless legal approach to sexual violence and sexual justice rooted in everyday hetero-patriarchy and structural inequality.

The predicament of translating terminology about sex from the Hmong language into English was also of paramount importance during Her's trial. At issue, specifically, was the contention of translating the word *mos* from Hmong into English to ascertain the truth of the events that transpired on March 14, 1990. In Her's appeal, his defense attempted to discredit the survivor's account by claiming that *mos* was incorrectly translated during the trial as "rape" instead of "wrestle."[16] According to the defense, Her and the survivor merely "wrestled" each other, rather than one sexually assaulting the other. Vang Pao Lee, a cultural expert for the defense, testified that the word *mos* was not translatable as "rape." Yet according to Michael Moua, a cultural expert testifying for the prosecution, *mos* can be translated as both "rape" and "wrestle," depending on the context. Another cultural expert for the prosecution, Sia Lo, testified that *mos* "certainly meant" rape in this context.[17] Yet Her's appeal suggested that there is no such thing as rape in his culture, and thus he could not have performed an act that does not exist. By translating *mos* as "wrestle," Her's defense painted a picture that was less graphic than that of the survivor's account. The cultural experts muddied the case with their contradictory claims of whether *mos* meant "rape" or "wrestle," in some instances enabling the conflation of the lack of terminology for rape with the nonexistence of rape.

The trial itself attempted to distinguish the subtle differences in meaning by situating the word *mos* in the context of the criminal trial. However, the question of whether *mos* should be translated as "rape" or "wrestle" extends beyond the technicalities of mistranslations in the legal context. What is at stake are the competing claims by Hmong cultural experts who were called into the criminal legal process as authenticators of culture and language, whose contradictory and inconsistent knowledge about Hmong's sexual norms became the basis of shaping ideologies about criminal sexual conduct. As demonstrated in *State v. New Chue Her*, interpreters and translators are not properly trained to be impartial arbiters of translation in the legal context. Rather, they are called into legal proceedings to operate as subjects who can present conflicting pronouncements about the fundamental sexual truths of a particular racialized polity and their consequent cultural differences.

Hmong cultural experts inadvertently become complicit in the racist and essentialist stereotyping and portrayals of their own communities through their expert knowledge about the "truth" of sexual relations within Hmong society. In many ways, cultural experts preserve the dominant narratives of culture already constructed through hegemonic institutions such as the courts and the law's epistemological archives. Drawing from Antonio Gramsci's concept of common sense, Stuart Hall contends that cultural experts, like other minoritized subjects, acquiesce to the same racist machinations that work to ideologically incarcerate them. Minoritized subjects who supposedly perform the work of counterhegemony within cultural relativist frameworks nonetheless inadvertently "purchase" racist ideologies in their own subjectification to commonsense narratives about themselves within the hegemonic structure.[18] Culturally "authentic" figures such as the "uncle" in the Her case aggravate the essentialization of Hmong as premodern when juxtaposed against a supposed neutral judiciary.

Thus, Hmong cultural experts perform the ideological work of perpetuating essentialist understandings of gendered and sexual subordinations in the "cultural defense." Volpp has cautioned against using the cultural defense in criminal legal cases because it risks relegating acts of violence to the realm of the insular community rather than identifying them as political acts that are dialectic with the dominant society.[19] In fact, the defense's claim that "there is no such thing as rape" in the Hmong culture and that there are no words to name or describe sexual assault and thus it does not exist marks Hmong as illiberal. However, the nonrecognition of rape does not signify its nonexistence. The state and prosecution doubly played on such claims when they argued that Hmong culture condones rape or, at best, creates the conditions in which rape becomes permissible. The cultural experts for the defense, in particular, rendered culture as a site where essentialist racist interpretations about Hmong can materialize, particularly because there is already an available legal archive of racial knowledge about Hmong as hyperheterosexual subjects.[20] Their interpretive testimonies were meant to be helpful in producing justice but were quite unhelpful in determining the truth of sex among Hmong. In sum, the impossibility, incomprehensibility, and irreconcilability of language to determine the innocence or guilt of sexual violence presents a conundrum for culture's place within US law in particular and the meanings that can be ascertained about racialized sexualities within US society more broadly.

Ultimately, the Minnesota Court of Appeals upheld Her's conviction. Judge Robert Schumacher determined that the prosecution "did not commit prejudicial misconduct" when assistant county attorney Schleh highlighted Hmong cultural differences about sexual violence and women's sexuality (or lack thereof) in her closing statement.[21] Ramsey County district judge Michael DeCourcy denied

Her's motion for a new trial on the basis of the appeals court's decision rejecting the defense's motion that racially inflammatory remarks and mistranslations during the original trial created impartial conditions for Her. While Judge De-Courcy admitted that misinterpretations and grammatical errors did take place during the trial, he claimed that the confusion and mistranslations of *mos* as "wrestle" were "immaterial" and "irrelevant" and were generally misinterpreted overall to benefit the defense and harm the prosecution.[22] Her's conviction for first-degree criminal sexual conduct and sentencing was upheld in January 1994.

A second, concurrent—and more dramatic—criminal sexual assault case astounded Hmong communities, journalists, and legal experts alike. The case involved twenty-nine-year-old King Buachee Lee, a community leader, real estate agent, and English-language instructor at the St. Paul Technical-Vocational Institute, who sexually assaulted two refugee women whom he was supposed to assist with finding employment. The first incident occurred on March 20, 1990, when a woman contacted Lee to drive her to apply for jobs. They met in the parking lot of the Technical-Vocational Institute, where she entered his car. He then transported her to a motel, deceiving her that an interview was going to take place. Instead, he sexually assaulted her. He threatened to murder her and her family if she told anyone about the incident. The following day, Lee called the woman and told her to meet him again at the Technical-Vocational Institute or else he would execute his threats. She complied with his demand and met him the next day at the institute, where in his car he sexually assaulted her a second time. The third incident occurred the following week, on March 26, 1990, when Lee met the first woman and a second, different woman in the parking lot of the Technical-Vocational Institute before their class was scheduled to begin. Lee demanded that the two women drive with him in his car to go and apply for jobs. The women refused to enter his car. However, they followed him in their own cars to a park, where the first woman immediately fled, knowing what Lee was about to do next. Lee forced the second woman to enter his car and drove her to his house. Once there, she refused his commands to exit the vehicle and enter his house. He then physically attacked and assaulted her in the car, inside his garage. As with the previous assault, Lee threatened to kill her and her family if she divulged information about what had transpired.[23] Neither of the women reported the crimes until two months later, in May 1990.

State v. King Buachee Lee was lengthy and muddy. As in *State v. New Chue Her*, both the defense and the prosecution in *State v. King Buachee Lee* infused innumerable elements of culture into their arguments in order to establish Lee's innocence or guilt. In the protracted and more publicized Lee case, the defense argued that the women had not been assaulted at all, mirroring similar claims made by the defense in *State v. New Chue Her*. Lee's own testimony insinuated that he and the women engaged in consensual sex and that what transpired were affairs that amounted to adultery. He claimed that the survivors wanted him to marry them during their affair. And because what had transpired between Lee and the women constituted adultery, a different route of reconciliation was needed outside of criminalization and incarceration, that is, if Lee was not innocent altogether. In an unsurprising twist, the survivors' own husbands believed that the survivors had indeed committed adultery with Lee. One survivor's husband even physically abused her for the supposed affair.[24] The fact that the women's husbands believed Lee provided credence for the defense in its claim that the events constituted adultery rather than sexual assault. Drawing supposedly from Hmong's sexual norms, the defense argued that a married woman's transgressive sexual promiscuity must be reconciled through a monetary payment from the woman's "lover" to the woman's husband rather than through criminalization of the male paramour. By exploiting cultural evidence to solicit the participation of the survivors' husbands in the trial as a measure of discrediting the survivors, the defense perpetrated both symbolic and emotional violence onto the survivors in a way that compounded the sexual violence they had already endured at the hands of Lee and their physical abuse at the hands of their husbands.

In another effort to discredit the survivors, the defense suggested that all parties drink a "curse water" that would spiritually compel them to disclose the absolute truth of what had transpired. This curse water was a mixture of chicken blood and water and, if consumed, would force the individuals to be truthful in their testimonies or else suffer the consequence of death that the "curse" would inflict. Drinking the curse water would have been akin to the individuals giving legal sworn testimonies after taking the stand at trial. The defense opted for a cultural relativist version of legal sworn testimony to ensure the trial would be fair to the parties as *Hmong*. The trial judge disallowed this maneuver by the defense, arguing that if any party refused to drink the curse water, there would be an implication that they were not telling the truth.[25] The conjuring of the curse water introduced elements into the trial already laden with puzzling and inconsistent dimensions of a supposed illiberal native culture. Not only did the scheme of the curse water draw from exoticism and orientalism, but it was also framed as a *Hmong* cultural maneuver aimed at producing justice by compelling the parties to disclose the absolute truths of the events that transpired in March 1990. At every twist and turn, their premodern culture is conjured as a totalizing force to make sense of Hmong as subjects enmeshed in the criminal legal system and to subsequently manage them in ways that the state might be unable to with any other population.

On the side of the prosecution, assistant Ramsey County attorney Clayton M. Robinson Jr. argued that Lee was a liar who abused his position in a "male-dominated native culture that accords few rights to women" in order to take advantage of the survivors.[26] The prosecution enlisted Nancy Donnelly, a white anthropologist from the University of Washington who had studied the experiences of refugee Hmong women, to testify that the survivors were terrified to report the crimes because they would compromise their reputation within their families and community. Donnelly explained, "Social reputation is the only thing a Hmong woman has to sustain her. Even her own clothes belong to her family; her jewelry belongs to her husband."[27] Donnelly declared that a Hmong woman's reputation is the only thing she can control, and thus it was rational not to be immediately forthright in order to preserve that reputation for as long as she can before it is inevitably tarnished and she thereby is left with absolutely nothing within her native culture. This claim also suggests that a Hmong woman has no entitlement to material goods such as clothes or jewelry, as she herself is considered an object. As such, she was certainly not entitled to ownership of her sexuality, thus promulgating her asexual status within the contexts of Hmong gender and sexual politics.

Furthermore, testimony from Ramsey County prosecutor Schleh corroded the case since she was a prosecutor in *State v. New Chue Her*. Schleh testified in *State v. King Buachee Lee* that the Her and Lee cases were similar in that both perpetrators were Hmong men in positions of power who victimized unsophisticated refugee Hmong women. In essence, Schleh's testimony identified the similarity in the two cases to be the ethnicity of the defendants, that is, both defendants were *Hmong* men. The appeals court found Schleh's testimony to be "improper racial and cultural stereotyping," since the fact that the defendants were *Hmong* men, in and of itself, was irrelevant.[28] This finding contradicts the decision from the earlier *State v. New Chue Her*, where the Minnesota Court of Appeals ruled Schleh's testimony *not* racially inflammatory. The courts cannot reconcile the racism evident in both cases, ruling in one that Schleh's testimony was not racially inflammatory and in the other that it was. Noting this inconsistency is important since the prosecution also relied on racialized representations of Hmong's constructed hyperheterosexuality to paint a picture of Hmong men as *especially* vicious because of the sanctions they receive from their native culture.[29]

A jury convicted Lee of three counts of third-degree criminal sexual conduct, and district judge Roland Faricy sentenced him to seventeen years and eight months in prison. In sentencing Lee, Judge Faricy stated, "This is a landmark case about the status of women worldwide, about sexual politics across cultures. I think the verdict will deliver an important message to the Hmong community as a whole."[30] Faricy's statement constructs a temporal gap between the supposed premodern Hmong culture and the supposed modern American judiciary, whereby Hmong need to be given accelerated lessons on the properties of sex and the legalities that circumscribe sexual violence in the United States. In essence, the modern liberal state disciplines the premodern and illiberal racialized other into sexual liberalism. The need to "deliver a message to the Hmong community as a whole" meant that not only is Lee guilty of sexual assault, but the entire Hmong community is also implicated in his crime. "Bad behavior," as Volpp calls it, in this sense is understood to be a collective pathology among an entire minoritized population.[31] Ultimately, Faricy's provocation effaces sexual justice for the survivors and instead exacerbates racial injustice for the entire Hmong people.[32]

In an unexpected turn of events, the Minnesota Court of Appeals overturned Lee's conviction in February 1992 on the basis of Schleh's testimony, which was deemed "improper and highly prejudicial."[33] However, the Minnesota Supreme Court reinstated Lee's sentence in a 5–2 decision in December 1992 and ultimately upheld Judge Faricy's sentence.[34] In making the decision and highlighting the intricacies of the case, Minnesota Supreme Court chief justice A. M. (Sandy) Keith stated, "The whole trial is one of credibility. Do you believe the two ladies, or do you believe the defendant? It's a very unusual case. It's a very difficult case, because we're dealing with people from another culture."[35] For Chief Justice Keith, the fact that Hmong are from a "another culture" rendered the case legally ambiguous and made it judicially difficult to assess the questions of sexual violence, women's sexual behavior, and legal justice for sexual assault survivors. The case is extraordinary because it highlighted the contradictory limits and possibilities with which culture, gender, sexuality, and the law are simultaneously intertwined and detached. Furthermore, legal measures are difficult to dictate regarding the terms of punishment for sexual violence among Hmong Americans because Hmong are understood in the legal context to exist on an unusual cultural terrain in which modern US law cannot reconcile and properly punish. Subsequently, Lee hastily fled to Thailand when he was momentarily freed after his conviction was overturned by the Minnesota Court of Appeals but before it was reinstated by the Minnesota Supreme Court. A manhunt for the fugitive ensued, ending in his eventual capture near Saraburi, Thailand, in 1998 and extradition to the United States in 2000.

Hmong men were posited in these two cases as "educated." They possessed degrees and jobs, which should ultimately denote the successful assimilation of the racialized refugee subject. However, contrary to the picture of successful assimilation within neoliberal multiculturalist discourses about Asian Americans as law-abiding, the deviousness comes through in their assimilated status (as being educated), which they co-opted to their advantage in order to commit these crimes. Their education is not used to reinforce their understanding of American law, to respect proper relations between teacher and student, or to signify their successful assimilation as upstanding citizen-subjects. Instead, their education and intelligence were represented as augmenting their heteropatriarchal power within their native culture. Thus, the crimes committed by Her and Lee were understood as exceptionally abhorrent in the court proceedings because they strategically sought justification from their native culture to excuse their crimes. Education is presented paradoxically as a tool of power and privilege, but also as a failure to achieve education's ideals as respectable and assimilated citizen-subjects. Instead, education represents the *almost* successful, but ultimately failed, assimilation of Hmong refugees into heteronormative, law-abiding, career-driven citizenship. The men's education status posits them as subjects-in-becoming that are neither victimized refugees nor properly assimilated proper citizen-subjects.[36] Their subject-in-becoming status enabled the discursive attachment of their identities as Hmong to heighten the hyperheterosexuality of their crimes. This ideological function in the usage of education-as-failed-assimilation further reinforces Hmong men's racial difference from the civility of whiteness and their status as perpetually unassimilable alien others outside the bounds of normalized heterosexuality.[37]

Both *State v. New Chue Her* and *State v. King Buachee Lee* exploited and distorted culture to make sense of sex, sexual behavior, sexual violence, and sex crimes among a minoritized population. Legal scholars William E. Martin and Peter N. Thompson, who studied the Her and Lee cases, contend that the two cases were mishandled by the introduction of "culture" into their arguments. Martin and Thompson state, "Cultural and racial stereotyping are pernicious, harmful tactics, and the effects of such practices are felt well beyond the immediate trial setting."[38] The prosecution and the media subsequently portrayed Hmong men's heterosexuality as violent beyond the boundaries of normalized heterosexuality due to its authorizations rooted in an essentialized native culture that affords no sexual agency to women. In this vein, Hmong men were able to strategically position culture in ways that elide the legal dimensions and definitions of sexual assault within the white supremacist judiciary.

Culture makes sense as a frame to understand racially minoritized others within the neoliberal multiculturalist order of the settler state. The prosecution's legal arguments depended on the vulnerability of Hmong women as subjects who possessed no sexual or political agency. The sexual violence they experienced was rendered more brutal when the women are indefinitely constrained through a premodern native culture that can be positioned opposite the contemporary judiciary. Because their supposed cultural sphere does not permit freedom of sexuality, the women were presumed to be believable victims, as they have no outlet to engage in sexual behavior. The binary logic of Hmong culture versus the criminal legal judiciary to address sexual violence explains how racialization operates through gender and sexuality to bolster the ideology of hyperheterosexuality and foreclose justice for the survivors. Judge Faricy defined Lee's case as "a classic example of a power rape—a man with authority and sophistication who took advantage of women who were unsophisticated and simply following the Hmong tradition of submissiveness."[39] Submissiveness here means Hmong women were not deemed subjects who have sexual desires. The women's repositioning toward judicial punishments and incarceration only serves to perpetuate their status as legible vulnerable subjects who can only achieve justice when the judiciary disciplines their perpetrators, who have already been ideologically constructed as existing in a criminal culture. Hmong women have no recourse for seeking justice to address their grievances within their own community and thus must seek recourse within the supposed impartial criminal legal system. Because both the defense's and the prosecution's articulations of Hmong's gender and sexual scripts were rather questionable in these cases, the judiciary gets the ultimate say in what constitutes Hmong's gender and sexual politics.

Furthermore, the women in the cases remain nameless. Throughout the ordeal, the public never heard the testimonies of the survivors, and they were never quoted in the *Star Tribune* or *Pioneer Press*. This namelessness and anonymity are indeed absolutely necessary for reasons of safety and confidentiality in the legal context. However, these measures perform the ideological work of rendering the survivors as hypervictimized subjects who have the unfortunate destiny of having been born voiceless *Hmong* women, precluding the use of testimony as justice.[40] Of course, this long portrayal of Hmong women as powerless has existed in historical and anthropological accounts of Hmong. As Chia Youyee Vang, Faith Nibbs, and Ma Vang write in the paradigm-shifting anthology *Claiming Place: On the Agency of Hmong Women*, "For contemporary Hmong women, a combination of subordinations imposed by those with different interests—such as Hmong experiences with French colonialism in Southeast Asian, Hmong struggles against the Lao state, U.S. military violence, refugee and diasporic experiences, and institutional inequities—produces their convoluted subjectivities. This complexity is often ignored in favor of centering analyses of power relations on their more easily targetable patriarchal social organization."[41]

The survivors were made more vulnerable through their refugee status. While the state incites violence to displace people and render them refugees, Hmong women's subordinated gendered status and political interpellation in the United States's racial caste system also paradoxically necessitates their rescue by the state.[42] These legal cases expose little about women's decisions to turn to the judiciary as a procurement of their empowerment and sexual agency in the age of liberalism. The refugee status works to bolster their vulnerability as unassimilated subjects who have no recourse to address injustice other than to turn toward the state, which, at its earliest inception, has been the apparatus that has produced and subsequently rescued the refugee subject from displacement and violence. As refugees, they lacked institutional knowledge and access to social services that may have assisted them in obtaining recourse after the crimes. Thus, the women being *Hmong women* and being *refugees* maneuvers a double vulnerability that translates to hypervictimization within law and representation. This gendered construction of the hypervictimization of Hmong women is posited against the hyperviolence of Hmong men, thus two sides of the same coin of hyperheterosexuality.

These two cases of sexual assault have been detailed by legal scholars of the failure of the justice system to address sexual violence even within a cultural relativist context.[43] Since the courts were dealing with "another culture," it became difficult to place Hmong into contexts of liberal justice because the courts wanted to consider Hmong's relevant sexual politics. However, this cultural relativist consideration of sexual violence committed by Hmong only works halfway through. Hmong culture subsequently becomes *the* site of oppression that is understood to have materialized the sexual violence in the first place. The hypocrisy of sexual liberalism at play here is that while the survivors are entitled to rights that are supposedly found in the United States, their rights are questioned through their perpetual status as victims within a hyperheterosexual culture. A cultural relativist approach is a double-edged sword in both cases because it is utilized to prove both the perpetrator's innocence and guilt. Thus, the racialized logics of gender and sexuality are further convoluted because there is no immaculate packaging of Hmong's gender and sexual politics for US law to cohere Hmong's racial difference. Legal cases about sexual violence are crucial to understanding racialization, gendering, and sexualization of minoritized polities and the larger ecosystem of sex. The antagonistic understanding of sexual assault lays bare the tensions that arise between the "legal" and "cultural" dimensions of gender and sexuality among Hmong and the difficulties they bear in relation to disciplinarian action by the state.

SENSATIONALIZING GANG RAPES

Clint Eastwood's 2008 film *Gran Torino* was the first Hollywood film to feature Hmong American actresses and actors and was also notorious for perpetuating stereotypes about Hmong Americans as gang members. Film critics lauded *Gran Torino* as a pathbreaking visibility opportunity for Hmong Americans. Some disagreed and criticized Eastwood's film for playing on racist stereotypes while reinforcing the white savior complex. In the film, actor Bee Vang plays the central character Thao Vang Lor. He represents the effeminate, hyposexual, Asian American male, while the gang members represent the other extreme of Asian American masculinity—hyperviolence. Thao's sister Sue (played by Ahney Her) is sexually assaulted by the gang members, including by her own cousin Spider (played by Doua Moua), in the film's climax, as a way to punish her for speaking out against and standing up to the gang. In a conversation between the anthropologist Louisa Schein and Bee Vang, they discuss the representations of sexuality and sexual violence in *Gran Torino*:

LS: Let's not forget that Asians are not only imaged as hyposexual . . . sometimes they are other kinds of sexually non-normative, especially when it comes to being patriarchal or menacing women.

BV: That's where the gang figures into the *Gran Torino* ensemble; and they even rape their own cousin.

LS: The transgression of the incest taboo being one of the most non-normative acts you can come up with, and a metaphor for all kinds of putative Asian perversity.[44]

Schein and Vang articulate that Asian American men, and specifically Hmong men, are not only racialized as lacking sexuality (hyposexualized); they are also racialized as possessing too much sexuality (hypersexualized). They possess excessive sexual appetites to the point of it being dangerous. Furthermore, Schein and Vang together with Va-Megn Thoj and Ly Chong Thong Jalao argue that the incestuous assault of Sue in *Gran Torino* represents a fashioning of Hmong women's sexual subjecthood. Sue initially appears asexual. However, the scene where Sue encounters several Black "thugs" on the street signals the beginning of her sexualization process. The concluding sexual violence she experiences at the hands of her own kinsmen extends the work of her sexualization, which began with the Black men and ends with Hmong men. As with the gendered and sexualized archetype of the refugee Hmong woman, Sue's gendered and sexual personhood oscillates between only two available binaries: her asexual and hypervictimized subjecthood. Schein, Thoj, Vang, and Jalao state, "This complementarity arguably blackens the Hmong gangbangers, aligning them with their African American seniors in sexual predatorship against women of color."[45] The culmination of Sue's assault at "the hands of men she knows well strips her of her dignity and renders her earlier invincibility a mere chimera."[46] Dominant representations of Black and Latino men in American visual media offer up accessible stereotypes about racialized gender and sexuality that also help to visualize "newcomers" such as Hmong Americans within *Gran Torino*.

Sexual violence is made more insidious and perverse through visual representation that is borne out of epistemologies about the hyperheterosexuality of Hmong culture. *Gran Torino* was not an isolated cultural production. Rather, it draws from selective knowledge about Hmong Americans, particularly of Hmong's alleged hyperheterosexuality filtered through the convergence of gang violence and sexual violence in order to construct a distinctive form of gang sexual violence, which plagued early representations of Hmong masculinity. Gang sexual violence is not imbued with the insidiousness of the "assimilatory" facets of Western education. Instead, gang sexual violence is fundamentally understood as barbaric acts perpetrated by premodern subjects outside the civility of whiteness. Thus, the specter of the "gang member" is racialized differently from the "educated rapist." Nonetheless, both figures are represented as unassimilated subjects, while their survivors' sexual agency is completely voided in order to exacerbate their hypervictimization.

Gang sexual violence in the 1990s was reported much more extensively compared to the kind of sex crimes emblematic of the Her and Lee cases. Starting in the 1990s and persisting into the 2010s, reports of gangs sexually assaulting very young girls endured as an archetype of Hmong and Southeast Asian men. In all the cases that appeared in local and national media, the young ages of the survivors and the gang membership of the perpetrators were emphasized. Like the trope that the historian Lisa Duggan writes about in her study of a nineteenth-century "lesbian lover" murder, in which the words "fiend," "brute," "maniac," and "crank" appeared in news headlines to mark lesbians as dangerous and to reinforce the boundaries of modern citizenship, the trope of the "gang member," "Hmong gang," or "Asian gang" was rampant in the press to produce racialized, gendered, and sexualized effects.[47] The narratives conveyed in most of the gang sexual violence cases followed a one-dimensional script: A very young girl or a few young girls were abducted, tricked, or lured by multiple gang members, were sexually assaulted, and then stayed silent for some time before reporting the crimes to anyone. They were ultimately shamed by their own family members and their native culture at large after divulging their experiences. The state apprehended the gang members; charged, prosecuted, and convicted them; and ultimately sent them to prison. Together, this singular narrative of gang violence with sexual violence rendered sex and sexuality as exceptionally violent, Hmong men and boys as more capable of perpetrating such violence due to their gang membership, and Hmong girls as hypervictims due to the overly stigmatized nature of any form of sex and sexuality within their native culture.

In a notorious case in late 1997, members of a gang sexually assaulted four Hmong girls—aged twelve to fifteen—after luring them to a secluded area through a telephone chat line in the Twin Cities. Two adults and five juveniles were charged and prosecuted in the aftermath.[48] Across the country in Fresno, California, in 1998, a gang sexually assaulted three girls aged twelve to thirteen in a motel room, during part of a fifteen-month period of sexual terror against Hmong girls in the region. The story appeared in the *New York Times*, and a subsequent *Los Angeles Times* article titled "Indictment Charges 23 Hmong with Series of Rapes" reported that a predominantly "Hmong gang" called the Mongolian Boys Society was responsible.[49] Felonies in this case included kidnapping, gang rape, aggravated assault, child molestation, terrorist threats, and false imprisonment.[50] One Associated Press article reported that defense lawyers for the gang members painted the survivors as liars because "it's not acceptable in traditional Hmong culture to have premarital sex."[51] Interestingly, this Fresno case also made headlines in both the Minneapolis *Star Tribune* and the St. Paul *Pioneer Press* in October 1999 because a thirty-one-year-old Minneapolis man was among the twenty-three arrested for the crimes.[52] The *Pioneer Press* article, titled "23 Charged in California Sex Case," quoted a police detective, who stated: "When these investigations are over, we will have incarcerated the major portion of the Mongolian Boys Society. But they are still recruiting, so we don't know when they'll stop."[53] The police detective's statement exaggerates the omnipresence of gangs as a constantly evolving and indefinite threat. Incarceration seems to be ineffective in stopping gang recruitment and membership expansion. Indeed, stereotypes of gang members and the specter of gang violence gain ideological traction through the gang's perceived status as a perpetual menacing force.

In July 1998, the *Star Tribune* reported a gang sexual assault involving Asian Crips gang member Wang Vang, sixteen-year-olds Tou Lia, Chia Vue, and Chia Vang, and two other juveniles aged fourteen and fifteen, who went on a "12-day initiation rampage" in the Twin Cities area, where they assaulted two girls aged twelve and fourteen and were subsequently charged with committing sex crimes for the "benefit of a gang."[54] Under the headline "Authorities Crack Down on Asian Gang Accused of Raping Hmong Girls," another *Star Tribune* article reported that the Asian Crips gang members knew that the survivors would never report the crimes because anything related to sex was heavily stigmatized in Hmong culture.[55] In September 1999, four teenage girls aged fourteen to seventeen went missing in Sheboygan, Wisconsin. They were discovered several weeks later in Detroit, Michigan. It was reported that ten to twenty members of a gang called the Bloods 116 abducted and subsequently sexually assaulted the teenagers. In November 1999, another two girls, aged eleven and thirteen, were kidnapped from St. Paul and transported to Detroit by Asian King Posse gang member Kong Meng Kue. The Associated Press reported that Kue was "an original member of the Asian King Posse" and that his role was "to lure young, female Asian runaways to go with him to Detroit, where they [were] forced into prostitution."[56] Kue later transported the girls to Indiana, where they eventually escaped and were sent back to Minnesota by local authorities.

Reports of gang sexual violence in Hmong communities continued well into the first two decades of the twenty-first century. A sexual assault of a fifteen-year-old girl in 2000 was reported as having been perpetrated at a Roseville, Minnesota, motel by members of an "Asian gang" whose members were from the Oroville Mono Boys and the Hmong Nation Society.[57] The Minnesota Gang Strike Force, a coalition of police officers across the state investigating gang-related criminal activities, noted that the Oroville Mono Boys' "main purposes [were] engaging in gang rape, assault of other gang members and drive-by shootings" and that there were about fifty members in the Twin Cities area.[58] In the Roseville motel sexual assault case, sixteen-year-old Jefferson Yang was first charged with criminal sexual conduct, in addition to possession of a firearm for the benefit of a gang, while four other suspects aged thirteen to seventeen remained at large. In 2009, four teenage boys, only one of whom newspaper articles named, sixteen-year-old Toua Yang, sexually violated a fourteen-year-old girl in St. Paul as part of a gang initiation and again for the benefit of a gang.[59] In 2011, news accounts indicated that nine suspects from the True Blood 22 and Blood Brothers gangs had assaulted a fourteen-year-old girl in St. Paul. The *Pioneer Press* reported: "The gang members had it all planned out. They would invite some girls to a party. They would get them drunk. And then, they would rape them. In November, a 14-year-old became their victim."[60] The most severe sentencing in this 2011 case was handed to twenty-five-year-old member Mang Yang in the form of twenty-five years in prison.[61] In assessing the difficulty of this case along with other similar crimes involving young victims, a St. Paul police gang investigator stated, "A big problem, especially in the Hmong culture, is that girls are afraid to come forward," because "they don't want to bring (perceived) shame on the family, so a lot of times it goes unreported."[62]

Gang sexual violence is branded as one of the most severe and sadistic forms of sexual violence. When a sexual assault occurs "for the benefit of a gang," the sentences are harsher and more unforgiving. In fact, under certain state statues, an enhancement penalty for a crime committed for the benefit of a gang can be imposed, making the sentence from five to ten years longer than if the crime were not labeled as such. The construction of masculinity and violence through a "gang member" is crucial here, as the ethnic studies scholar Lisa Marie Cacho articulates at length: "Gang-related crime is even classified as belonging to a different class and caliber of violence than the very same crimes committed by nongang members. . . . As a result, both how we make sense of gang membership and how we make gang violence make sense have consequences that extend far beyond actual gang members and their territories."[63] Gang membership and violence supersede the gang members themselves into something larger by amplifying dominant racialized, gendered, and sexualized narratives about who is a "gang member." The fact that these crimes all took place in metropolitan areas also reinforced dominant conceptions of racialized urban spaces linking space, race, gender, and crime. For claims of racialized sexual violence to perform their ideological work, Hmong men who commit sexual violence must be cohered and conflated as "gang members" in order for the violence to be processed cognitively within the larger racialized social field of knowledge.

In fact, various conflations are occurring all at once and reflect what Cacho has called a "de facto status crime."[64] A de facto status crime captures how racialized bodies and statuses, such as Mexican migrants labeled as "illegal aliens," Arabs as "terrorists," or Southeast Asian Americans as "gang members," constitute their identity categories "as not only illegal but also innate, inherent, and inherited."[65] Thus, a "gang member" is very much defined through the conduct of violence as much as through an assigned group status or embodiment. Labeling a sexual assault as a "gang rape" renders the crime more monstrous precisely because any crime committed by a "gang member" is deemed more criminal than the very same crime committed by others without the label. It is not a surprise, then, when Black, Latinx, Asian, Arab, and Indigenous men and boys participate in gang activity given that they embody a de facto status crime on the basis of their identity category, rendering their gang activity as primordial rather than rational.[66] "Hmong" is easily conflated with "gang member" to render the sexual violence committed by gang members as racial and thus necessitates their surveillance, incarceration, and elimination. How gang violence makes sense in the dominant imagination reveals that it is also a form of racializing sexual violence—hence, the hyperheterosexuality of sexual violence.

The sensationalism of gang sexual violence is a recurring theme in US media culture. Sensationalism of sexual violence operates as an "archive of violence" in that its hypervisibility works to expose corruption, abuse, and scandal, but also to exploit suffering in the service of capitalism.[67] The social and political power of sensationalism enables the visibility of certain forms of violence while hiding others by discursively constructing and upholding raced, classed, gendered, and sexualized ideals of normative citizenship. While sensationalism is certainly not unique to the media narratives about Hmong gang sexual violence in the contemporary era of sexual harassment and assault scandals in media, educational, and sports industries, its function as a cultural, theoretical, and political strategy reinforces discernments of Hmong's supposed cultural pathology when conjoined with existing epistemic archives about sexual violence. In the gang sexual violence cases, the news media clearly documented the very young ages of the survivors in order to render them as hypervictims. The article titles included words like *girl* or *teen* to sensationalize headlines, such as "Adult, 4 Teens Suspected of Raping Girls as Gang Initiation," "Alleged Gang Leader Gets

11-Year Sentence in Girls' Rapes," and "Man Gets 25 Years in Rape of Girl Who Trusted Him—Sentence Is the Most Severe So Far in Case."

The construction of a violent and hypersexualized gang member must also exist at the expense of a hypervictim. Children, girls, teenagers, and women make excellent victims in which representations about violence can elicit strong affective responses. In the articles, the survivors mainly were twelve-year-old girls, one girl was thirteen, and another girl was a fifteen-year-old. In the case of the missing girls from Sheboygan, their ages and gender, along with racialized ideas about the perpetrators' de facto status crime of being "gang members," were clearly explicated to magnify their victimized status. As one article about the Sheboygan girls narrates, "The four girls tell frightening stories about being held against their will by members of a gang called Bloods 116 who assaulted them while threatening them with guns and a leather strap."[68] Sensationalism accentuates the violence of sex crimes as much as it produces a palatable victimized subjecthood. In these cases of gang sexual violence, Hmong girls are afforded a hypervictimized status distinct from other girls of color—most notably Black and Indigenous girls—whose victimhoods are not legitimized (and are in fact denied) by the law or media. The specificity of Hmong girls' victimization is intimately attached to Hmong's positioning as hyperheterosexual subjects unwilling to bestow on women and girls the freedom of sexuality or sexual agency. Whereas claiming victimhood continues to be nearly impossible for Black girls even as they encounter interpersonal and police violence or for Indigenous girls who are missing or murdered and rendered invisible, for Hmong girls' victimhood is hypervisible through a racial frame that coalesces meanings about race, gender, and culture idiosyncratic to Hmong's racial, gender, and sexual formations under the rubric of hyperheterosexuality.

When King Buachee Lee and New Chue Her committed their crimes, the media portrayed them as educated Hmong men who tricked and assaulted recently resettled refugee Hmong women. In an article in the *Star Tribune* the prosecutors in the Lee case claimed, "The survivors have faced extreme disgrace in the Hmong community as poor, uneducated women pitted against an elite, financially successful college-trained man."[69] The survivors' "disgrace in the Hmong community" is heightened in order to ideologically highlight the stigma around sex among Hmong. This sense of "shame" that survivors experienced was also present in the discourse and reporting of gang sexual violence. In the chat-line sexual assault cases, a *Pioneer Press* article quoted assistant Ramsey County attorney Chris Wilton as saying, "A lot of these young girls who get raped are not sure if they should come forward because of the stigma that surrounds a raped Hmong woman. No longer are they 'pure' in the sense that they're a virgin, which in some parts of the Hmong community is very important. We have some young girls thinking, 'What if I come forward? I may not get married.'"[70] Hmong culture is conflated with gang sexual violence to crystallize the notion of a minoritized culture as violent. At its core, the representation of sexual violence among people of color and minoritized communities exposes the contradiction of the state of sexual violence in American culture. While sexual violence is condoned or ignored when committed by all kinds of people in US society, including police officers, politicians, university administrators, religious leaders, and college athletes, this form of violence is not racialized in the ways we understand the very same crimes committed by people of color. Branding certain communities' crimes as "cultural" and thus as *essential* justifies racist refugee and immigration policies, surveillance, police brutality, incarceration, and ideological violence levied against them. In contrast, sexual violence committed by whites in carceral, educational, religious, or sporting institutions receives the benefit of being seen as exceptional and individual.

The conglomeration of meanings about race, gender, sexuality, and minoritized cultures of violence perhaps is encapsulated best in one more notorious example of sexual violence among Hmong Americans. In 2005, an infamous four-part exposé about sexual violence among the Twin Cities Hmong community was published in the *Star Tribune* under the title "Shamed into Silence."[71] Part 1 chronicled the story of an unnamed girl who was sexually assaulted by a gang when she was twelve years old. Members of the Asian Crips gang transported her to Battle Creek Park in St. Paul and later to a park in the city of Cottage Grove, Minnesota, where they threatened her with a gun and assaulted her as a form of initiation into their gang. She was assaulted again at a motel a few days later. When she returned home, a relative noticed her limping and assumed she had engaged in sex. The relative proceeded to shame her by calling her a slut. Eventually, ten people were arrested and charged in her case. The authors of the article wrote, "Secrecy and shame keep survivors from coming forward, and authorities believe there are many more crimes undetected. So police search for possible survivors."[72]

Part 2 of "Shamed into Silence" described the story of a ninety-six-pound, twelve-year-old sixth grader named "Ka" (pseudonym), who was drugged, pimped, and assaulted by various gang members, including a man as old as thirty-five years. The article stated that along with the fear that reporting the assault would lead the perpetrators to harm her again, Ka was "worried that her family might demand that she marry one of her attackers, a traditional Hmong resolution."[73] Part 3 recounted the story of a white American woman, Lynnette Hedlom, who spotted a twelve-year-old Hmong girl in her driveway. The girl had run away from home and subsequently encountered a gang, who assaulted her. Hedlom wanted to call the police, but the girl objected, fearing the shame and humiliation it would bring her. Yet Hedlom called the police anyway. In explaining why the survivor objected to Hedlom calling the police, the article stated: "Hmong have a highly patriarchal society. Girls who lose their virginity outside of marriage are devalued; the community scorns them and their families unless the girl marries the rapist. By contrast, some families and clans will rally to protect the males accused of rape or paying for child prostitutes."[74] The series goes to some length in part 4 to use the "culture clash" model as an explanatory framework for why girls run away, how gangs are formed, and why survivors of sexual violence experience shame in their native culture. It quoted many Hmong cultural experts about sexual attitudes and norms to confirm the validity of the culture clash model. For example, Der Her, a volunteer coordinator with Ramsey County's Sexual Offense Services, was quoted, stating, "The [Hmong] culture also shames females for having sex before marriage—even if they're raped. Their male counterparts aren't shamed."[75]

The characterizations of the girls doubly victimized by gang members and then subsequently their own culture greatly affected *Star Tribune* readers. One response published in the newspaper's Letter of the Day section demonstrates these ideological effects on readers:

> By and large, American Catholic families and farm families do not arrange a forced marriage after a girl is raped. Nor do they call girls sluts or say they deserved being raped. In this country, the idea that a woman or girl deserves being raped went by the wayside a very long time ago. For crimes such as these to become so widespread, a certain environment needs to be created. The survivors interviewed for this article made reference time and again to the shame and blame that they would be subjected to by their families after their brutal rape. They mentioned family members attempting to force a marriage after a rape to save family honor. These are cultural factors that have helped create the current problem. As the only elected Hmong senator, [Mee] Moua should be leading discussions in the Hmong community to change these undesirable aspects present in the Hmong culture. The

problem needs to be acknowledged before it can be solved. If the rest of the Hmong community is as unwilling to look at these cultural realities as Mee Moua, this is a problem that will persist to the detriment of Hmong girls.[76]

The reader's response offers a glimpse into the mentality of the general readership to reveal beliefs about the supposed gender and sexual pathologies among Hmong. The reader draws from an existing archive of racialized meanings about Hmong—in contrast to "American Catholic families" and "farm families"—as sexually backward and as detached from the national body politic. White bourgeoisie understanding of sexuality among people of color suggests that "cultural factors" are the main elements to explain sexual violence. In turn, the reader posits this phenomenon as a "Hmong problem" only to be resolved by Hmong community members and elected officials. Furthermore, the reader does not suggest that she herself, non-Hmong individuals, or larger restorative justice or social service institutions participate in addressing this phenomenon. In fact, dominant media and larger institutions of power, including judicial systems, in US society lack the compulsion to support survivors in general even as sexual liberalism purports women to have sexual and legal rights.[77] The reader's accusation that the Hmong community is "unwilling to look at these cultural realities" reveals how sexual violence is compartmentalized as a Hmong "cultural reality" rather than a social problem rooted in multiple micro and macro systems of oppression and structures of power. The conflation of culture and race completes the ideological work of hiding relations of power that enable the proliferation of sexual violence in the broader US society while maintaining racial domination through the stereotyping and incarceration of people of color.

Nowhere in the four-part "Shamed into Silence" exposé do reporters mention whether the survivors received justice. The perpetrators were charged and sentenced to long prison terms, while the survivors perpetually lived in shame. The focus on the carceral sentences of the perpetrators sensationalizes punishment rather than gesture toward justice for survivors. In fact, Hmong girls' victimization is exacerbated by their status as "runaways." The "Shamed into Silence" series posits Hmong girls as runaways in order to explicate the violence they experience. In part 4, it states: "In traditional Hmong households, girls stay home, care for siblings, cook and clean. But in the United States, these girls sometimes rebel. They yearn to do what their American friends do, they say—go to the mall, go to the movies. Many girls run away."[78] In a racist article titled "The Violence of Hmong Gangs and the Crime of Rape," published in the *FBI*

Law Enforcement Bulletin, "Asian gang expert" Richard Straka, a St. Paul police sergeant, espoused that some runaway girls may end up staying with the gang. Cacho, in her analysis of the article, argues that Straka's portrayal of Hmong girls as runaways ironically perpetuates further symbolic and ideological violence by rendering survivors themselves as deviants.[79]

Indeed, Straka reinforced the hyperheterosexuality of Hmong culture by denouncing the violence of gangs who forced girls into prostitution, only in turn to denigrate the survivors as prostitutes. When the de facto status crime of "prostitute" is applied to girls who are kidnapped or who join gangs, then their victimhood is removed to rationalize their own sexual subjugation. Straka privileges comments from readers who blamed Hmong women and girls for their own victimization, with one reading: "The girls themselves were gang members, too, a lot of people disagree with the girls for charging the boys with raping them. We, as parents, would want to put them both into jail. Not everyone believed the girls."[80] While it is the case that survivors are rendered asexual victims of their culture in most of the reporting of gang sexual violence, they can also be constructed as the opposite: unsympathetic players (runaways or prostitutes) complicit in their own victimization. The culture framework enables the survivors in many gang sexual violence cases to claim victimhood when the law and media seeks to blame Hmong cultural and racial difference for social pathologies, but the frame of gang membership can flip the script to preclude Hmong girls from claiming victimhood on the basis of assumptions about their own sexual deviancy.

The namelessness and facelessness of the survivors means they are forever invisible because they continue to be relegated to the background of this sensationalism. Their suffering is heightened, but their humanity and lives are never revealed. In a sense, their facelessness enables their hypervictimized and deviant runaway status to be used as a stand-in for their marginalization. The education scholar Bic Ngo writes that the "Shamed into Silence" series highlights the culture clash model of immigrant identities by emphasizing the intergenerational conflicts between Hmong children and their parents.[81] The culture clash framework within the series also makes visible the fact that, besides cultural difference, no alternative explanation is given for why girls might become runaways. The "Shamed into Silence" series ironically silences and expunges the humanity of the survivors by fabricating Hmong girls as unwilling victims of gang sexual violence, problematic runaways who are to be blamed for putting themselves in harm's way, and, most importantly, asexual victims of their native culture.

The discourse analysis that I have presented exists in tension with the very real instances of sexual violence perpetrated by Hmong Americans. Survivors are the ones who are ultimately harmed through the material and ideological violence that they experienced throughout these entire ordeals. Sexual violence across various communities in the United States is surely a pervasive problem, as are the ways we understand and make sense of that same violence. In both the Her and Lee cases and the gang sexual assault cases, survivors were harmed by men and boys who were inculcated within heteropatriarchal masculine norms that perceive women as objects to be violated. Yet these same survivors were doubly harmed through the discourse of hyperheterosexuality, which anchors their gendered and sexual victimhood in Hmong's cultural differences and excessiveness divorced from larger power structures that enable and condone gender-based violence across various interpersonal, legal, social, institutional, and political contexts. That is, the discourse of hyperheterosexuality as an ideological structure forces a compulsive understanding of sex, sexuality, sex crimes, sexual behavior, and sexual violence among Hmong as rooted in their own cultural pathology. The multiple material, ideological, and discursive violence at the intersections of Hmong's racialization, gendering, and sexualization ultimately exists at the expense of survivors. In so doing, my critique of the culture concept as a limited framework that aids and abets the discourse of hyperheterosexuality also reveals that justice is ultimately not achievable for survivors through such frameworks.

The anomaly of Hmong's racialized status lies in the instability and impossibility of legal interpretations of sex and sexual violence and its entwinement with the concept of culture. These representations are powerful and everlasting and shape the very ways Hmong imagine themselves and how others imagine Hmong as premodern subjects that are troubling for sexual liberalism and feminist articulations of sexual justice. In this way, the ideology of hyperheterosexuality produced through institutions of power can implicitly and explicitly compel and demand that minoritized subjects acquiesce to its controlling power. Hyperheterosexuality positions gender and sexuality as the nexus of Hmong racial formation and produces dominant knowledge about Hmong that extends the controlling images of Asian American gendering and sexualization through and beyond Asian American women's hypersexuality and men's hyposexuality. Hyperheterosexuality at large remains a fictitious discourse, but one that carries with it serious material and ideological consequences for people of color and minoritized polities. It remains a system of knowledge that allows for hegemonic ideologies about who is and is not a criminal or a citizen and what is or is not an aberrant sexuality. This epistemological system of racialized gender and sexuality bourgeons within multiple dimensions, across various social fields, to complicate minoritized and racialized sexuality in the United States. Thus, these images continue to proliferate into the contemporary moment as evidenced by *State v. New Chue Her*, *State v. King Buachee Lee*, and the gang sexual assault cases and help to modify and codify knowledge about Hmong as hyperheterosexual subjects that transfigures other historical and contemporary Asian American racial, gendered, and sexual formations.

CHAPTER 2

Legislating Conjugalities

THE MARRIAGE BILLS IN MINNESOTA

Hmong Americans in the late 1980s and early 1990s were encountering numerous obstacles to belonging and social citizenship in the United States. Most notable were impediments pertaining to the benefits of legal marriage. Many Hmong American couples were wrongfully filing joint tax returns as non-legally married couples, and they could not access benefits such as health insurance and Medicaid, veterans' services, child support, joint parental rights, inheritances, asset division, hospital visitation rights, marital and family leaves, survivor payments, and pensions, since these benefits are intimately attached to legal marriage. In short, couples who were in respectable, monogamous, heterosexual, and long-term unions were excluded from the material rewards of heteronormative legal marriage more broadly, even though they themselves and those around them genuinely believed them to be "married." In the state of Minnesota, traditional Hmong marriages are not legally recognized because Minnesota does not recognize common-law marriages.[1] In other words, traditional Hmong marriages are not legally binding in Minnesota despite the wider Hmong community recognizing the unions as socially and communally binding. The conundrum of legal recognition is further muddied by Hmong's practices of non-legally recognized kinship formations that are deemed hyperheterosexual, such as plural marriages or so-called underage marriages. Hmong's status as racial outsiders whose "cultural" practices of marriage are incompatible with legal marriage structures in the United States renders Hmong a political dilemma for state-based liberal formations of gender, sexuality, marriage, and equality.[2] Furthermore, Hmong Americans' desire for state recognition of their traditional marriages and wedding ceremonies endangers them to the voyeurism of the state by exposing the vulnerabilities of their intracommunal politics and subjecting them to state racism that is conjured through the frame of hyperheterosexuality. Ironically, Hmong practices of kinship also expose the hypocrisies of liberalism and of recognition itself by calling into question the state's unwillingness and failure to fulfill its promises of racial equality for minoritized populations.

I analyze a series of bills that were introduced in Minnesota by both non-Hmong and Hmong American politicians from 1991 to 2006, known collectively and colloquially as the "Hmong marriage bills" or simply "marriage bills," to show how the discourse of hyperheterosexuality shores up in a different arena of law, namely, the legislature.[3] The bills sought the legal recognition of Hmong's traditional marriages and the legalization of their wedding processes in order for Hmong to avoid having to conduct a civil ceremony at a court to solidify the legal status of their marriage. In seeking this legal recognition, supporters of the marriage bills envisioned that the state would bestow belonging and social citizenship on Hmong through the legalization of their traditional marriages so that they could ultimately access the material rewards ascribed to monogamous legal marriage in the United States.

Marriage presents a fruitful domain in which to examine how those who are ostensibly incompatible with modern configurations of what the state deems to be "acceptable" or "unacceptable" for inclusion, recognition, and belonging may confront the contradictions of their political status as minoritized populations in the United States. Additionally, marriage is about access to rights as much as the exclusion of rights based on normative metrics of being and embodiment. Marriage is a system of recognizing the normativity of the citizenry and an allocation of social citizenship in the form of material rewards based on that recognized normativity. In the context of Hmong's involvement in the United States' secret war in Laos and their subsequent resettlement in the United States as political refugees, Ma Vang has argued that the state's bestowing of legal citizenship on Hmong refugees represents a neoimperial relationship whereby the state simultaneously affirms and disavows Hmong's presence. This selective relationship between Hmong refugees and the state through a politics of recognition reproduces an unequal relationship between Hmong and the US government. Bestowing legal citizenship on Hmong refugees for their "sacrifices" in the secret war constitutes a "reward" rather than an ethical obligation of repayment.[4] Hmong's desire to access the rewards of marriage can be situated in their continuing quest for state recognition of their histories, Indigenous soldiering for the state, and unique cultural differences in a multicultural United States, all stemming from their participation in the secret war in Laos. Yet Hmong's quest for state recognition of their traditional marriages engenders racist perceptions about their kinship practices that trouble the politics of recognition and question the feasibility of inclusion itself.

Even though legal marriage has been historically promoted and fostered as a citizenship-making process since colonial times, legal marriage is not always entirely liberating, as would become evident to Hmong Americans throughout the saga of the marriage bills. Marriage is a way for states to exert governmentality, particularly for people of color. Black marriages in the immediate post-emancipation era are one example demonstrating the perils of legal marriage. The historian Tera W. Hunter notes that particular legislation such as the Civil Rights Act of 1866 was implemented to bestow Black individuals with the power to contract marriages, but the act also mandated their subjection to heteronormative patriarchy found within normalized heterosexuality by provisioning that Black men, as newly established heads of households, engage their families to work as "free laborers" in the post-emancipation economy, which would ultimately benefit their white former slave owners.[5] Black intimacies during the pre-emancipation era were considered too messy, informal, and largely "unknown."[6] Whites feared that newly freed Black individuals who were granted the personhood of contracting civil unions but who did not "stabilize" their conjugal relationships might jeopardize the operations of local economies, as the patriarchal nuclear family became the paramount social unit in which labor was organized and divided. Thus, the rationale goes, allowing Black people to contract their marriages and instructing them on proper gender and sexual proprieties would alleviate the disruption of the economy as these individuals transitioned from slaves to free persons. Additionally, the feminist scholar Amy L. Brandzel argues that "while marriage rights offered an opportunity for African Americans to claim humanity and some sense of belonging and respect within U.S. structures, immersion into heterosexual marriage norms of citizenship allowed for another avenue through which white supremacy could police African American behaviors."[7]

On a grander scale, marriage is understood as central to the vitality of the nation itself. Marriage is considered so sacred that initiatives such as marriage-counseling services have been established within the past century to rescue deteriorating marriages in what the historian Rebecca L. Davis calls the "search for marital bliss."[8] Many marriage proponents argue that successful marriages among responsible and respectable adults can "anchor individuals to social values and enable them to set down roots in their communities."[9] Thus, marriage—particularly marriage among free persons—is carefully crafted and maintained through legal structures, indoctrination of gender and sexual norms, and initiatives to save failing marriages in order to foster the economy, prop up communities, and preserve a homogenous nation through the maintenance of capitalist social values. Bestowing formerly disenfranchised Black individuals with the "freedom" and legal power to contract marriages also meant interpolating them into the heteronormative capitalist nation. That is, the policing of minority sexual behaviors and conjugalities extends the white heteronormative colonial power that has dehumanized minoritarian subjects in the intimate sphere within the past two centuries.

Legal recognition of minoritized kinship structures as "marriage" invites state involvement in minority intimate relations. Racial and gendered violence shores up when belonging and social citizenship is framed in the form of legal, state-sanctioned marriages, even for heterosexual monogamous couples. In essence, inclusion through the legalization of marriage for some is inevitably an exclusion for others. While feminist and queer studies scholars have critiqued, expanded, and transformed marriage over the past half century, one thing has persisted: a sustained investment in marriage as a process of assimilation, belonging, and citizenship. For Hmong, hyperheterosexuality constructs them as racial outsiders vis-à-vis legal marriage, even as the state claims to want to recognize them as a unique cultural group in a liberal multiculturalist United States.

Through close analysis of the bills proposed in the 1990s and the first decade of the twenty-first century in the Minnesota legislature, committee hearings and testimonies, news articles, opinion pieces written by keys players, and interviews with the key players themselves throughout the saga of the marriage bills, I demonstrate the competing manifestations of culture and its implications on Hmong American racial, gendered, and sexual belonging. Specifically, the tropes of polygamy and underage marriages haunt Hmong Americans' belonging by juxtaposing their heterosexual kinship practices against heteronormative legal marriages. The culture concept and its attendant practices of marriage are constructed as inherently incompatible with heteronormative legal marriage in the United States, and thus the lack of a modern sexual legal personhood comes to stand in for Hmong American racialization. Hmong Americans' intracommunal politics further endangers their claims to belonging and social citizenship by exposing the conflicting gendered and sexual dynamics of culture and its precarious position within law. In the case of the marriage bills, key players, including

Hmong American legislators, non-Hmong legislators, and community members, articulated culture in contradictory ways that complicated Hmong Americans' understanding of gender, sexuality, and marriage. On the one hand, non-Hmong legislators and some Hmong Americans themselves understood Hmong practices of polygamy and so-called underage marriages as regressive and exploitative. On the other hand, Hmong Americans sought to defend their culture from the accusations of gender and sexual exploitation by illuminating the racism and fallacy of hyperheterosexuality. The dominant understandings of hyperhetero-sexual kinship formations nonetheless rendered Hmong as culturally different to reveal the state's fundamental inability to include racially minoritized polities deemed too transgressive in state-based belonging. Ultimately, the contestation over Hmong's supposed backward practices of kinship led to the demise of the bills both in the 1990s and in 2003–2006.[10]

THE MARRIAGE BILLS IN THE 1990S

Sometime in late 1990, community leaders held a meeting at the Wilder Community Center in St. Paul, Minnesota, with Representative Andrew J. Dawkins to initiate a bill that would allow Hmong Americans to conduct traditional marriages but would also subsequently render the traditional marriages as legal "in their own way."[11] Dawkins then introduced House File (H.F.) 91 in 1991 in the seventy-seventh Minnesota legislative session on behalf of his Hmong American constituents.[12] H.F. 91 would have imparted on traditional Hmong marriage practitioners the power to sign marriage certificates for Hmong couples at their traditional wedding in order to "legalize" the traditional marriages. At its core, H.F. 91 was intended to demonstrate that the law and Hmong culture could coexist.[13] This coexistence between the state and minoritized populations is crucial for the management of these same populations in contemporary US society. In the post–civil rights movement era in the second half of the twentieth century, in what Howard Winant has called a "rupture" or "break" in the explicitly white supremacist global racial order, the state needed to radically shift from an overtly racist legal agenda to a "non-racist" one in order to announce itself as progressive. That is, the United States recognized that "racial equality" must be a national and long-term goal if it was to be legitimated as a powerful nation in the eyes of the rest of the world. The state must affirm itself as flexible and open to all sorts of possibilities regarding minoritarian subjects and cultures.[14] This post–World War II "break" ushered in new phases of racial liberalism, which entailed bestowing rights on minoritized populations in the hopes of preventing further social unrest stemming from state racism and cementing the state's reputation as inclusive and democratic.[15]

State recognition and inclusion converges with Michel Foucault's theorizations of power as a set of social relations in which the state and other hegemonic social structures concomitantly invest in social difference rather than quelling it.[16] This form of state power is no longer just exclusion, as seen in legalized racial discrimination, immigration exclusion, and segregation throughout the first half of the twentieth century. Instead, state power in the postwar and post–civil rights movement era is characterized as a racially liberal form in which the state sought to distribute rights to previously disenfranchised peoples through legislation such as the Civil Rights Act of 1964, the Voting Rights Act of 1965, and the Immigration and Nationality Act of 1965 and through landmark Supreme Court cases such as *Brown v. Board of Education* in 1954 and *Loving v. Virginia* in 1967.[17] In affirming Hmong's unique "cultural differences" in their practices of marriage, the state is enacting a form of productive power that seemingly avows Hmong personhood but also questions it. The state's willingness to entertain the legal recognition of Hmong's "cultural differences" appears as state benevolence toward racial difference.

In the context of equal rights and the coexistence of state and minority cultural differences, Dawkins cited Quakers, Baha'i, Buddhists, Hindus, and Muslims as groups whose right of solemnizing and legalizing their own traditional or religious marriages Hmong Americans could replicate.[18] Because these religious groups are already afforded this right, Dawkins wanted to ensure that the law could also demonstrate flexibility, parity, and equality for another minoritized group such as Hmong.[19] In turn, the state would also crystallize its status as a truly liberal multicultural entity that is tolerant and equal toward its diverse polities. Dawkins later stated in an interview that passing the marriage bills would have "expressed our diversity and our willingness to accept all sorts of cultures, ways, and traditions, and especially something as solemn as a marriage ceremony."[20] The state's liberal multiculturalist politics is even more suggestive in the case of Hmong Americans and marriage, as marriage is considered to be the most consecrated human formation in the eyes of the state. Both Hmong Americans and the state had something to gain by engaging each other in this legitimization dance, despite a complicated mesh of power dynamics that would soon come to jeopardize this inclusionary project.

Without the marriage bills, Hmong Americans who wished to have the state legally recognize their marriage would have to undergo two separate ceremonies that would formalize their marriage: a traditional wedding at their home and a civil ceremony at a court. Traditional Hmong wedding processes usually entail that the two marrying individuals perform an extensive and complex premarriage negotiation and wedding ceremony, including a formal request from the groom's family to the bride's family; negotiation of a dowry, popularly known as the "bride price"; determination of the costs of the wedding ceremony itself; and several religious rituals to welcome the bride into the groom's household. However, they must then shoulder the extra measure of signing a marriage license and legalizing their marriage in a civil ceremony at a later date in front of a state-certified officiator, requiring additional time, money, and inconvenience.[21] For Hmong Americans, both processes are seen as valid ways to initiate and commence a marriage, whereas only the civil ceremony is legally binding in the eyes of the state. H.F. 91 would have addressed this issue to bridge this "cultural clash" by demonstrating that Hmong culture could come "into the fold of Minnesota law" by "legalizing" traditional Hmong marriages.[22]

H.F. 91 mandated that "two Hmong elders" acting as two Mej Koob could solemnize a marriage. A Mej Koob is typically a male elder who volunteers to negotiate a marriage between the bride's and the groom's families. There can be one or two Mej Koob from each side of the families. The Mej Koob resolves the predicaments of how the bride will leave her family for marriage into the groom's family and settles disputes pertaining to clan rivalries or past resentments between the two conjoining families and their extended families. Furthermore, the Mej Koob discusses the terms of the dowry that the groom's family may provide to the bride's family to ensure that the bride will be treated with respect and love once the marriage commences. The Mej Koob subsequently determines the terms of the wedding ceremony itself, from the purchase of the pig for the wedding feast to the selection of songs and poetry to be sung during wedding rituals and how long the wedding ceremony itself will last. For a marriage to be legally recognized, H.F. 91 required that a marriage license be filed with the county with the signatures of the two Mej Koob, the couple, and two witnesses aged sixteen years or older who were present during the traditional Hmong wedding. Ultimately, the two Mej Koob designated as the legal "solemnizers" could sign the marriage license and deliver it to the district court.

Dawkins galvanized support for H.F. 91 among other legislators. One was Senator Linda Berglin, who introduced a companion bill, Senate File (S.F.) 107, which eventually received a hearing by the Judiciary Committee on February 6,

1991. During the committee hearing, it was clear that an underlying function of this bill was to facilitate the assimilation of Hmong Americans into a legal conjugal status, extending from the fact that social service workers had discovered girls who were being "forced" into so-called underage marriages within Hmong American communities. James Coben, a law professor at Hamline University who had helped Hmong Americans understand the marriage bills, testified at the Judiciary Committee hearing, stating, "The idea is, by giving authority to the traditional leaders in the community to solemnize, that carries with it also, the obligation to solemnize appropriately. And actually, it does provide . . . criminal penalties if you do choose to solemnize a marriage that is inappropriate. . . . I think there's a genuine interest on the part of the [Hmong] leadership to make sure that they assimilate as best as they can into Minnesota culture and at the same time retain what is best of their own culture. I think that's a very admirable goal."[23] Coben's statement underscores the need to bestow on Hmong Americans the "gift" of legal marriage in exchange for legal compliance, even as his testimony seemingly highlights the "admirable goal" of cultural balance.[24]

Hmong Americans were not immediately privy to the surveillance and assimilatory underpinnings embedded in the bill because they were mostly focused on the benefits of the bill and not on the criminal consequences of it. What began as a process of legally recognizing and honoring Hmong's cultural differences suddenly appeared in the Judiciary Committee hearing for the first time to have potential criminal consequences. Coben's testimony revealed that the bills were not solely about expanding the purview of marriage to embrace an assortment of marriage practices among Minnesota's diverse populations. Indeed, it was also about transmuting traditional Hmong marriages to align with existing legal norms. Taken together, Coben's authority as a law professor and his nomenclature designating "inappropriate" Hmong kinship practices as "culture" established both the legal and ideological tone for painting Hmong as a racialized group whose "cultural" practices of marriage and kinship were troubling for state recognition of racial difference. Coben's statement demonstrated that legal inclusion of Hmong's traditional marriages simultaneously presented the possibility of both recognition and criminalization.

Testimonies from the Judiciary Committee hearing also revealed that disagreements existed among Hmong Americans themselves on the meanings of marriage and the legal ramifications of the bills. The question of whether legally sanctioning traditional Hmong marriages — and by extension Hmong culture — may also inadvertently sanction underage marriages and whether endowing the Mej Koob to legally solemnize only those "appropriate" traditional Hmong marriages in compliance with Minnesota law could mitigate gender and sexual oppression became prominent points of contention in the committee hearing. Choua Lee, executive director of the Lao and Hmong Women's Association and a proponent of the marriage bills, testified at the hearing: "Even in this country, practices [such as bride kidnapping and underage marriages] still exist because we don't have any law to follow. So, a lot of people just do what they feel is right because they have been practicing in the past, so they feel that it's right for them to practice what is right for them, that marriage arrangement. And I like to encourage and also to support that, as Hmong women, that we don't have enough say in the Hmong marriages. With this, making this legalized, perhaps this will eliminate some of the problems for the Hmong women."[25] For individuals such as Lee, the bills represented one technique to eradicate "problems for the Hmong women," such as alleged bride kidnappings and young girls entering into marriages. Lee's comment demonstrated how the mode of entering into a marriage (by being kidnapped) and the age of the party (underage girls) do not align with the consenting nature and legal age requirements of legal marriage in dominant US society. In short, Lee understood the bills as providing Hmong Americans a "law to follow" to ensure that Hmong women "have enough say in the Hmong marriages" so that they can have a sense of recourse when they find themselves in these "inappropriate" marriage arrangements.

However, some unnamed Hmong American individual women and women's groups lobbied politicians, including Dawkins's colleague Representative Kathleen Vellenga, to oppose the bills. Contrary to Lee's interpretation of the bills, the unnamed Hmong American women and women's groups argued that the bills would lead to the *increase* of underage marriages within their communities. Vellenga urged Dawkins to withdraw the bills because they were too controversial and were causing internal strife among Hmong Americans themselves, many of whom were Vellenga's constituents. In essence, non-Hmong politicians such as Dawkins and Vellenga carefully negotiated the terrain of Hmong American intracommunal differences by presenting a neutral stance on the bills in order not to fracture their constituencies.[26] Ultimately, both H.F. 91 and S.F. 107 failed to pass in the Minnesota legislature due to the unresolved problems raised during the Judiciary Committee hearing.[27] Dawkins directly stated, "It was the community that killed the bills."[28] His poignant observation demonstrated the shambolic collusions of both state and Hmong American intracommunal politics in meditating gender and sexual relations among minoritized subjects in the United States. Questions over minority culture and its status in the United States, particularly the status of Hmong Americans' supposed exploitative hyper-heterosexual kinship practices, haunt attempts to assimilate Hmong Americans into the modern state through legal recognition and their quest for belonging.

REVIVING THE MARRIAGE BILLS IN THE NEW MILLENNIUM

The marriage bills were reanimated in the Minnesota legislature in the new millennium and played out from 2003 to 2006. At about the same time, Mee Moua was elected to the Minnesota Senate in 2002, becoming the first Hmong American state senator in US history. Dawkins approached Moua in January 2002 and suggested she reintroduce the marriage bills because doing so was important to Hmong Americans. Moua's election signaled a historical moment where Hmong Americans could more forcefully lay claim to belonging and social citizenship by joining the system. By the early years of the new millennium, the demographics of Moua's district on the east side of St. Paul (District 67) consisted overwhelmingly of working-class immigrants and refugees, the majority of whom were Democratic-leaning Hmong Americans. Hmong American mutual assistance associations also became prominent entities during this period. Hmong American Partnership, the largest Hmong American social service organization in the United States, flourished after its relocation to St. Paul's east side, in District 67, in 2001.[29] The organization's financial growth and its focus on facilitating refugee naturalization processes through citizenship training, civic engagement, and voter registration coincided with Hmong Americans' rapid political rise to demand full belonging and social citizenship through propping up their own political candidates. The sociologist Yang Lor has convincingly demonstrated that the large Hmong American population enabled the development of an empowered racialized group consciousness, which propelled Moua to victory.[30] Thus, Hmong Americans' geographic and demographic strength and their subsequent political momentum in the early years of the new millennium provided a crucial opportunity for them to revive the marriage bills.

Moua accepted Dawkins's proposal to reignite the bills in part because it was "really important for [her]," as a Hmong American, "to help shape the narrative" of the marriage bills.[31] The demands of Hmong Americans to revive the bills corresponded with this political moment in Hmong American history to reshape the bills in their favor in an antiracist and culturally relevant fashion. To achieve this antiracist version of the bills, Moua framed her position as a civil rights attorney who understood the state as needing to fulfill its obligations of equal protection under the law for all citizens.[32] Moua explained, "I looked at [the marriage bills] from a lens of civil rights and equal access and equal protection, for a protected class of people or for a minority community."[33] The legal scholar Patricia J. Williams states that "rights rhetoric has been and continues to be an effective form of discourse" for marginalized and minoritized subjects, namely because it affords them at least some sliver of agency to enact social change in destabilizing racism.[34] Moua's move toward a rights rhetoric also meant ensuring that the bills did not criminalize traditional Hmong practices of kinship. Considering the law's treatment of Hmong Americans as hyperheterosexual criminal subjects, Moua rightfully sought to intervene in the racializing and criminalizing processes that the bills would propagate. She stated, "I looked at the criminal implications of the language of the bills very closely. And I was trying to write the language so that it did not trigger a criminal penalty for the people in my community."[35] Moua comprehended the marriage bills as a maneuver to gain rights—and to access the rewards that accompany such rights—as much as a move to protect Hmong's status as a minoritized population from discrimination and racism.

Moua introduced S.F. 3368 in the Senate on February 21, 2002. S.F. 3368 dictated that "two Hmong Mej Koob," one chosen by the bride's family and another chosen by the groom's family, should officiate a traditional Hmong wedding.[36] Because of the centrality of the Mej Koob to traditional weddings, Moua included in S.F. 3368 the presence of *two* Mej Koob as the legal officiators of the marriage. In a sense, Moua's maneuver advanced greater egalitarianism between the two parties, because both the bride's and the groom's families would have decision-making powers in selecting their own Mej Koob. The notion here is that the Mej Koob would represent the interests of their respective parties to ensure full neutrality in negotiating the marriage. This strategy was feminist because it sought to improve gender equality through the representation of the bride, the groom, and their respective families in historically male-dominated marriage negotiations and wedding ceremony processes.

S.F. 3368 additionally contained a retroactive clause, whereby marriages that occurred prior to the passage of the bill could also be legalized if those marriages were contracted in Minnesota and the persons at the time could legally contract their own marriage. This meant that individuals who wished to legalize their existing traditional marriage would have to be residing in Minnesota and must have complied with the Minnesota law of being able to contract to marry at the time in which they inaugurated their traditional marriage. Under Minnesota law, both parties can contract their own marriage only if they are eighteen years old or above, or between sixteen and eighteen years old with the consent of their parents or the court. Moua's version of the bill, however, was extremely limited in scope in determining the legal statuses of both past and future marriages. The retroactive clause in S.F. 3368 excluded all current Hmong Americans whose marriages did not occur in Minnesota at the time in which they contracted their marriage. It also excluded all those marriages in which both or either of the parties were under the age of sixteen, or those who did not receive parental consent to marry between the ages of sixteen and eighteen at the time in which they contracted their traditional marriage.

The bill's retroactive clause meant that even though a couple may now be well into adulthood and happy about the course of their traditional marriage, the state of Minnesota will not legally recognize their traditional marriage on the grounds that they did not meet the terms and conditions of Minnesota law at the time in which they contracted their marriage. The retroactive clause would have validated only marriages that already legally exist in the first place (heterosexual, monogamous, of legal age, and occurring in Minnesota). Furthermore, the retroactive clause would not legalize marriages from other states that recognized common-law marriages. It is not clear whether a marriage legalized under the retroactive clause would become legal if the couple were to relocate to a different state. Additionally, it remains unclear whether the retroactively recognized marriages would be acknowledged as legal on the federal level for the couple to receive federal benefits such as social security.

Hmong Americans immediately debated the bill before it received any kind of hearing in the Minnesota legislature. Most noteworthy of the opposing ends of the ideological spectrum were cultural nationalists, who viewed state recognition as beneficial by bestowing the gift of legal solemnization on the Mej Koob, and feminists, who believed that the Mej Koob should be held criminally liable for the "inappropriate marriages" that they supposedly knowingly solemnize in the name of culture.[37] Hmong American women wanted an avenue to address gender and sexual exploitation within marriages. They contended that the bill did not contain language that would assuage hyperheterosexual kinship formations, namely, polygamy and underage marriages. Instead, feminists feared that the bill would, at best, fail to provide sanctions for women and girls who are victims of these practices and, at worst, empower the Mej Koob to negotiate and officiate these "inappropriate" marriages that subjugate women and girls. A day after its introduction and referral to the Senate Judiciary Committee, Moua retracted S.F. 3368 from consideration and vowed to let the issue "ferment in the community to see whether the community might have some agreement" on the bill in order for it to be reintroduced in the future, which it was, as S.F. 827, one year later, on March 13, 2003.[38] Moua addressed these divisions among Hmong Americans in an opinion essay published in the *Asian Pages*, in which she vowed to work with both sides to mitigate these tensions, stating, "Compromise is the essence of a great policy, and I believe there is room for compromise on this legislation."[39] In what started as the premise of how to structure the coexistence of culture within the law, the marriage bills proliferated into an uncertain deliberation about Hmong's gender and sexual politics and its volatile status within US law.

Another Hmong American politician was elected to the Minnesota legislature, on November 5, 2002. Cy Thao became the first Hmong American in the Minnesota House of Representatives and, upon taking office on January 7, 2003, introduced H.F. 707, the companionate version to Moua's new S.F. 827. Thao was part of the 1990s lobbying efforts to compel Dawkins to introduce the original bill and thus saw his own rise to the Minnesota legislature as "fixing" what he considered to be unfinished business.[40] Contrary to the original claims of feminists that the bill would harm women and girls, Thao utilized the lexicon of women's rights to rationalize introducing and passing the marriage bills once and for all. Thao explained:

> I had an aunt [who] was married in [the] traditional sense. She never went through the legal [marriage]. And so, when she and her husband divorced, she got nothing. They are not married, and none of [their belongings and properties] were [legally] hers. Everything was under his name. She walked away with nothing. And to me, that was big enough for me to say, "Let's fix that. Let's allow the traditional Hmong wedding to be legalized." And if their marriage is legal, she could go to court and argue, "We did have a legal [marriage]. It is recognized here in the statute. So legally, I am married to him, and legally, I have every right to these assets." So that was my intention all along.[41]

The competing vocabularies of "women's rights" and "women's empowerment" presented a double bind for Hmong Americans. On the one hand, Thao witnessed the unequal dimensions of a traditional marriage not sanctified by law. He conjured law as a remedy to these "cultural" impediments to women's belonging (equal treatment under the law) and social citizenship (equal access to property ownership). Thao's gesture aligns with the civil rights frame insofar as it considers the legal personhood of women and their entitlement to property under the liberal terminology of rights. That is, since Hmong culture purportedly afforded very few rights to women, legal sanctions could ameliorate these inequities within Hmong culture. In essence, Thao's framework and rationale in introducing the House companion bill in fact aligns with the forms of feminist thinking that his opponents claimed the marriage bills lacked.

Thao's H.F. 707 excluded the retroactive clause found in Moua's S.F. 3368 and rendered the bill more ambiguous regarding who can solemnize traditional marriages. In short, Thao's version of the bill jettisoned the requirement of two Mej Koob solemnizing the marriage and, instead, simply stated that "marriages may be solemnized among Hmong by the Mej Koob, according to the form and usage of Hmong culture."[42] This ambiguity at once seems to decentralize the Mej Koob as the subject who can solemnize traditional marriages, but it also suggests that Hmong Americans can have more control over how to solemnize and ultimately "legalize" their marriages in ways that are not concretized in law. Attaching an ambiguous framing of "culture" to the language of the bill operates as a strategy that may preemptively enable Hmong Americans to claim the bill as their own with minimal interference or input from non-Hmong legislators. Deploying the hazy language of "the form and usage of Hmong culture" could suggest that only those truly knowledgeable about Hmong wedding and marriage negotiation procedures or religious rituals can determine how the bill will be implemented on the ground. Yet this maneuver of rendering culture ambiguous ironically opened it up for debate within the legislature itself. Hmong Americans also immediately deliberated the merits and pitfalls of H.F. 707 as it proceeded to committee hearings.

The implications of the ensuing debates between Hmong and non-Hmong—and among Hmong Americans themselves—reflect the difficulties and paradoxes of political recognition of cultural difference in the context of multiculturalism and racial and sexual liberalism. How does culture factor into questions of inclusion? What are the stakes of recognition, and how might such political projects serve or harm the interests of a minoritized polity such as Hmong, particularly women? In retrospect, Moua readily assessed the dangers of recognition after witnessing the fallout from her original S.F. 3368. She stated, "To [those individuals who wanted this bill], I said, 'Be careful what you ask for. There is some value to being left alone.' Nobody ever asks for government regulation, particularly when you are a protected class in this country. You are always already overregulated. So really, be careful what you ask for. I was worried about having government interference in our cultural activities as a people."[43] Moua straddled the borders of being an antiracist legislator by consecrating Hmong American social and political interests in law while negotiating the politics of recognition in order to evade "government interference." Moua's critique of the politics of recognition reflects her understanding of culture's fraught position within state-based inclusionary projects that have historically meant to manage racial difference. Moua's knowledge that minoritized polities and their modes of life are "overregulated" means that culture and its attendant gender and sexual politics are not neutral concepts that can be easily absorbed into the state. Thus, debates about the merits of the marriage bills represent larger questions about how, why, and whether Hmong's marriage practices can (and should) be "legalized" to align with state-based concepts of kinship in Hmong Americans' quests for belonging.

NARRATIVES FROM THE COMMITTEE HEARINGS

The House Civil Law Committee conducted a hearing on H.F. 707 on March 25, 2003.[44] The hearing included Thao's explanation of the bill, testimonies from Hmong American community members who both supported and opposed the bill, and inquiries from non-Hmong committee members about the bill. Thao defended H.F. 707 by casting off his critics who argued that the bill did not address inappropriate marriages among Hmong Americans. Thao stated:

> H.F. 707 will allow members of the Hmong community to solemnize marriages, of marriage ceremonies conducted in the Hmong tradition. Now this will enable the Hmong, the person facilitating the ceremony, called the Mej Koob, to sign the marriage certificate at the conclusion of the ceremony, much like a priest would for Catholic ceremonies. . . . This bill does not exempt the Hmong community from other statutes of the marriage laws. Actually, it makes the Hmong community conform to Minnesota marriage statutes. . . . Opponents also say this bill will legalize underage marriages, force girls into marriages. There are statutes in the marriage laws that prohibit these practices. . . . Now under current law, no one can be forced into marriage under section 518.02, titled "voidable marriages," for persons knowingly officiating and solemnizing illegal marriages, who can be charged with a misdemeanor.[45]

Thao's testimony exposed the complexities of Hmong kinship within law. He evoked the illegality of practices such as coerced or underage marriages to ensure that Hmong communities understood they were not receiving special treatment as a protected class. Additionally, Thao assured the committee that Hmong would "conform to Minnesota marriage statutes" because there are already laws in place designed to prevent nonconsensual and non-legal marriages across the board. These are laws that all persons must adhere to, including those possessing current solemnization powers, such as Catholic priests.

Thao also mitigated the accusations of Hmong's hyperheterosexuality by alluding to existing race-neutral statutes, namely, "voidable marriages," that already exist in the Minnesota constitution. Existing statutes aimed at nullifying "illegal" marriages do not necessarily name "Hmong marriages" as constitutive of the statute's prohibition. Thus, Thao cautioned the need to implement additional restrictions to the marriage bills, arguing, "We already have [anti–human trafficking or child abuse laws] and programs. I myself spawned a lot of those programs and got money to address child trafficking. The laws are in place. We do not need new laws. The matters that they are concerned about are already protected. So, say someone was forced to get 'married' at fifteen. We could just use that [voidable] underage statute to [penalize a member of the party]. We do not need a Hmong marriage bill."[46] In essence, Thao critiques the redundancy of criminalization *specific* to Hmong Americans when race-neutral "voidable marriages" statutes that do not target any specific racial group or culture already exist.

Two proponents testified in support of Thao's bill. Sher Lee, president of the Hmong Cultural Center in St. Paul, stated, "As a person who grew up in this country, I organize the Hmong Cultural Center to educate the old things to the new people who grew up in this country. And as president of the Hmong Cultural Center, I [would] like to see this bill pass, to maintain the Hmong marriage tradition and also to support this country."[47] Lee's statement addresses the bill's potential to recognize traditional Hmong marriages as unique and argues that it may lead to more cross-cultural understanding between Hmong and non-Hmong. Furthermore, his claim that passing the bill would be a form of Hmong people supporting the United States solidifies his understanding that the bill could ensure Hmong participation within US legal structures through a politics of recognition. Ai Vang, who identified herself in the hearing as a private citizen, testified: "I am a Christian, and my husband still practice Hmong culture. When we got married, my pastor was not willing to get a marriage license, to sign on the marriage certificate because we go through the Hmong tradition. So, the bill will help the couple [go] through Hmong tradition, and I'm here to support this bill, I think it will really benefit the community."[48] In many ways, H.F. 707 and the marriage bills as a whole sought to rectify marriages such as Vang's, whose religious officiator refused to sign the couple's marriage certificate and transform the marriage into a legal union. Vang's marriage could have been legalized if her pastor or priest had been willing to solemnize, sign, and file a marriage certificate with the court, *or* have a Mej Koob officiate her marriage by following the same procedure. Since the Mej Koob did not possess such legal powers, and her pastor was not willing to file the marriage certificate, Vang probably saw her marriage as not fully formalized until she and her husband both legally filed their marriage with the court themselves.

The bill's opponents consisted primarily of Hmong American women and non-Hmong legislators. Self-identified concerned private citizens Ka Vang, Pacyinz Lyfoung, and Out Vang were opponents of the bill, whose testimonies were recorded in the committee hearing's archives.[49] Lyfoung, although she identified herself as a private citizen during the hearing, was the founder and previous executive director of Asian Women United of Minnesota, an anti–domestic violence advocacy organization. In general, the women criticized H.F. 707 for its lack of input from Hmong American women. They argued that the bill did little to prevent men from engaging in polygamy, would not deter parties from entering into underage marriages, and would not safeguard women and girls from being coerced into nonconsensual marriages. Their critiques as to *who* was forcing women and girls into unwanted marriages were unclear, as was whether their critiques of underage marriages concerned the marriages of two individuals under sixteen or the marriages of girls under eighteen to older men. Nonetheless, they wished for more language in the bill to provide recourse for when women and girls encounter these forms of exploitative kinships. Ultimately, questions remained: How would the bill address some of the hyperheterosexual kinship practices among Hmong, such as polygamy and so-called underage marriages? If the marriage bills affirmed that Hmong Americans are prohibited from engaging in illegal marriages, what additional tools could be provided to ensure Hmong Americans would follow the law? Furthermore, are additional statutes prohibiting or nullifying "voidable marriages" specifically for Hmong necessary as part of the marriage bills themselves? For the women who testified during the committee hearing, these questions informed their view that legalizing traditional Hmong marriages meant sanctioning women's and girls' oppression, further evidencing Hmong's fraught cultural politics of gender, sexuality, marriage, and equality within law.

Potential answers to some of these inquiries can be gleaned through the private citizens' testimonies. Ka Vang began the testimony by articulating her opposition:

> I am a Saint Paul resident, a Hmong woman, and an American citizen. I'm here to state that I oppose the Hmong marriage bill. It was very difficult for me to come here today to oppose this bill since so many Hmong women who oppose this bill have been publicly harassed and even intimidated. But I come here at risk, because I don't believe this bill had adequate community input, particularly from Hmong women and the people who really, it affects most, the Hmong Mej Koob. This bill cannot address a four-thousand-year-old issue such as polygamy, underage marriages, or forced marriages.[50]

Lyfoung testified next and stated her opposition at length:

> Will there be money to educate the Hmong community about the new law, to let women know that they have this remedy, to let the men know what the consequences of their actions will be? Will there be money to train the systems, law enforcements, and the court systems about this law, so that it will be implemented and enforced? Will there be money . . . to accommodate all the new cases of men who violate the law and would be punished for breaking this law? What kind of [compensation] will this statute be willing to award to women who have been victimized under the Hmong marriage bills? . . . Without the provisions, this bill cannot deliver on all its promises, and it will just be a mockery giving false hope, and empty promises to Hmong women. . . . It is not possible for this kind of bill to resolve thousands of years of gender inequity. Because it is the shotgun solution to legalize some kind of marriage, and not change the fact that polygamy, false marriage, and underage marriage will still be happening.[51]

Finally, the hearing concluded with Out Vang's passionate testimony:

> I am opposed to the Hmong marriage bill, because the Hmong cultural marriage practices are oftentimes harmful to girls and women. As you've heard the many testimonies, there are underage marriages, forced marriages, and polygamy. The Hmong people come from a patriarchal society, where women do not have much of a voice. . . . If this bill were to pass, how can we expect

Hmong women to be treated fairly? This bill does not give accountability to the parents, nor the Mej Koob, the go-between, who are, by the way, all men. These Mej Koob can be any men the parents choose. They don't need to have any legal training. And furthermore, this bill does not give the intended parties a say in their marriage, especially the brides, the Mej Koob and the parents marry them, but she can't really say yes or no. She has no voice.[52]

Vang, Lyfoung, and Vang demonstrated in their testimonies that they understood marriage as a sexual contract, whereby contracting the marriages further exacerbates its exploitative dimensions.[53] Legalizing traditional Hmong marriages meant the state is somehow *sanctioning* its exploitative components. That is, these individuals saw practices such as polygamy, underage marriages, and nonconsensual marriages as fundamental practices constitutive of "Hmong marriages," expressed in a way that the legalization of "Hmong marriages" becomes conflated with the legal sanctioning of these abusive kinship formations. The women hoped the marriage bills would do more than legalize existing structures of traditional Hmong marriages. They wanted a reform that would render conjugalities such as polygamy and underage marriages legally unacceptable and would provide accountability measures for those solemnizing such unions.

The testimonies from Vang, Lyfoung, and Vang reflect the long-standing discourse of hyperheterosexuality that has been ideologically linked to "Hmong gender and sexuality," "Hmong marriages," or even "Hmong culture" writ large. The women's testimonies replicate the prevailing power of hyperheterosexuality in shaping public consciousness about Hmong kinship and intimacy. Practices such as plural marriages, marriages not rooted in consensual love, or marriages whose participants are under legal age or age of consent have come to define "Hmong culture" in much the same way that the supposed condoning of sexual violence has come to be conflated with gender, sexuality, and culture among Hmong Americans, as demonstrated in chapter 1. In this strand of discourse, Hmong's marriage practices are mutated to an extreme to the detriment of women and girls, who have no power or agency in their sexuality or sexual desires. On the one hand, patriarchy among Hmong Americans within marriages is constructed through the hearings as even more damaging to women and girls than "normal" heterosexual legal marriages. On the other hand, Hmong women and girls are constructed as perpetual victims of their own culture, rendered more oppressed through their contract in something as sanctified as marriage. While Vang, Lyfoung, and Vang rightfully meant their testimonies to be sincere grievances of problems found within their own ethnic community and assumed that the context of a legislative committee hearing was a reasonable avenue to express such grievances, the reality is that a government committee hearing is far from being a neutral legal space.

In testifying "against their culture," Hmong American women had their concerns co-opted by a non-Hmong legislator and committee member, Representative Dick Borrell, who remarked to Lyfoung: "What I'm struggling with here Ms. Lyfoung, is our constitution requires that we give equal protection under the law and it occurs to me that in the Hmong culture, there is no equal protection for citizens under the law. And we're struggling with how do we bring this to a conclusion where you fall within the constitution and are equally protected?"[54] Borrell's statement underscores the paradoxes of Hmong's subject position within US legal domains. First, Borrell's statement presents a hyperbole for the state's claims to racial equality. The reason why Hmong Americans wanted the marriage bills in the first place was because they were excluded from equal protection under the law in accessing the material benefits supposedly guaranteed to all under the banner of "equal rights." Borrell's comment underlies how hyperheterosexuality renders logical Hmong's exclusion from US legal heteronormativity. Second, a conundrum emerges such that non-Hmong individuals are positioned to potentially alleviate the gendered and sexual pathologies within Hmong American communities.

Borrell's comment that Hmong culture does not provide equal protection for citizens under the law and that he is struggling to bring Hmong women and girls into a system of equal protection away from their native culture reveals that he recognized Hmong culture's inherent inequality, but that there seems to be little procedure in which to democratize it. Read in this way, the committee hearings operated as a way to invite the legal apparatus to discipline and reform a premodern hyperheterosexual culture rather than as a means to include Hmong's unique cultural differences in the law under the rubric of racial liberalism. Hmong are further situated as differential subjects both as racially other and as ethically incompatible with the moral righteousness of one very selective component of US liberalism that presumably affords equality to all. The fact that this was playing out in the committee hearings did little to assist the committee members to position social reform outside of law. Thus, while those who supported H.F. 707 situated their testimonies within a framework of liberal multiculturalism where Hmong culture is the site of a secure location for respectable married citizens, the opposition situated their critiques of culture as a location where gender and sexual exploitation is institutionally sanctioned in ways that further crystallize narratives of Hmong's purported criminal and undemocratic hyperheterosexuality. Understood in this way, culture is rendered as a highly unstable concept that does little to serve Hmong American interests in the legal domain. More importantly, it is revealed to be an enormously insecure and vulnerable foundation for claims to belonging and social citizenship in the United States more broadly.

The Senate Judiciary Committee heard testimonies on Moua's S.F. 827 on April 8, 2003, in which Ilean Her, a Hmong American attorney and executive director of the Council on Asian Pacific Minnesotans, emerged as the biggest opponent of the bills in the entire chronicle of the marriage bills.[55] This committee hearing signified a crucial shift in the life of the marriage bills, as Her ultimately became the opposition's most influential witness. Her's testimony mirrored that of the previous women in that she desired a pathway for women and girls to rectify exploitation within polygamy and underage marriages allegedly rampant among Hmong. That pathway lay in mandating that the Mej Koob become obligated mandatory reporters of "illegal" marriages that they themselves or other Mej Koob whom they know have officiated. Her stated in the committee hearing: "The reality is that the form and usage of Hmong culture results in the under-aged, forced, and polygamous marriages that are real in the community, that do in fact happen. . . . My concern is that, sometimes, it is not people's desires, and it is not people's will. But it is done to them."[56] Her's testimony suggested that bestowing the Mej Koob with legal solemnization powers *reifies*, rather than *rectifies*, the contractual oppression of marriage, which essentializes Hmong kinship and culture itself as fundamentally exploitative and rooted in gender and sexual violence. Her's statement conflates culture with race to construct an image of Hmong as a polity whose gender and sexual politics and kinship practices are antithetical to modern US heterosexual marriage norms, where Hmong marriages operate as an oppressive imposition on women and girls rather than a system of consensual choices. The unidirectional construction of the form and usage of Hmong culture as *resulting* in inappropriate and harmful marriages that are *real* establishes an ideological narrative—framed as a form of "truth" about Hmong marriages—that perpetuates the dominant notion of Hmong as hyperheterosexual subjects. Her continued to testify on behalf of the state's opposition throughout the next two years, which rendered her testimonies problematic mainly because they were utilized by non-Hmong legislators to proffer up criminal penalties for Hmong.

The opening up of culture in this way forced Moua to defend the purpose of S.F. 827 and Hmong people at large. Moua was called on by Senators Thomas M. Neuville, Wesley Skoglund, and John Marty to "explain" how Hmong culture could be transformed through the addition of provisions within S.F. 827. Neuville was one individual who was completely opposed to polygamy and plural marriages in both the "legal" and "traditional/unofficial/common-law" sense. In the hearing, he asked Moua: "How would your culture react if the bill said, once you have a marriage solemnized through the cultural method that was authorized, you can't have, not only can you not have any more legal marriages, but you can't have any more traditional, non-solemnized ones either?"[57] He positioned Moua as a statesperson initiating a bill, but also as an authentic voice who could speak about the prohibition of plural social relations within Hmong society and who sits outside of the state. Moua and Thao were originally state officials but became nonstate, authentic subjects informing the state about their racialized native culture. Neuville's question enacts the device of making illegible social relations that are both formally and informally plural. Thus, while the state does not prohibit the formation of common-law or plural "unofficial" marriages, Neuville enacts a maneuver to suggest that plural marriages within both legal and non-legal domains be prohibited.

Frustrated by the repeated accusations of hyperheterosexuality that the Judiciary Committee members were espousing about Hmong's alleged rampant polygamy and underage marriages, Moua passionately exclaimed:

> I am not a proponent of polygamy in my community, nor am I a proponent of underage marriages in my community. I am actually one of the most outspoken people in my community given my position, to try to change it. So don't mistake my [position], but I also want to let this committee know, and the people who want to be on the record and the people who are here to hear this, that the Hmong culture is not, Hmong marriages are not all about underage marriages and polygamy. That is a very, very minor aspect of it, and yet that's the aspect that gets talked about, gets reported in the newspapers, and gets really all of us going as we start looking at it.[58]

Moua's exclamation reveals the pervasive power of the discourse of hyperheterosexuality within the social imaginations of both Hmong and non-Hmong. Her lamentation that plural marriages or marriages of teenage girls constitute a minor element of Hmong marriages yet are the aspect that is most spectacularized represents how certain configurations of intimacy and kinship among

Hmong come to represent the totality of "Hmong marriages." Moua recognized that the ideology of hyperheterosexuality is proliferated in media outlets to sensationalize Hmong's cultural and racial differences and props up a selective and distorted account of Hmong kinship. In fact, these particular nonnormative conjugalities come to stand in for "Hmong marriages" even as the original concerns of the marriage bills were targeted toward *normative* marriages involving long-term heterosexual, monogamous, adult couples who could contract their own marriages.

Paradoxically, the marriage bills generated further problems rather than resolving what they sought to rectify in the first place. Three years later, during the 2006 legislative session, Skoglund introduced S.F. 2403, which sought to curb "underage marriages" in Hmong communities that, he argued, would result from the passage of Moua's and Thao's bills. He said that he acted on behalf of his own Hmong American constituents who had advanced this particular concern to his attention over the previous three years, most notably Her and other, unnamed Hmong American women. Four amendments proposed in Skoglund's S.F. 2403 introduced culpability measures for the Mej Koob. The amendments were (1) the Mej Koob would have to be mandatory reporters of the marriages that they solemnized; (2) accountability measures would ensure that the Mej Koob must know Minnesota laws regarding "persons capable of contracting" marriages and "prohibited marriages" such as polygamy; (3) Hmong marriages would have to comply with Minnesota law, and, as explicitly stated, the Mej Koob could not solemnize "underage marriages"; and (4) "child neglect" would be broadly redefined to include scenarios in which a parent allows a child to enter a marriage without the child's consent, including the usage of culture or religion to do so.[59]

Blong Yang, a Hmong American attorney who closely monitored the marriage bills, understood Skoglund to be engaging in racist behavior when he sought to legally curb what is already nonexistent within the law.[60] When all Americans, including Hmong Americans, are already legally forbidden from entering into these particular "prohibited marriages," Yang wondered, why had Skoglund brought it up in a legislative bill if not to single out Hmong for their *traditional* practices external to the law?[61] Yang further pointed out that Skoglund's own bill was impractical because such culpability measures for the Mej Koob cannot be implemented at all due to the fact that "prohibited marriages" such as polygamy and underage marriages are considered legally nonexistent unions.[62] According to Yang, the legal definition of marriage in Minnesota already prohibits anyone from engaging in bigamy because it defines bigamy as a person engaged in two *legal* marriages. *Bigamy* is the legal term in which an individual contracts a marriage with another individual while legally married to another. However, "polygamy" can and does transpire among Hmong Americans vis-à-vis a legal marriage and a traditional marriage, or two or more traditional marriages, which are both seen as legitimate forms of marriage by Hmong Americans but not by the legal system.[63] Yang shows that Minnesota law recognizes only the legal marriage and voids the existence of the traditional marriage altogether, thus rendering nonexistent the bigamous/polygamous marriage. In the same logic, an "underage marriage" cannot exist at all at the de jure level. There is no such notion within Minnesota law as "underage marriage" because the law automatically nullifies the marriage of anyone younger than sixteen years of age and renders it legally nonexistent.

However, individuals who are "underage" (meaning under sixteen years old) can contract and enter into unions among Hmong Americans and subsequently present such unions as "marriages" to the larger community, which in return readily recognizes the unions as such. The regulation of "underage marriages," then, does not necessarily attempt to rectify existing law to prohibit such unions, but rather attempts to use law to regulate such practices within Hmong society altogether, regardless of whether it makes legal sense or not. As such, Skoglund's bill to outlaw underage marriages or prevent "prohibited marriages" such as polygamy is both a maneuver to prevent the individuals from legally entering into such unions *and* an attempt to rupture the larger Hmong polity from recognizing such unions as "marriage" altogether. Because the state fundamentally does not recognize the existence of these conjugal practices, it simultaneously cannot regulate something that is not legally present or not legally recognized, other than to target what Yang understood to be informal behavior and de facto forms of intimacy and sociality among a minoritized population. Hmong culture and other so-called orientalist cultures do not exist under the law because they are viewed as incompatible with legal/Western standards of humanity and personhood. The possibility of accepting and dealing with cultural differences or diversity is unachievable in this flawed liberal framework. Hmong become, quite literally, legally ungovernable subjects within the context of gender and sexual liberalism and kinship regulation in the United States.

Even with Skoglund's bill not legally withstanding, the Judiciary Subcommittee on Family Law nonetheless conducted a hearing on his S.F. 2403 on March 3, 2006. During the committee hearing, Skoglund articulated the reasons behind introducing his amendments: "There's been a real tragedy of underaged girls being married. Girls who are thirteen, fourteen, fifteen years of age being married to men two, even three times their age in the Hmong community."[64] The hyperheterosexual nature of Hmong culture comes to haunt and structure Skoglund's understanding of Hmong's intimacies and kinship, compounded by his collusion with the state to criminalize and penalize Hmong Americans for engaging in these practices. Committee members once again relied on Her to reveal the gendered and sexualized truths of Hmong culture when considering whether girls under the age of sixteen provide consent to enter marriages. A committee member asked, "Ms. Her, in the Hmong culture, can thirteen- or fourteen-year-olds give consent? Are they deemed old enough to give consent for marriage?"[65] Her responded, "A woman does not have to consent, and her consent is not even sought. Her family does the negotiating for her. And I have seen, and I've witnessed where a woman, not just a teen, teens and older women, where they do not want to enter into marriage but because the family thinks it's in the best interest of the young girl, maybe she's pregnant, maybe she went out late with a boyfriend, and she doesn't want to get married."[66] The lack of knowledge on the part of the non-Hmong committee member reveals that a particular form of knowledge regarding Hmong's suspected hyperheterosexuality is accepted and circulated, yet simultaneously remains an extremely fraught episteme, therefore leaving more questions for non-Hmong than answers.

Ultimately, Skoglund's S.F. 2403 is also about saving women and girls from their culture, as he ended the hearing by stating: "We're going to be helping some young girls so they can grow up with careers, futures in America. I have gone to several [Hmong community] meetings. I've been to a meeting, I couldn't tell you, one hundred fifty, two hundred people were there. . . . And when I left, three young women followed me down the steps and they're chasing me, . . . well, they're college women. And they were telling me you've got to keep on doing this, you've got to save these girls, you've got to do this, their futures depend upon it."[67] Skoglund's usage of educated Hmong American women's insistence that he be the one to "save" young girls from being married off so that they can have viable careers and futures in the United States absolves him of perpetuating rescue narratives about racialized hypervictimized feminized subjects while establishing the space in the committee hearing for the continued demonization of Hmong as criminal hyperheterosexual subjects.[68] Scholars have demonstrated that rescue narratives perform powerful ideological work because the concept of "saving" women and girls of color is situated within a longer representational and discursive history of women and girls of color as hypervictims of their pathological cultures.[69] The question of women's treatment in so-called regressive cultures enables the intervention of structures such as the state and ideologies such as white saviorism to infiltrate minoritized communities in the name of gender equality. This ideological maneuvering of rescuing racially feminized subjects enables the waging of war against and criminalization of the racial other, and particularly men of color, as the primary procedure of recourse for women and girls of color.

In a subsequent *Minnesota Public Radio News* article, Skoglund stated, "[The Hmong marriage bills would] give [the Mej Koob] the authority to marry, but then with that authority, give them the same responsibility that every pastor, rabbi, everybody else who has the authority to perform a marriage has. They must become mandatory reporters. . . . These 13-year-olds, 14-year-olds and 15-year-olds are being forced into marriages that we wouldn't allow anybody else in our society to have to go into. I'm saying it's wrong and we should stop it."[70] Here, Skoglund assumed that allowing traditional Hmong marriages to exist as a legal practice would simultaneously sanction prohibited practices such as polygamy and underage marriages. Furthermore, Skoglund's amendments attached extra reminders for the Mej Koob and parents who "neglect" their children through the usage of their own culture or religion. In short, the Mej Koob and parents were to be tasked with knowing and understanding Minnesota legal codes regarding marriage and child neglect beyond common knowledge. The Mej Koob were expected to be experts of Minnesota state law on marriage if they were to become legal solemnizers of traditional Hmong marriages.

Some committee members argued that this expectation was not an undue burden unique to Hmong Americans, with some individuals later justifying these provisions that solemnizers of all backgrounds must understand Minnesota laws regarding persons capable of contracting a marriage. In practice, however, many Mej Koob are elders who are knowledgeable in complex wedding ceremonies and rituals but are not literate in the English language or do not understand convoluted family law. Moua reflected on these provisions by arguing that the role of the Mej Koob is mostly a symbolic and goodwill gesture in which a family must formally supplicate in order for the Mej Koob to agree to participate in a wedding in the first place. She explained, "In order for [a person to agree to volunteer and serve as] a Mej Koob, you need to come and kneel to him and beg for his service. And then you are going to say to the Mej Koob, 'Oh, and by the way, if you come and do this, then you will be criminally liable.' My father and all the Mej Koob will refuse to do the ceremonies."[71] The requirement of the Mej Koob to become mandatory reporters and experts on marriage law is utterly unrealistic, and the fact that the Mej Koob's goodwill volunteerism comes with a high level of criminal risk and liability would all but discourage Mej Koob from participating in wedding negotiations and ceremonies altogether, thus potentially fracturing Hmong wedding ceremonies and marriage processes on a broader scale. And because the Mej Koob not only performs the wedding ceremony but also resolves clan rivalries or familial animosities that extend beyond the impending marriage itself, the criminalization of the Mej Koob and the Mej Koob's potential refusal to participate in this process in essence entail a larger fragmentation of Hmong sociality beyond the issue of marriage.

Representative Michael Paymar introduced the final iteration of the marriage bills, H.F. 3674. Two final hearings for H.F. 3674 occurred on April 3 and 6, 2006—both of them more argumentative than previous hearings. In the hearings, Thao, Her, and other concerned Hmong American community members testified both in support and in opposition of the bill, often reiterating the same narratives and arguments from the previous hearings, but this time with a more contentious tone.[72] Paymar mirrored Skoglund's perspectives on the saving of Hmong women and girls from their culture, stating, "Our intent is to protect underage people, and especially girls, in the Hmong culture from being forced into marriages. . . . While I do not want to impose my views on any culture, people of any culture who reside in our state are expected to comply with our laws. While we are a quilt of woven cultures, and while we respect individual customs, the state has a duty to ensure that our children are protected."[73] The discourse of hyperheterosexuality is powerful in this session because it further entrenches the fictitious image of Hmong girls as hypervictims who are ubiquitously oppressed by their native culture. Paymar's rhetoric of a "quilt of woven cultures" within liberal multiculturalism cannot reconcile the alleged illiberalism of certain premodern cultures that harms women and girls. This narrative is ultimately abetted by Her, who continued to perform the role of state expert on exploitative marriages among Hmong Americans. In a sense, Her's testimonies may contain certain validities to the occurrence of de facto polygamous marriages or marriages between individuals under sixteen years of age. However, the ideological dimensions of these discourses render the rescue narratives as more in service of state intervention and criminalization of communities of color rather than in service of gender equality or justice for survivors who may experience exploitation in "prohibited marriages."

Additionally, Skoglund's and Paymar's newly introduced bills and their focus on (and targeting of) Hmong culture also entail what Leti Volpp has argued is a form of assimilation, which was the intention of the original 1991 marriage bills. Volpp argues that using the notion of "culture" is not necessarily aimed at changing the culture of the minoritized population itself, but rather is directed at assimilating immigrants. She takes up the example of arranged marriages to cement her argument.[74] Within arranged marriages, the *entering into* a marriage is the most significant element of all, as it centralizes the notion of "consent" to contract a marriage.[75] States demand that immigrants discard their practices of arranged marriage as a strategy of assimilation. Yet the state has a compelling interest to curb these "cultural" practices as a form of limiting immigration to the United States rather than denouncing the actual practice itself. Because immigrants may use arranged marriages as a strategy to attain legal citizenship, Volpp demonstrates that "arranged marriage functions as a particular trope for immigrant culture; restricting arranged marriage has worked to restrict minority communities from gaining citizenship."[76]

Thus, demonizing the marriage and kinship practices of immigrants operates as a form of gatekeeping to exclude them from legal citizenship as much as it functions as a form of biopolitical management that assimilates them into state-based heteronormativity. In dominant discourse, Volpp argues, Mormon fundamentalists who practiced arranged polygamous marriages in the past, for example, are understood as religiously different, whereas communities of color who have the same practices are understood as racially, ethnically, or culturally different. To be sure, minoritarian subjects fashioned as religiously different can also be construed as racially different (e.g., Muslims). However, certain subjects retain their religious differences in ways that do not implicate them within ideologies of racial difference. This discursive positioning of "religious difference," "cultural difference," or "racial difference" enables states to accommodate certain groups but not others in their practices and allows for states to determine which groups are assimilable and worthy of recognition and inclusion and which are not.[77] In sum, whether the state's inclination to recognize Hmong's unique cultural differences is genuine or not is not as important as its subsequent attempts to criminalize, surveil, and assimilate Hmong Americans for engaging in what it deemed "prohibited marriages" external to ideologies of women's empowerment and rights within sexual liberalism.

The media headlines that purported Hmong to be pathological subjects provided credibility to the assimilationist arguments presented by non-Hmong legislators. The testimonies of the non-Hmong state legislators and that of Her revealed how assimilation comes to stand in after displaying Hmong's gender and sexual politics in front of the state. Her spoke of the "bride price" when she described traditional Hmong wedding ceremonies in the Committee on Public Safety Policy and Finance hearing on April 6, 2006, which prompted Representative Rob Eastlund to immediately ask her, "What is the average bride price in Minneapolis and St. Paul?" She replied, "The average bride price is four to seven thousand dollars."[78] Eastlund promptly responded, "The last thing that I just want to comment on is the four thousand, the seven thousand average payment. I mean, I understand that cultures are different. But we don't buy and sell people. And I really am struggling with this issue, personally. I just think that's [such] a huge issue that we need to address it. The way I see it is, if Hmong people want to be part of American culture, maybe that's the part of their culture they have to leave behind."[79] The marriage bills were designed to transport the premodern Hmong into a modernity vis-à-vis assimilation so that they could be included in systems of heteronormative capitalism through legal marriage. The "bride price" that is part of a traditional Hmong wedding ceremony is considered an unacceptable form of monetary and capital exchange assumed to operate in a human-commodity market, but the benefits and financial capital attached to modern US structures of marriage — such as tax benefits, inheritances, pensions, settlements — are upheld as moral, natural, and desirable. Hmong's alleged hyperheterosexuality, this time being understood by Eastlund as buying and selling women through the concept of the "bride price," disguises the ways heteronormative legal marriage in American culture is also fundamentally even more of an exploitative financial contract. Assimilation is crucial to the device of recognition and inclusion, yet Hmong's purported hyperheterosexual conjugal and kinship formations also mark the impossibility of their recognition, inclusion, and assimilation.

Many Hmong Americans had become increasingly frustrated at the repeated racist accusations of their culture as hyperheterosexual. Moua and Thao had grown to resent the marriage bills altogether throughout the years, with Thao proclaiming during the committee hearing: "Throughout our history, there are two things that people are willing to die for: land and religion. Now this country was founded by people who left because they were [persecuted for] their religious beliefs. And I strongly feel this bill attacks my religion."[80] One Hmong American attorney, Sia Lo, passionately testified during the committee hearing, stating, "We're not here for early marriages! No one wants that! Ms. Her is an attorney. She's Hmong as well. But she has never been forced to marry. She's an attorney and well successful. My sister is an attorney. Senator Moua is an attorney. If the

Hmong were that oppressed about women, these young professionals would never be here today, or be successful if they are!"[81]

The conflicting testimonies of Her and other Hmong Americans who testified over the life of the marriage bills evidence the instability of culture as a more general concept, but certainly as it pertains to marriage and Hmong's quest for belonging. Over the saga of the marriage bills, Thao and other Hmong American community members modified their claims, arguing that the Mej Koob is *marginal* to a wedding ceremony and overall traditional Hmong marriages. This shift from the desire to imbue the Mej Koob with legal solemnization authority to now declaring that the solemnizing power is unnecessary because the Mej Koob is peripheral within traditional Hmong marriage and wedding ceremonies represents Hmong Americans' attempts to destabilize the perceived hyperheterosexuality of Hmong culture. This maneuver renders the very concept of culture as fraught and highly unstable. In fact, Thao had proposed to Skoglund, Marty, and Her "behind the scenes" that his original bill be amended to eliminate the solemnization powers of the Mej Koob altogether and instead simply requesting that any six witnesses at the wedding sign the marriage certificate. Yet Skoglund, Marty, and Her all rejected his proposal. Thao reflected on this process, stating, "I told them my concern. The last thing I want to do is have a Mej Koob go to prison, but we could avoid that by just making six members of the wedding party [sign the marriage certificate]. But they did not want [that] either. At the end of the day, I think they really looked forward to punishing the Mej Koob."[82]

In many ways, the legislation of the marriage bills repositions the question of women, gender, and sexuality in Hmong America into public discourse and domains. In what is supposedly an operation to alleviate the private matters of marriage and its subsequent benefits, the conversations about Hmong kinship and conjugal formations were ironically very public. Dominant society derives a great mixture of pleasure and disgust from viewing gender and sexuality in American culture, depending on whether the object of viewing and thinking is considered normative, deviant, or perverse. Minoritized gender and sexuality is understood as deviant and becomes a never-ending spectacle for the viewing and judgment of the dominant class. The marriage bills enabled Hmong's supposed hyperheterosexuality to be viewed by all, subsequently cementing narratives about it into a state archive. In the Foucauldian sense, power is enacted over and over again through a series of confessional regimes. Hmong Americans continually confessed and addressed the pathologies of hyperheterosexuality in the service of the state through the committee hearings. The politics of gender and sexuality is proliferated to a wider viewership through these confessional apparatuses rather than being contained. Hmong Americans are subjected to a voyeuristic and confessional regime from the state in which it is not that the case cannot be absolved and resolved by the state but that it remains unresolved for the purposes of voyeurism and spectatorship of racialized others. When the bills come up for debate, they enter a confessional command where Hmong Americans must disavow their hyperheterosexual practices, but nonetheless are recuperated into this system of confession about gender and sexuality that ultimately casts them as premodern and illiberal.

At its core, the confusion for Hmong Americans, non-Hmong, and the media writ large lies in the instability and flexibility of "culture." For subjects such as Her, Moua, and Thao, the contestation also relied on who is the more "authentic" Hmong voice, each contradicting the other on the "truth" of gender and sexual relations among Hmong. The anthropologist Uma Narayan has succinctly problematized the concept of the "authentic insider" by parlaying criticism of "primitive" cultures among the insider's own people. In that sense, dominant players within the so-called Western society assign the function of giving a critical perspective to the authentic insider.[83] However, the very conferral of authenticity to the female subject who speaks for her culture also means that the dominant culture can readily withdraw that title of authenticity.[84] Thus, who speaks for culture, and who is deemed the bearer of truth about a culture's treatment of women and girls specifically, and politics and practices of gender and sexuality more broadly? Moua pointedly critiqued this authentic insider paradigm, stating, "So why is it that these white men get to pick a Hmong woman's version of truth versus another Hmong woman's version of truth? And then they get to choose winners and losers? I refused. I'm not going to subject my community to that."[85] Moua's critique reveals how the "truth" about gender and sexuality within any given culture can oscillate between various authentic speakers within a state apparatus such as a legislature or a public committee hearing. Consequently, what may be stable in the mode of testimony may be rendered unstable at any given point within a field of power.

This attempt at legally recognizing traditional Hmong marriages turned out to be more problematic than what Hmong Americans had hoped for. The marriage bills inevitably failed altogether in Minnesota's legislature due to disagreements about whether to include the amendments proposed by Skoglund and Paymar or to rewrite them altogether from scratch as suggested by Thao.[86] In essence, the death of the marriage bills signified Hmong Americans' refusal to continue subjecting their modes of life to the gaze of the state, particularly that of non-Hmong legislators who perpetuated the demonization of Hmong Americans through the frame of hyperheterosexuality. Ultimately, however, all versions of the marriage bills failed to pass during Moua's and Thao's tenure in the legislature and remain unresolved just like their 1991 predecessor.

BEYOND THE "FAILURE" OF THE MARRIAGE BILLS

Ultimately, the failure of the marriage bills to pass in the Minnesota legislature substantiates my claim that there is a fraught understanding and enactment of culture as it concerns gender and sexuality in the current phase of sexual liberalism that enacts profound violence if deployed in uncritical ways. Because of the historical and ongoing distortions and misrepresentations of "Hmong gender and sexuality," "Hmong marriages," or "Hmong culture" as hyperheterosexual within law and media, it has become difficult, if not impossible, for Hmong Americans to seek belonging and citizenship through legal marriage as racialized subjects within a liberal multiculturalist frame. In seeking for their unique culture to coexist with the law so they could access material benefits, Hmong Americans inadvertently found themselves being subjected to racist stereotyping and criminalization regarding their kinship practices. Failure to pass the marriage bills should also be understood within the context of Hmong American *monogamous* relations that are nonetheless unrecognized by the state. Moua's retroactive clause that excluded all common-law marriages performed within the Hmong tradition that did not conform to legal citizenship but nonetheless contained all facets of a monogamous, long-term, respectable, and heterosexual marriage problematizes the very notion that only "prohibited marriages" are conundrums for the state. In fact, Hmong Americans whose marriages occurred in transitional or liminal spaces (such as the highlands of Laos, the jungles as Hmong fled war, or nonnational spaces such as refugee camps that no longer exist) may not be "legal" in the sense of a nation-state recognizing them as marriage contracts. Thus, Moua's retroactive clause does not fully encompass the totality of even traditional *heterosexual* Hmong marriages that transcend nation-based legalities. In sum, a multiplicity of kinship practices among Hmong continue to symbolize the ungovernability of Hmong kinship practices as a whole.

The history of the Hmong marriage bills in Minnesota reveals two important lessons on the entanglement of ideology, law, race, gender, sexuality, marriage, and culture. First, dominant understandings of Hmong gender and sexual politics as manifested in their traditional practices of marriage are perceived to be antithetical to mainstream US structures of legal marriage. In this sense, non-Hmong legislators conflated culture with race and exploitation in order to sensationalize nonnormative kinship formations such as polygamy and underage marriages. Second, Hmong Americans themselves have a very volatile comprehension of "culture." The understanding of the concept of culture as an essentialist trait fundamental to a particular people is an extremely limiting framework to understand the histories; religious beliefs; political activities; identities; familial, social, and kinship practices; or gender or sexual politics and practices of any particular group. Conflating culture with any of the aforementioned concepts enables a racialized blanket ideology to emerge that ultimately imperils communities of color. Hmong Americans' quest to be included in the material rewards of heteronormative monogamous legal marriage ultimately transmuted into a spectacle that sensationalized the nonnormative kinship practices purportedly rampant in their communities. The transformation of the state's objective to interpolate Hmong Americans in social citizenship concomitantly reveals the state's inability to include Hmong Americans who are deemed too culturally and racially transgressive. These two lessons uncover a larger composition about the entangled politics of race, gender, and sexuality and ideologies about cultural and racial difference that structure minoritized belonging in the United States.

CHAPTER 3

Queering
Spirituality

CRITICAL IMAGINATIONS
BEYOND RETICENCE

In 2002, the *Fresno Bee* published a special report titled "Lost in America," which documented eight Hmong American teenage suicides in Fresno, California, in the early years of the new millennium.[1] One story in the report, titled "Embracing the Forbidden," documented the suicides of seventeen-year-old Pa Nhia Xiong and twenty-one-year-old Yee Yang. Xiong and Yang were a lesbian couple who bound themselves together and plunged into Millerton Lake because "their love would never be accepted by their families or the Hmong community, which strictly forbids homosexuality."[2] The author and *Fresno Bee* staff journalist Anne Dudley Ellis introduced the string of teenage suicides in the special report by articulating a profound message linking queer suicides to a repressive native Hmong culture to establish a "culture clash" among refugee parents and their American children:

> Hmong parents grieve for a lost generation . . . the teens are among the first generation to be raised in America. Their parents had hoped they could restore honor and pride to a displaced people, but the teens struggle to balance their American lifestyle with Hmong traditions. Hmong parents, raised in a primitive, agrarian society, expect their children to follow and respect their culture. They also want them to succeed in American society. Sometimes these expectations conflict, sometimes with tragic results. Perhaps no other ethnic group immigrating to the United States has come from a society so different. In America, Hmong parents have no road map for raising

their children. Consider what a minefield the teen years can be for U.S.-born parents, and picture a Hmong refugee trying to navigate these issues. . . . Troubled romances appear to be the cause of at least half of the Hmong teen suicides, an indication of how blending the Hmong culture's strict rules about dating and American practices can have disastrous results.[3]

Ellis positioned "troubled romances," such as same-sex relationships, as the site of conflict between Hmong's stringent regulation of sexuality and "American practices" of freedom of sexuality. The *Fresno Bee*'s binary construction of Hmong as a displaced "primitive, agrarian" refugee population who are among some of the most peculiar newcomers and the United States' reputation as a supposed liberal society that is tolerant and accepting of various forms of sexualities and intimacies emphasizes Hmong's racial difference through the rubric of "culture."

The *Fresno Bee*'s framing of Xiong's and Yang's suicides as a consequence of Hmong culture's inability to name, accept, or contend with queer identities, sexualities, desires, practices, intimacies, and configurations is used to explain the hyperinvisibility of queerness while rendering hypervisible the native culture's role in this forced invisibility. The illegibility of queerness in the Hmong consciousness is purportedly due mainly to the absence of words in the Hmong language to name subjective experience, as the special report further elaborates: "There is no Hmong word for 'I feel.' There is no Hmong word for 'depression.' There is no Hmong word for 'suicide.' . . . It is the story of how a road to a better life in the United States has led unsuspecting Hmong refugees into a bewildering culture clash, endangering their values and their children's lives."[4] Xiong and Yang were "lost" in their parents' eyes because they were lesbians, who had traversed outside the sexual boundaries of their native culture.[5] Being lesbian is rendered as being unrecognizable to the parents, who are conflated with "tradition." Queerness is understood to be a shattering force that fragments the reticence of the nuclear family unit. In other words, queerness is represented as compounding the disruption in harmony that Hmong are already experiencing as displaced refugees. Their parents' and community's repressive response—or its inaction—to queerness then resulted in Xiong's and Yang's suicides.

Chapters 1 and 2 demonstrated how Hmong's assumed hyperheterosexuality—that is, sexual crimes perpetrated against women and girls framed as "cultural" and inappropriate marriage practices such as polygamy and underage marriages framed as incompatible with liberal multiculturalism's mechanisms of recognition and inclusion—is fashioned as exploitative, damaging, and criminal contrasted with white normalized heterosexuality, kinship formation, and intimacies in the contemporary United States. The racialization and sexualization processes of minoritized polities in the United States have transmuted to include queerness as a central component. In the current phase of queer liberalism, scholars have demonstrated how lesbian and gay subjects within the mainstream have been afforded visibility, representation, and civil rights, particularly through the decriminalization of sodomy, the overturning of "Don't Ask, Don't Tell" to permit lesbian and gay people to openly serve in the military, the legalization of same-sex marriage, the proliferation of lesbian and gay characters in popular culture, and the ascent of lesbians and gays into local, state, and federal government positions in the twenty-first century. In this vein, the increasingly liberal attitudes and their attendant politics of inclusion have enabled queerness to become "normal" in mainstream US society.[6] It is in this context of the supposedly increasingly liberal attitudes and policies toward lesbians and gays that those who are constructed as intolerant of homosexuality are construed as backward and illiberal.

It is significant to note, however, that the current phase of queer liberalism deployed in the racialization of minoritized polities remains deeply uneven and inconsistent. Queer liberalism—the ideological bedrock of lesbian and gay freedom in the United States—is strategically deployed to invoke notions of equality and sexual progressivism at the expense of those whose embodiments do not align with normalized homosexuality. That is, the invocation of queer liberalism only goes so far in delivering rights to those described by Lisa Duggan as homonormative—white, wealthy, and cisgender.[7] The current phase of queer liberalism in the United States remixes imaginaries of recognition and inclusion of those whose embodiments support both normalized heterosexuality and homosexuality to construct some subjects as worthy of possessing rights and others as not. Queer liberalism, like the supplementary appendage of sexual liberalism, performs an ideological function of racializing, marginalizing, and criminalizing minoritized subjects such as trans people, immigrants, refugees, the poor, and women of color. Hmong are one community whose history of refugee migration and apparent cultural-sexual deviancy becomes a discernable subject whose experiences can be deployed to further reinforce a strategic—and very exclusionary—formulation of queer liberalism in the contemporary United States.

Hyperheterosexuality also plays another key role in Hmong's racialized construction: the heightened homophobia purportedly extensive in Hmong culture that forces the erasure and deaths of queers. Unlike dominant discourses of racialization that imagine Asian Americans—and particularly Asian American men—as possessing deficient masculinities (i.e., gay), hyperheterosexuality positions queerness in Hmong America as an impossible subjectivity against their heightened masculinities. Thus, queerness is figured strongly as a racializing optic to marginalize Asian Americans, while Hmong Americans' queerness is fashioned as constrained. Hyperheterosexuality distorts queer identities, experiences, and practices in ways that untangle Hmong Americans' complex intersectional subjectivities. The discursive formation of Hmong Americans and Hmong culture as not fully queer (friendly)—as only hyper*heterosexual*—is constructed as oppressive to lesbian and gay Hmong Americans, to the point where lesbian and gay Hmong American youth are experiencing death. Whereas women and girls are harmed through Hmong's "cultural" attitudes about sexual violence and marriage practices, queer people are positioned as victims of their own culture through its apparently "strict" prohibition of queer sexuality. The hyperheterosexuality of culture is not just about men dominating women and girls, but also about how straight people control and erase queer people. This strategic positioning of queer people within the racialized optic of hyperheterosexuality reveals the operation of multiple modes of power. First, hyperheterosexuality is juxtaposed against US liberal multiculturalism and sexual liberalism's ideologies of heteronormativity that position Hmong as a racially degenerate population. Second, Hmong's cultural homophobia is positioned as antagonistic to queer liberalism's discursive formation of homonormativity that renders Hmong as a sexually regressive race. Hyperheterosexuality is assigned and contained within the domain of racialized minoritarian sexualities in ways that not only disfigure Hmong's place in the United States's system of multicultural belonging but also fail to deliver justice for Hmong Americans who do experience patriarchal, queer, and trans violence within their own ethnic communities and society at large.

There is certainly a grain of truth to the existence of homophobia among Hmong Americans, as there is within any given community. I acknowledge the invisibility of queer Hmong Americans; however, like other forms of violence against queer people, invisibility is a much more complicated form of power that cannot solely be cohered through the framework of minoritized people's cultural and racial differences or supposed sexual and queer illiberalism. Instead, reticence—as one distinctive form of silence, disavowal, and inaction manufactured through the heterosexual family unit—forces queer invisibility and extends the ideological powers of hyperheterosexuality across the domain of queerness.

In turn, queer Hmong Americans navigate their forced invisibility by critically imagining a radical queerness that refuses the racial logics of hyperheterosexuality and the sexual and queer logics of liberalism to craft an existence that can persist above and beyond reticence.

LOST REFUGEES, LOST QUEERS

The *Fresno Bee* report represented both refugees and their American-born children as "lost." Being lost, in this sense, is a state in which the subject becomes imprisoned. Being lost in the world is a feeling of being unsettled. One can be lost in the woods, where no one else is around to witness one's condition. One can also be metaphorically lost in a way where one becomes invisible to everyone else. Being lost is to not be seen. It is a modality of being unrecognizable to others. One is lost when there are no clear directions to follow in the temporality of life. The feminist scholar Sara Ahmed attaches the feelings of being "lost" with experiences of disorientation in the world. Lost subjects are phenomenologically "out of place" within space-time.[8] More importantly, however, is that Hmong refugees' state of being "lost" is also attributed to their paramount experiences of "loss" during the United States' secret war in Laos. The medical anthropologist Mai See Thao explains that resettlement in the United States signified a "loss" for Hmong refugees, whereby the objects of loss constitute "a social life where one is socially valued, mobile, young, and youthful," "Laos and the once autonomous region of Nong Het where Hmong leaders emerged for a time," and "a Hmong sense of sovereignty and a Hmong Kingdom."[9] Hmong's losses during and in the aftermath of the secret war in Laos produce their suspended orientation toward that object which cannot be named as a loss.[10]

Hmong refugees' displacement across the globe means their proximity to their objects of desire—be it social value, mobility, youth, beauty, or autonomy—becomes ambiguous, paradoxical, and even impossible. Additionally, racism expunges Hmong refugees from the national body by disorienting them from approximating "American" space. Hmong refugees' state of being "lost" is pathologized through their loss, a suspended affect that skips over mourning and into the territory of melancholia.[11] The feeling of being "lost" is transferred onto the second-generation teenagers, who are unable to overcome the bind of their own lost refugee parents. Being lost—and living in perpetual loss—is a multigenerational phenomenon constitutive of the refugee's political condition, but it is also ideologically fashioned as their inability to be properly incorporated within the linear temporality of refugee resettlement and assimilation into the nation-state. As refugees who were displaced both physically and mentally, the parents are unable to comprehend "modern" youth issues of gender and sexuality. The lack of parental guidance—hypoparenting—leads youth astray as "lost." Being labeled "lost" concretizes the refugee as a temporally suspended subject existing in a past that is historically fixed. This fixity establishes the ideological construction of past losses and the attempts to recover them as "precipitat[ing] despair, because such narratives are . . . not only illusive but also elusive."[12] Thus, the refugee condition functions as an epistemic and symbolic structure that crystallizes the essentialism of both parents and children as lost subjects of history.

Hmong's grief from their forced participation in the United States' secret war was never officially mourned by the state or by refugees themselves.[13] Secrecy displaced Hmong's history and structured the epistemological frame utilized to underscore Hmong racial formation in the United States, glossing over their official losses to deny them a rightful path toward mourning.[14] Instead, secrecy as an epistemological structure imposes an incoherent and pathological state of melancholia onto Hmong refugees and renders their loss as unrecognizable. They are simply "lost."[15] The *Fresno Bee* doubly entangles and conflates Hmong's histories of displacement and loss to their conditions as refugees and marks these dynamics as constitutive of them becoming lost as they transition from premodernity to modernity. In their inability to overcome their displacement and melancholic losses, they are ultimately represented as lost within the modernity that is queer liberalism.

The state of being refugees and being lost aligns with the displacement and then subsequent saving of refugees to bolster discourses of state rescue and liberation. However, there are also contradictions found within discourses of liberalism toward refugees. Queer of color critique suggests that this liberal discourse toward the racial other positions them outside the realm of the normative even though liberalism was designed to enfold them into normativity in the first place.[16] Refugees are imbued with a diminished belonging insofar as they are divested from the "rationality" of the Western citizen-subject. Therefore, in the *Fresno Bee*'s "Lost in America" report, the idea of Hmong as refugees augments their racial otherness, which rationalizes Hmong's parental failure—and, by extension, Hmong culture's failure—to steer their children toward model minority success within heteronormative and homonormative US capitalist society. As such, any failures arising from resettlement in the United States come back to the refugee status and the refugees themselves, either as the parents who fail to understand their own children's contemporary identities and sexualities or as the children who cannot reconcile conflicting forms of belonging between their native Hmong and the newly discovered American worlds. Xiong's and Yang's suicides reveal these contradictory meanings about refugee displacement and resettlement to propagate the dominant narrative of Hmong as lost subjects of history. The *Fresno Bee*'s "Lost in America" strategically constructs this narrative of a static refugee temporality to establish a grander and more targetable ideology of Hmong's inherent homophobia in contradistinction to the modernity of queer liberalism to cohere Xiong's and Yang's suicides.

QUEER UNINTELLIGIBILITY THROUGH RETICENCE

A more complicated theorization of queer invisibility and violence within minoritized communities is needed beyond the framework of cultural difference rooted within racial hierarchies perpetuated through queer liberalism. Taiwan-based queer theorists Jen-peng Liu and Naifei Ding argue that violence against queer and trans people is a reality present in various societies across time and space, certainly in the so-called West, but also in Asian and Chinese social worlds, including Chinese America. They explore the concept of "reticence" as an aesthetic, rhetorical, and moral force of silence, inaction, and even tolerance that maintains the normative social order and contributes to the invisibility and deaths of lesbian and gay subjects. They argue, "Reticence deploys its peculiar force as rhetoric, narrative deployment and aesthetic ideal, as well as model behavior and as a mode of speech. In these various forms, reticence simultaneously hides yet displays and deploys an ineradicable force and effects."[17] Thus, reticence is both the lack of vocal communication and an aesthetic structure of power that dictates the directives of sexual morality, character, and behavior through "saving face" or "not recognizing" queer sexuality. Read as a form of "tolerance," reticence is deployed, for example, when Chinese parents may know that their child is lesbian or gay but choose not to antagonize (but also not to recognize) their child's queerness as a method to maintain harmony within the familial social unit or larger extended kinship system. They "tolerate" what is otherwise intolerable.[18] Liu and Ding contend that such deployment of the micropolitics of reticence in everyday life sequesters queerness into the realm of the unspeakable.[19] Similarly, the anthropologist David A. B. Murray has situated "homophobia" as a set of unequal power relations that are manifested in myriad ways across space and time, including indifference, dismissal, or other more sinister variations of "tolerance," such as "embracing the sinner but not the sin."[20]

Reticence also illuminates how not acknowledging queerness works as a force of invisibility within Hmong social worlds. Reticence is a system of dogmatic disavowal that renders queer subjects unintelligible through aesthetics of spirituality and cosmology. This supposition, however, diverges from the racial caricatures that the *Fresno Bee*'s "Lost in America" report portrays, whereby lesbian and gay subjects are interpolated within an arrangement of essentialist "cultural" assumptions about Hmong homophobia to bolster state ideologies of queer liberalism. That is, mainstream representations of Hmong as perpetually homophobic are clouded in racialized terms and reproduce a racist epistemology of "culture" that does not address the power structures of reticent repudiation. My rejection of the framing of the *Fresno Bee*'s "Lost in America" report and its story about Xiong and Yang concerns its propositions that rely on oft-narrated and easily targetable binary paradigms of cultural and racial difference. It is not the homophobia of rejection rooted in Hmong's inability to name queerness but rather the everyday practices of discursively skewing queer sexuality rooted in a micropolitics of reticence within spiritual and cosmological discourses that implicate queer slow death and what the queer theorist Eric Stanley calls "death-in-waiting."[21] In fact, parsing out the complexities and contradictions of reticence in turn may also dislodge the processes of slow death and death-in-waiting embedded within queer liberalism that can cultivate a racially minoritized queer subject formation rooted in life and empowerment.[22]

One example that demonstrates how reticence shores up to force queer invisibility is Bic Ngo's article "The Importance of Family for a Gay Hmong American Man: Complicating Discourses of 'Coming Out.'"[23] In the article, Ngo interviews a gay man named Fong (pseudonym) and situates his experiences of identity and experiences of "agency" within the heterosexual family structure. Ngo utilizes this framework to argue that Fong resists the Western and white paradigm of "coming out" as an individualistic and neoliberal act of freedom to account for the well-being and wishes of his family. Fong was able to negotiate his queer *and* Hmong identities by marrying a woman, something that his parents sincerely desired. This in turn supposedly led his parents and his wife to eventually accept him as gay later on, while "saving the face" of the entire family in the grander scheme of things. Ngo challenges portrayals of Hmong as homophobic by reading queer Hmong American experiences within the family unit as antiracist and empowering. This reading also suggests that Hmong families are indeed "tolerant" of queer sexuality. I appreciate Ngo's agentic reading of Fong's marriage to his wife as a way to "save face" and preserve the harmony of the heterosexual family unit through a Hmong-specific framework. However, Ngo's analysis situates Fong as having agency *within* an essentialist culture by reinforcing reticence through the concept of "saving face," which is supposedly inherent in various Asian societies.[24] It appears as if nothing "has been changed or disturbed; at least not on the surface" for Fong and his family.[25] Fong's unacknowledged material, symbolic, and psychological sacrifice of performing a compulsive heteronormativity to save the face and safeguard the harmony of the heterosexual family unit reinforces his unintelligible queer subjecthood.

Although agency may exist within the heterosexual family unit, this perspective reifies Hmong culture as unchanging and static. I am certainly interested in how queer Hmong Americans live, negotiate, and survive within oppressive and destructive structures, including the heterosexual family unit, as much as how institutions such as the heterosexual family unit are complicit in perpetuating queer slow death and death-in-waiting. Ultimately, I am interested in how queer Hmong Americans can "forge another paradigm, other models of thinking, acting and feeling enabling and empowering non-reticent acts and feelings, allowing non-reticent lives to articulate the challenging legitimacy of their spaces."[26] In other words, how might non-reticent acts of refusal—of imagining other forms of sociality that do not implicate the entire heterosexual family unit in a compulsory heteronormativity—enable a more capacious formation of intimacy and queer intelligibility?

Central to my version of queer of color critique is the rhetorical deployment of culture—and specifically spirituality and cosmology—as a means of reticent violence. A scenario of the reticence of spirituality and cosmology is demonstrated in a passage in Ngo's article in which Fong recounts how he complied with his family's wishes to "cure" his gayness through religious spiritual ceremonies carried out by shamans. Fong, in his own words, states that the shaman had provided a rationale for his "defect": "[The shaman] said that when I came to earth to be born my bridge was broken and they wanted my parents to go find . . . my dad's sister, which is my aunt, one of her jackets for me to wear so that I can be cured. They actually did that but it didn't work."[27] While Ngo's analysis is valuable in demonstrating that Hmong families may be more "tolerant" of queerness than had previously been expected, it inadvertently essentializes culture because it passively centralizes many supposed Asian familial and cultural ethoses that are in fact complicit within reticent disavowal. Furthermore, it does not completely address the ways that queer sexuality has come to be understood as "taboo" and aberrant in various Asian social worlds, including Hmong spaces, through spirituality, cosmology, and the aesthetic structure of "saving face." Fong's testimony reveals the reticent forces of spirituality and cosmology that undergird the repudiations of queerness. Reticence is simultaneously a form of tolerance, harmony, agency, and familial cohesion as much as it is a form of forced invisibility, unintelligibility, and renunciation of queer subjectivity.

Liu and Ding have critiqued gender, feminist, and queer theories of the so-called Third World that present decolonial versions of queer sexuality by positing the West as introducing homophobia into its cultures while absolving its own idiosyncratic internal homophobias. They state, "A gender studies that seeks to privilege pre-modern categories and concepts of gender over and against both 'Western' modern gender relations and 'Western' feminism is just as problematic as a queer theory that seeks to claim the absence of homophobia and homosexuality in a would-be post-colonial decolonized present."[28] Such deployments of reticence are precisely the effects of queer violence that go under the radar to relegate lesbian and gay subjects to the realms of slow death, death-in-waiting, and actual death by spectralizing and aestheticizing queer sexuality as disarticulated ghosts. This relegation dematerializes queer sexualities and subjectivities in the contemporary moment and instead foregrounds an afterlife that promises a freedom "in the next life." Queerness is forever deferred in the hopes of a hypothetical redemption in the future.

RETICENCE, SPIRITUALITY, COSMOLOGY

The "Embracing the Forbidden" story ultimately brings readers of "Lost in America" to Xiong's soul release ceremony.[29] The author writes, "[Xiong's mother] will no longer dream of her daughter because her spirit has been released. She believes her daughter's spirit is in a baby boy, born to a neighbor the day of the ceremony. This is good, her mother says, because Xiong talked about wanting to be a boy so that she could have more freedom."[30] Not only does the story misrepresent the process of rebirth by assuming that the release of the spirit brings about a feeling of closure and that Xiong's mother "will no longer dream of her daughter," but it also foregrounds the mother's statement of reticent spirituality and cosmology. Xiong's mother is using a particular epistemology of the rebirth process in order to come to terms with Xiong's death and her queer sexuality. Xiong's mother understood Xiong's queer sexuality as an inversion of gender. This is not a new understanding of queer sexuality. Read in this way, queer sexuality is rendered as a "sexual inversion" that posits a body-centric version of queer sexuality by casting it as being born in the wrong body.

The notion that Xiong may have wanted to become a boy—since she was a woman, lesbian, and sexual invert during this lifetime—provides meaning to her loved ones to comprehend and understand life after death, and particularly that of the tragic passing of their queer child. However, it posits an impossible framework for the flourishing of multi-varied genders and sexualities that cannot be neatly pigeonholed into the framework of gender inversion; it also does not appreciate being lesbian as a legitimate mode of subjectivity on its own terms. The death of one's child is an extremely painful event. It is not my concern to diminish the very real grief of those close to Xiong or Yang in the aftermath of their untimely deaths, as their deaths have also affected us queers who are still violently living and who are undergoing death-in-waiting. Xiong's mother was able to utilize a meaningful and logical framework to contend with her daughter's suicide by turning to cosmology as a means to cohere Xiong's queerness.

Cosmology is a major property of Hmong spirituality and is used to make sense of life and death. Hmong's understanding of cosmology affirms that the dead matter. The anthropologist and mortuary expert Vincent K. Her demonstrates that in dominant Hmong cosmology, *ntuj* (upper realm), *ntiaj teb* (earth), and *dab teb* (spirit world) are all interconnected. These realms are intertwined where the souls of the deceased travel to be born and reborn. Entities within these realms are affected by how their souls transition from one realm to the next. These domains are not deserted spheres to which the "dead" are coldheartedly relegated, but rather they are booming with movement, affect, sensation, creativity, and warmth. Yet because these realms and the journey that the deceased must undertake to travel from *ntiaj teb* to *ntuj* in order to *thawj thiab* (be reborn) may be interpreted as harsh, the living descendants of the deceased continue to sacrifice animals as offerings of food to guide the deceased through this cycle of birth and rebirth.[31] Hmong social and spiritual life is governed by this cycle of the wandering, traveling, and constantly shifting world of souls pursuing birth and rebirth, in which the dialogic relationship between the dead and the living continues to inform Hmong social practices. The souls wandering in *dab teb* thus haunt how the living continue to exist on *ntiaj teb*.

Hmong funeral rituals consider this cosmological process of birth and rebirth when executing specific funerary acts, such as playing the traditional *qeej* (bamboo reed) instrument. A deceased individual's soul is released from *ntiaj teb* through the singing of *zaaj qhuab ke*, a funerary ritual ballad that guides the deceased to retrieve their amniotic sac buried on the grounds of their birth, thereby releasing the soul to travel to *ntuj*. The deceased's soul will then be permitted to be reincarnated again once they have travailed in the dangerous spirit realm and reached *ntuj*. Unlike in Christianity, which purports that human souls go to stay in heaven (presumably forever, and thus they can encounter their deceased family members decades down the line), in Hmong cosmology, people's souls go to the upper realm with the goal of being reborn. Once the souls have reached *ntuj*, they must negotiate with the guardian of *ntuj*, Yawm Saub, regarding their rebirth. Yawm Saub interrogates the souls to inquire about their life and the circumstances of their death on *ntiaj teb*. Once ordained and released by Yawm Saub, the souls then can be reborn again. In some narratives, Yawm Saub also prescribes *daim ntawv noj ntawv haus*, or simply *daim ntawv*, for the souls to be materialized upon their reincarnation as physical human beings. *Daim ntawv* may be understood as the provision of the souls' destiny ordained by Yawm Saub and carried out in their next physical lifetime.[32]

In some interpretations, souls are rendered as babies, who may have the power to choose their families. For example, in her well-celebrated book *The Latehomecomer: A Hmong Family Memoir*, the author Kao Kalia Yang theorizes this process of rebirth in an agentic fashion:

> Before babies are born, they live in the sky where they fly among the clouds. The sky is a happy place and calling babies down to earth is not an easy thing to do. From the sky, babies can see the course of human lives.
>
> This is what the Hmong children of my generation are told by our mothers and fathers, by our grandmothers and grandfathers.
>
> They teach us that we have chosen our lives. That the people who we would become we had inside of us from the beginning, and the people whose worlds we share, whose memories we hold strong inside of us, we have always known.
>
> From the sky, I would come again.[33]

In Yang's version, babies float within *ntuj* as the process of rebirth begins. It is not an easy task to call babies down from *ntuj* because of the lengthy process by which the deceased need to be guided through the rebirth process. However, Yang also indicates that it is the babies themselves who "have chosen their lives," signaling a self-fulfilling prophecy of rebirth. This perspective complicates dominant cosmological sensitivities of the world, because it destabilizes Yawm Saub's provision of a preordained life. Yawm Saub is not essentialized as preordaining life, but rather it is the subjects being rebirthed that have chosen their destinies. Yang's iteration that the souls of babies "have always known" their destinies as they descend to be reborn again into physical humans reveals new feminist understandings of the cosmological processes in the (re)invention of Hmong lives on *ntiaj teb*.

Her has also acknowledged this flexibility by stating that *daim ntawv* is not a deterministic scripture. The souls can negotiate with Yawm Saub about their life provisions before their rebirth.[34] Her's admission confirms Yang's version of the souls as agentic in choosing their own destiny before being reborn and challenges the notion that queer Hmong Americans have no agency in crafting their lives. Xiong's mother's understanding of queer sexuality is situated within this framework of cosmology that indexes the simultaneous processes of birth and rebirth, of babies coming and going, and provides her metaphysical tools to follow Xiong's path from her violent suicide to her ultimate redemption as a baby boy in her next life. In Xiong's mother's view, Xiong's memories of her previous life were carried with her, which transformed her queer sexuality into heterosexuality in the form of a presumably straight man in the next lifetime because Xiong was free to choose this path of life that she supposedly had always wanted.

IMAGINING A QUEER COSMO

I was invited to share my research and participate in a spiritual meditation on politics with a women's dance group in August 2016. I narrated Xiong and Yang's story and the perspective of Xiong's mother on queer sexuality and the agentic rebirth process, when the participants asked me to share a bit about my research. One participant asked, "If her mother thinks she will be reborn into a boy in the next life, then what did she think Xiong was in this life?" This participant's poignant critique suggests the violence of ghosts and the so-called afterlife as an essentialist interpretation of cosmology used to deny the materialization of queerness in *this* life. The participant urged me to consider whether in *this life* it is possible to engage a queer and feminist materialist practice that does not simply relegate queer people to the realm of ghosts in deferring their full potentiality at the "threshold of obliteration" and into the *next life*.[35] That is, must queerness be intelligible only through its suspended temporality within the various cosmological realms? The participant was concerned that the dematerialization of queer subjects problematically romanticizes cosmology for the purpose of an "agency" that decentralizes Xiong's material queerness without taking responsibility for the violence that compelled Xiong and Yang to end their lives in the first place. The participant argued that spirituality should be not only ghostly but also material. Spirituality and cosmology should provide flexibility for the flourishing of queerness in all phases of this life, in the afterlife, and in the next life.

Cosmological renderings of social and spiritual life have their limits in accounting for the materiality of gender, sexuality, and queerness in *this* life.[36] My conversations with queer Hmong Americans reveal the reticent politics of the cosmos that delegitimize and render illegible queer identities, subjectivities, and material embodiments. Khoua, a twenty-five-year-old bisexual man, told me: "I worry about if my family disowns me, when I die, where does my soul go? . . . How should I come out to my parents and my family? If I do, worst-case scenario, if they disown me, kuv cov dab [my spirits], what am I gonna do? When I die where does my soul get sent to?"[37] The act of "disowning" a queer child is serious because it denotes the severing of the child and their soul from the protective household. Cosmology is deployed as a tactic of delineating the boundaries of spiritual belonging. It also marks a form of reticence because the queer child's soul may potentially disrupt the harmony and aesthetics of the spiritual household. Khoua's distressing quandary suggests that this spiritual disownment, often accompanied by and manifested as a physical expulsion from the home, is simultaneously an amputation of one's soul from the household (presumably forever), whereby it disconnects one from the spiritual and social benefits of having a funeral arranged when one passes away.

Thus, as refugees are figuratively lost in America, the queer soul will also be spiritually "lost" (*poob zoo*) in the afterlife and cannot *thawj thiab*. Being lost, whether psychologically, spiritually, or figuratively, constitutes the oppressive power structure that defines the precarity and unintelligibility of queer Hmong American and Hmong refugee life in the United States and beyond. Therefore, in Khoua's case, the act of disowning will disconnect the queer child's soul from accessing communication with *ntiaj teb* upon death. Not only does this severing cause a presentist impossibility ("what am I gonna do?"), it also renders illegible a future ("where does my soul get sent to?"). In the end, the afterlife itself remains inarticulate and *thawj thiab* becomes impossible ("where does my soul go?"). Thus, this trifold temporality of the present, future, and afterlife establishes a despairing metaphysical predicament for the queer child. The profound conundrums conjured through my conversation with Khoua irradiate this spiritual violence and reticent political, rhetorical, and aesthetic work.

Spirituality and cosmology are also used to "explain" one's queerness as a "sick," "negative," "defective," or "false" soul. Keng, a twenty-year-old gender-nonconforming heterosexual man, recalled when his mother rationalized his gender nonconformity through the framework of the cosmos. Keng recounted: "My mom stated to me, 'Koj tus plig yeej yug los ua tub, tabsis koj lub cev tsis yog [Your soul was born to be a boy, but your body was not].' I responded, 'Okay, that doesn't make a lot of sense.'"[38] Keng further described a situation that infuriated him when one of his aunts, who is an experienced shaman, arrived at his home and informed him about his soul. He stated, "She told me, 'I looked into your soul—when you get older, you're never going to be happy. You're just going to get older, and you're just going to look at life and ask, 'When am I going to die?' She said the afterlife for me is not going to be good either. I was pissed, so I just left."[39] Keng's anger and disavowal of how his soul is unhappy reveals how spirituality is deployed as a reticent tool to cognize, discipline, and disarticulate gender-nonconforming bodies. Since the ultimate desire of a soul is to *thawj thiab* and not to *poob zoo* (be lost) or wander restlessly in the afterlife, the notion that Keng's soul in the afterlife is "not going to be good," that his soul will be despondent and cannot be reborn, thus operates as the ultimate form of disparagement and condemnation. The impossibility of his soul to *thawj thiab* after death functions as a disciplining tactic and a shadowy force of reticent disavowal to induce spiritual nonbelonging.

In my conversation with a twenty-eight-year-old bisexual woman named Pakou, she revealed to me her mother's understanding of both her and her sister's bisexuality and her sister's partner's transgender identity. Pakou described how her mother comprehended queer sexuality through cosmology, referencing *daim ntawv* as a provision preordained by Yawm Saub:

My mom [talked] about my sister, who is also bisexual, and her partner, who is transgender. My mom was very much against their relationship. And she kept saying that my sister's partner daim ntawv los yuam kev [has a mistaken provision]. He was supposed to be a man, but he chose the wrong person to be reborn into. He has the female sex. And that creates a stigma on their relationship.

Because my mom is a shaman and she has these abilities, she says my sister can't be having these kinds of things [her queer sexuality] interacting with my mom's spiritual gift. Because my sister's bisexuality will phiv nws cov dab neeb [infringe on her household spirits]. And my mom said that anything that my sister does may be a stigma and can wreck her altar, and the altar can make you sick.

So, my mom had to be very cautious about these things. I didn't fully believe in what my mom was saying, but as I grew older, I started believing it more. And then my sister started to ua neeb [become a shaman], and then I started to experience spiritual phenomena too. Sometimes, it's not real, sometimes it's real, maybe I'm schizophrenic, I don't know. I start questioning things.[40]

Pakou's mother explained that the provision Yawm Saub had ordained for her sister's transgender partner was a "mistake" and thus will foster a social stigma that can be detrimental to the spiritual energy and "wreck her altar" containing the household spirits. In this way, Pakou's sister's bisexuality and her sister's partner being transgender were understood to be a form of anti-reticence that will disturb the harmony of the household because they will "phiv nws cov dab neeb [infringe on her household spirits]" and make them "sick." Her mother seeks a spiritual and cosmological explanation of her sister's bisexuality and her sister's partner's identity as transgender in order to uphold the harmony of the household at all costs. Yet her mother's understanding also skews their queerness and forces their unintelligibility by targeting it as a potential source of spiritual pathology ("sickness"). The mother's authority as a shaman compounds her usage of spirituality and cosmology to render queer subjects as "mistaken" subjects—which in turn implies the existence of "correct" counterparts, presumably cisgender heterosexuality. Pakou, her sister, and her sister's partner occupy an ontologically precarious status within the dominant interplay between spirituality, cosmology, and subjectivity.

In another conversation, with Mai Tooj, a twenty-eight-year-old lesbian, I learned about how she conceptualized the messiness of the so-called present life and the afterlife. Mai Tooj stated strongly,

Why do you have a big problem if next tiam [that is, in your next life], koj yuav mus ua poj niam thiab ne [you can become a woman]? And, if I'm correct, that [in] the afterlife, the other side of the world, gender means nothing, then what's the big mothafuckin' deal? So where did this whole notion come from? Like Native American Two-Spirits, some people are totally fine with them being queer because they can live between different spirit worlds.

So if there is a queer Two-Spirit shaman, woman or man, the whole Native community accepts them, it's not a problem. So then what's the big deal, if you put it in that perspective? What's the big fuckin' deal?[41]

Mai Tooj's zealous musing articulates an afterlife that allows men to be reborn into women, or vice versa, thus why is it such a "big mothafuckin' deal" to allow this interchangeability of gender and sexuality within the upper realm (*ntuj*), the current material life on earth (*ntiaj teb*), and the spirit world of the afterlife (*dab teb*)?

While Mai Tooj's critique is situated in the apparent metaphysical contradictions between *ntuj*, *ntiaj teb*, and *dab teb*, whereby *ntuj* and *dab teb* are presumably less rigid realms of possibility yet constantly interact with and engage *ntiaj teb*, then why is it that queer genders and sexualities seem to be so rigid in this supposed flexible and dialogic relationship? Mai Tooj's critique of this contradiction reveals the ways spirituality and cosmology operate as an aesthetic construction to delegitimate queer sexuality. More importantly, it reveals the fraughtness of Hmong's spiritual worldviews about and formations of gender and sexuality, which perhaps can be cracked open to account for queerness. Furthermore, Mai Tooj alludes to her understanding of the Indigenous concept of "Two-Spirit," whereby the subject can simultaneously embody a multiplicity of "spirits" and flexible ways of being that traverse the material world *and* the spirit world, thus indexing the interactivity of such domains. Without essentializing or romanticizing Two-Spirit or Indigenous ways of knowing and embodiments of gender and sexuality, it is important here to ruminate on Mai Tooj's critique as a way to illuminate spirituality and cosmology as limited frameworks for understanding queerness, while also hinting at the potentiality of a Hmong-specific imagination of the world through cosmological frameworks of gender and sexuality that can penetrate through the shroud of their current forced invisibility and ontological precarity.

Spiritual and cosmological sites reveal forms of nonbelonging and authorize particular epistemologies about souls and their intersection with gender and sexuality and its consequences for identity and subjectivity. In the midst of their reticent disavowal, queer Hmong Americans seek alternative modalities of knowledge that affirm the totality of their being and embodiment. They seek empowering readings of their modes of existence that do not render their queer souls as deficient. Queer Hmong Americans enact a politics of spirituality and cosmology through what I call their "critical imaginations," which understand the soul as a figuration of complex elements outside of the deficient reading. In this way, by reclaiming spiritual and cosmological modes of being, queer Hmong Americans challenge their forced invisibility under the curtain of hyperheterosexuality to reveal that their enactments and epistemologies of spirituality and cosmology are not completely antagonistic with queerness.

FOSTERING AND ENACTING CRITICAL IMAGINATIONS

My conversations and interviews with queer Hmong Americans are complicated, because while they question the supposed "cultural" elements that define Hmongness, they may also embrace these same elements and render them as queer. In many instances, however, queer Hmong Americans showed ambivalence or even uncertainty about how to deploy a liberatory spirituality and cosmology. That is, how do they simultaneously embrace the emancipatory facets of "culture" that resist racist essentialisms while also questioning the violence of this same "culture" that coerces their erasure within the dogma of hyperheterosexuality? I encouraged my participants to imagine how the abstract of "culture" shores up in their lives in material ways. Most interviews revealed that queer Hmong Americans intimately experience "culture" through the domain of spirituality and cosmology—specifically, the ways spirituality and cosmology are deployed to delegitimize their queer sexualities and identities. However, the ways spirituality and cosmology are utilized to repudiate, misrepresent, or explain queer sexuality, while unjust, are also not definitive. Contrary to how the ideology of hyperheterosexuality skews Hmong's sexual forms that claim a definitive gendered and queer subjugation, queer Hmong Americans revealed to me that they are in fact (re)fashioning visible selves in ways that thus far have been inconceivable and incomprehensible to the larger community and certainly not yet discernible to feminist and queer theorizing of cosmological subject formation. Queer Hmong Americans hold on to these frameworks to also make sense of themselves and generate alternative meanings about their queerness in a myriad of creative ways in accordance with their interpretations of the cosmos. Their ruminations require a self-reflexivity about what it means to be born and live "wrongly" in the cosmos with which they are familiar. Drawing from the feminist scholar Gloria Anzaldúa's theories of spirituality and the imagination, I demonstrate how queer Hmong Americans practice critical imaginations to dream alternative modes of being that deconstruct hyperheterosexuality and challenge reticence within their families and communities.

Anzaldúa's theories of spirituality have enabled feminist, queer, and critical race and ethnic studies to flourish beyond the positivist methodologies of Western Eurocentric scholarship. Concomitantly, Anzaldúa's concept of the imagination is intimately attached to spirituality in her scholarship. She uses a variety of concepts to reposition how we can imagine social change, from the ways in which the soul and spirit are formulated in the world of dreams to how these imaginations can be implemented in the outer world. Imagination enables the envisioning of what is yet to come, according to Anzaldúa: "Whatever occurs back in the external world first occurs in the imagination."[42] Yet Anzaldúa's multifold worlds are not always so seamless. She writes, "All my escape modes had problems: I couldn't be in the outer world all the time because that was painful. I couldn't be in the inner world all the time because that was painful, too."[43] Thus, Anzaldúa became adept at switching into various modes of consciousness. Imagination should not be romanticized as completely free of pain and anguish. The process of imagination can be agonizing, compelling the subject to constantly shift consciousness in order to recover from this intense psychological labor. Imagination requires deep mental contemplation and reflective labor in ways that are not always perfect but nonetheless offer productive avenues to visualize the world anew.

Yet one thing remains certain. Anzaldúa understood that alternating states of consciousness are empowering "when we shift our stance from the perceptual to the imaginal."[44] Similarly, the queer performance theorist José Esteban Muñoz demanded that we envision queerness as a future project, that "queerness is not yet here but it approaches like a crashing wave of potentiality."[45] Thus, the imagination is a powerful metaphorical concept to dream about a world not yet present, a world where we can "process feelings, traumas, negativities resulting from gender, racial, or other oppressions" and "mourn those losses" in a way that nourishes and heals the soul, even in ways that are unexplainable.[46] The crashing wave of potentiality will then commence once the vision is cultivated, processed, nurtured, and finalized in our imagination. Extending this to my concept of "critical imaginations," I argue that queer Hmong Americans struggle to enunciate a definitive configuration of spirituality and cosmology, and thus they leave open their imaginations in order to maintain the shape-shifting dimensions of identity and subjectivity in responding to their forced invisibility within hyperheterosexuality. Therefore, critical imagination is the "ability to spontaneously generate images in the mind," yet not fully concretizing those images in order to preserve an imagination that is simmering on the horizon.[47]

Rather than reject the soul, queer Hmong Americans problematize the soul to render abstract its meanings for future usage. In other words, "imagination is the realm of the soul, and the psyche's language is metaphorical."[48] In this sense, subjectivity is constructed and reconstructed in relation to what is critically imagined. Subjectivity is translated into experience through a series of creative gestures that remake knowledge and reveal reality to be a composition of that very same creative gesturing—critical imagination, if you will.[49] Critical imaginations, then, unsettle notions of cultural authenticity and radically reveal the limits of authenticity in discourses about identity and subjectivity and their intersection with gender and sexuality. That is, queer Hmong Americans' critical imaginations confront the fallacy that violence is fundamentally embedded in their native culture and precipitates their deaths and death-in-waiting.

Critical imaginations are evident in my interviews and conversations with queer Hmong Americans. In my conversation with Pakou, she revealed that she does not wholeheartedly believe in spiritual teachings and frameworks. However, as she grew older, she understood her mother's position, precisely because she herself was maturing into her own spiritual being. In this way, Pakou understood "culture" generally as a fragmented dynamic and malleable force amenable to reinterpretation. While Pakou's shaman mother was transfigured as the "authority" of spirituality and cosmology within the household, Pakou's questioning of her mother's teachings—"Sometimes, it's not real, sometimes it's real, maybe I'm schizophrenic, I don't know. I start questioning things"—demonstrates her rejection of the supposed truths of the spiritual and cosmological explanations of her, her sister's, and her sister's partner's queer genders and sexualities. However, she is ultimately ambivalent, using the word *schizophrenic* to designate the irregular going-betweenness and back-and-forthness of Hmong ways of knowing. Skepticism of this system of knowledge does not mean Pakou rejects it, but she calls into question its truthfulness as an explanation of her, her sister's, and her sister's partner's queerness. Pakou's shifting relationship and ultimate ambivalence toward her mother's deployment of spirituality enables a queer disruption of the rigidity of the cosmos as an overdetermining structure of nonnormative sexualities.[50]

Queer Hmong Americans also critically question the ways spirituality and cosmology are expended as disciplining tactics. In doing so, they offer evolving interpretations of the intersections of queer invisibility, spirituality, and cosmology. Pa Houa, a twenty-six-year-old pansexual woman, recalled her upbringing to me. She had run away from home as a teenager to live in the home of an abusive man, who regularly assaulted her. He fathered her first child soon after she moved in with him. Her abusive partner's mother also lived with them, and she found an excuse to be condescending toward Pa Houa on a nearly daily basis. Pa Houa eventually returned to her parents' home, only to discover that her return was not a welcoming event, due to her disobeying them, running away, being a domestic violence survivor, identifying as pansexual, being a teenage mother, and fracturing their family unit. Pa Houa's relationship with her parents became deeply strained and disjointed because of her rebelliousness and nonnormativity. After her maternal grandfather passed away in 2010, her mother forced her to consult a shaman to explain why the entire family was experiencing paranormal activities. Pa Houa's mother suspected that she was the cause of the family's unnerving paranormal experiences and ongoing disharmony. Her mother was also interested in having the shaman "explain" her rebelliousness and pansexuality. They ultimately learned from the shaman that these paranormal signs were indicative of Pa Houa herself likely becoming a shaman. The shaman also revealed to her why she was "rebellious" in her teenage years, as Pa Houa remembered:

> After my grandfather passed, my mom took me to go receive spiritual readings from shamans. They told me that the reason why I grew up so rebellious was because kuv nyob tsis taus qhov chaw [I don't have a home], [and] kuv muaj kuv cov dab neeb [I have had shamanistic spirits] since I was five years old. My soul was so destructive because it didn't have a home. So, growing up, I never cared much for Hmong religious beliefs. Because I think I'm an atheist. I don't really believe in anything. I didn't really believe in religious gatherings like hu plig [soul calling], or whether any of it really works. And I never really cared for it. I never really cared to do anything church-related either.[51]

Pa Houa's disbelief in the ways her soul was exploited to explain her rebelliousness is enlightening. In many ways, these systems of beliefs are used to simplify youth subjectivities and struggles in the United States. When so-called spirits are the only explanation, it renders invisible other political and socioeconomic structures that contribute to youth rebelliousness and insurgency. This usage of the spirits may also perpetuate neoliberal claims of personal and spiritual livelihood through the notion that it is the soul within the individual that is misplaced, displaced, or unplaced rather than larger sociopolitical dynamics that perhaps contributed to the spiritual displacement. Pa Houa was skeptical about whether or not the spiritual readings or soul-calling ceremonies "really work."

Despite this apparent disavowal, Pa Houa revealed her subjectivity to be more complicated. She told me that after her grandfather's death, she further experienced a series of unsettling dreams, which led her to accept that she might truly have been chosen by the spirits to become a shaman. She also began to believe that perhaps her misplaced soul did indeed lead to her rebelliousness. As Pa Houa stated, her "soul was so destructive because it didn't have a home," and therefore she was seen as lost.[52] Yet she embraced this narrative of her lost soul as a sign for her to find her way back home in order to accept her ultimate calling as a shaman. I also asked her if having the unsettling dreams affected her in a negative or positive way, to which she responded: "It did impact me in a positive way. I've had other paranormal experiences before. But I just thought it was just a thing that adults always tell you, that's why you see paranormal activities. I always thought it was always that way. It's so complicated and scary and weird."[53] Pa Houa's slow and evolving process of beginning to believe in her misplaced soul as an explanation for her rebelliousness and pansexual identity begs the interrogation of how systems of spirits and the cosmos are oppressive, but also liberatory, when queer Hmong Americans struggle over their meanings and are given complete and untethered freedom to interpret and embody spirituality on their own terms. Pa Houa's nonnormativity as a rebellious pansexual teenager who ran away from home and became pregnant disrupts the politics of reticence through her refusal to surrender to her parents' expectations of peace and harmony. She was traumatized to see a shaman, who claimed that her soul was displaced, but she ultimately found peace with her parents after her own relationship toward spirituality evolved into one that is more ambivalent and ambiguous. Pa Houa's spiritual transformation from not "really believing in anything" to now accepting that she might become a shaman represents how she converted her anti-reticent acts of rebellion into acts of reconciliation through critically reimagining her place as a queer subject within the shifting world of the cosmos.

By critiquing the essentialism of what has dominantly been understood to constitute Hmong cosmology, queer Hmong Americans can deconstruct and then subsequently critically imagine a flexible space for spirituality that dislodges hyperheterosexuality as the prevailing interpretative framework of Hmong gender and sexual politics. Since hyperheterosexuality purports Hmong's cultural forms to be monolithic, static, and oppressive, what becomes more powerful is when queer Hmong Americans articulate the instability of gender and sexuality through their interpretations of so-called cultural frameworks of spirituality and cosmology. This critical imagination is lucidly demonstrated in my conversation with Nhia, a twenty-five-year-old gay man, who has struggled for years to articulate a version of his soul that is anti-essentialist, flexible, ambiguous, and queer. When I asked him how spirituality has enabled him to come to terms with his understandings of his own sexuality, he responded:

> I legitimately thought about this for a while. For myself, I don't know what my plig [soul] looks like.[54] I don't know, I guess I don't believe in shamanism or animism at all. I don't know what to believe. But, in terms of my plig, I don't think there's a gender for it. I never imagined it as an image of myself. There is your soul, it looks like you, or at least that's what was communicated to me. But to me, I have a plig, but it doesn't look like me. I don't know what it looks like. I know it's kind of feminine for me. I don't think it's a man. And that's where I left it. But it took me a long time to get to that point. To be okay, to get to that. I know it's really simple and I just said it, but it took a long time. I don't see it as a man, but I also don't see it as an image of a human. It's not an animal either. I guess it's just a light or something. I don't know. I just don't see it as a human form, at least in the terms in which we imagine it. It's not humanoid. Sometimes old folks would say, oh nws nqa tsab ntawv tsis yog lawm os [he has a wrong life provision]. I imagine some queer or trans folks would think about that. I was supposed to nqa daim ntawv poj niam [bring the provision of a woman], tabsis nqa tau daim ntawv txiv neej lawm na [but instead brought a provision of life for a man]. Maybe that saying is just more of an expression in trying to communicate and explore gender identity, rather than actually finding an actual frame for identity.[55]

Nhia's struggles with this articulation speak more to the fractures of an essentialist formation of the soul than to what has been understood in dominant Hmong cosmology. The racist view would posit Hmong's expressions of spirituality as exotic, yet inflexible, as to render queer deaths and death-in-waiting. Nhia's struggles over the form and meaning of cosmology reveal that he is attempting to critically imagine a spirituality for himself that does not abandon animism as wholly unworthy despite his disbelief in most of its tenets. Rather, his testimony reveals how he is living *in this life* as a subject who does not strictly embody a gendered, masculine or feminine, "soul" despite his "incorrect" life provision ordained by Yawm Saub. In fact, Nhia gestures toward a posthumanist understanding of queerness that leaves open the possibilities of reading spirituality and cosmology queerly. This strange turn provides possibilities of reading beyond the male-female and body-soul dichotomies and positions queerness as posthuman.

Nhia's critical imagination of his soul as "a light" leads to a position of him not as a defective subject, but as a complex subject who may not neatly fit in the normative paradigms of a gendered or humanist cosmology. Nhia's queerness is complex because he resists static arrangements of spirituality and cosmology and their relation to sexuality, while also struggling to not exoticize spirituality as an extension of "culture." That there are no words in the Hmong language to name or describe queerness is not incongruous in this instance, as it seems queerness is unnameable and indescribable to begin with. There is an inarticulability about his queer existence that ultimately works to "reinterpret history" and "shape new myths" about subjectivity.[56] Additionally, Nhia's contention that sometimes the supposed "provision," which oftentimes might be read as strict or essentialist, is not necessarily a means to an end for interpreting queerness. Rather, it is just another paradigm of subjectivity that queer and trans Hmong Americans can creatively reappropriate or contingently utilize in their own self-discoveries of what queerness means as they experiment with their identities as second-generation children of refugees.

Queer Hmong American critical imaginations are perhaps most ingenious and concrete when creatively conjoined directly with animist religious practices. This is the case with Siv Yis, a well-respected twenty-three-year-old queer shaman master, who has refashioned much of religious scripture to queer animist practices. Moving from the world of dreams within the inner world and implementing it in the outer world, he creatively interprets the *ntsuj* (soul) and the *plig* (spirits or minor souls) in ways that queer spirituality and cosmology. Siv Yis carefully explained to me in our conversation that the *xyw* (totality of the self) is a constellation of twelve *ntsuj* and twenty-four *plig*. The *plig* are the smallest fragments of the self, which Siv Yis equates to "cells" in the body. Thus, when an individual *poob plig* (loses their soul), they will not die, as that is only a small particle of the totality of the self, although they may fall sick. Taken together, the phrase *ntsuj/plig* (souls and spirits) also constitutes the various essences that encompass the *xyw*. The *ntsuj/plig* are the vivacious organs that constitute Hmong metaphysical life.[57] Similarly, the anthropologist Jacques Lemoine's own shaman master Xyooj Tsu Yob described the twelve souls as "expressing a crucial aspect of human psychosomatic life."[58] Siv Yis distinguishes between a variety of *ntsuj/plig*, stating,

The ntsuj is neutral, while all the plig are a mixture of feminine, masculine, and those that are in-between. Some ntsuj/plig are chickens, pigs, or cows. There are also a variety of plig, including plig qaib (chicken spirits), plig noog (bird spirits), plig nyuj kab (pull cow spirits), plig nyuj kaus (mooing cow spirits), plig qoob plig loo (harvest spirits), plig nplej plig txhuv (rice stalk and rice grain spirits). When someone is queer, Hmong people can say they are more balanced because they can control a variety of feminine and masculine [energies]. We talk about spirituality being balanced. [Thus], queer folks are more [whole], more balanced, more spiritual.[59]

Siv Yis is often called on to "explain" queerness to elders in a multiplicity of contexts, including one in which family members performed a Christian exorcism on their gay son. Siv Yis recounted, "They put the Bible on his head. They are screaming in his face."[60] When this exorcism did not work, Siv Yis was called on to offer an animist interpretation, which was then readily accepted by the individual's parents. Siv Yis stated, "I broke it down to his parents. I said nws tus plig zoo nkauj [their spirit is beautiful], or nws tus plig zoo nraug [their spirit is handsome], or nws tus plig muaj ib tsom li no [their spirit has a quirk and is different]."[61] While the dominant interpretation of Hmong culture may deem its spiritual and cosmological elements to be oppressive to queer Hmong, an individual like Siv Yis problematizes this interpretation by revealing the constellation of parts that comprise the self, not in strictly gendered terms, but in ways that are posthuman. Furthermore, Siv Yis intervenes in Christian homophobia by offering Hmong epistemologies of queerness, revealing that one Hmong-specific way of knowing queerness is the liberatory episteme—not the oppressive one—as in this particular scenario.

What Lemoine's shaman master Xyooj Tsu Yob may describe as the "vegetative souls" and "unstable souls," and what Siv Yis characterizes as souls/spirits that are grounded in cycles of harvest, rice, and animals, for Hmong souls/spirits are not strictly static or even gendered. They in fact fluctuate in alignment with one's sociopolitical environment. So, when a particular *plig* is lost—say, the *plig qoob plig loo* (harvest spirit) becomes lost—then symptoms of illness may include loss of appetite, as it corresponds to the social condition of exhausting one's food reserves or experiencing famine. A shaman must therefore call on the individual's *ntsuj/plig* by buying "a new (symbolic) stock of food wherewith to sustain [the individual's] life."[62] In sum, Siv Yis describes the soul as more expansive and capable of being adversely affected by a host of sociopolitical and metaphysical dynamics across the cosmological dominions of *ntuj*, *ntiaj teb*, and *dab teb*, rather than relegating any deficiency of the soul to the singular individual.

Siv Yis argues that reframing the *ntsuj/plig* in this way—as a fleeting soul impacted by sociopolitical forces—enables Hmong folks "to respect [the queer person] because [the *ntsuj/plig*] is so precious and holy." He added, "They then will not judge the individual. It helps them humanize the [queer] person. [Queerness is] not a deformity and it is not an illness."[63] In Siv Yis's interpretation, queerness is not a bodily dysfunction or sickness, as has been understood in Western biomedical history. Rather, what is causing the "illness" of the subject is a social condition, such as *homophobia*. That is, the *plig* can "become lost through wandering or fright from traumatic events such as displacement or an accident, leaving the body weak and prone to sickness" and not through any kind of deformity within the subject themself.[64] It is the conditions made unlivable in the world for all minoritized subjects, particularly refugees and queer people, such as war, forced displacement, refugee resettlement, poverty, or famine, and an amalgamation of interpersonal, reticent, and state-based homophobias that generate Hmong refugee and queer Hmong American disempowerment, death, and death-in-waiting. Consequently, Siv Yis's expert knowledge fundamentally challenges the essentialism of hyperheterosexuality, particularly the element of homophobia that exists against the backdrop of queer liberalism. Instead, the critical imagination in his head and within the cosmic realm and his subsequent enactment of these imaginations in the outer world affirm queer Hmong Americans' epistemologies of spirituality and cosmology, and their overall senses of selves.

Queer Hmong Americans' critical imaginations and simultaneous refusal and reception of the explanatory powers of spirituality and cosmology deconstruct the inscrutability of cosmology as the "truth" of naming and understanding queer sexuality. In the case of Xiong and Yang, their deaths only became legible for Hmong when reincorporated through the system of cosmology and for non-Hmong when repackaged into a voyeuristic "ethnic" display of religion presented in the *Fresno Bee* report. Thus, when cosmological fundamentalism is deployed as an expounding reticent force, queer Hmong Americans resist the narratives of their bodies and souls as "incorrect" or as a "mistake." Taken in this way, they challenge the essentialist framings of queer sexuality as inherently "wrong." This mirrors the critiques of biological and bodily essentialisms that are used in discourses of biomedicine and sexology to reify queer sexualities and trans embodiments as needing to be "fixed," oftentimes through death. Queer

Hmong Americans' reframing of these explanations also reincorporates them into Hmong-specific epistemologies that empower them when they are given opportunities and wide-ranging liberty to critically imagine the intersections of gender, sexuality, spirituality, cosmology, and subjectivity on their own terms. Doing so means that they can create empowering modes of existence in *this life* for themselves and not always defer them to the next life.

My argument thus complicates Hmong ways of knowing about gender and sexuality to highlight the hidden reticent forces in their deployment that facilitate queer slow deaths, skew queer sexuality, and deny the agency and livelihood of queer Hmong Americans. The spiritual ramifications are liabilities because of the incapacity to bestow queer freedom through cosmology, but such spiritual and cosmological frameworks also offer some possible rationalizations for "unexplainable" and complex phenomena such as ethnic and queer subject formation. However, more importantly, we cannot hold on to cosmology's emancipatory powers if we fail to scrutinize its reticent poetics of disavowal that dematerializes queerness, relegates queer people to the realm of ghosts, and masks such a realm as "agentic" without interrogating its aesthetic structures of power. Queer Hmong American critical imaginations expose the ways hyperheterosexuality works to exaggerate Hmong's gender and sexual politics and practices through cultural and racial difference while constricting Hmong-specific forms of queerness under the current phase of queer liberalism.

REFIGURING LOSS AND REORIENTING STATES OF BEING LOST

This chapter has woven together three interrelated components through a critical reading of an infamous report written about Hmong American youth suicides in the early years of the new millennium coupled with interviews and conversations with queer Hmong Americans. First, I scrutinized dominant narratives of refugees as lost subjects of history as they are juxtaposed alongside the suicides of two queer Hmong Americans to illuminate how this ideological positioning enables an uncritical coherence of Hmong refugee and Hmong queer subjectivities in the United States. Second, I utilized a queer of color critique to interrogate cosmology's role in denying queerness through its reticent politics in ways that bolster the dominant narrative of Hmong culture as oppressive to queer people, while I also pushed back against uncritical narratives of freedom within discourses of queer liberalism. And third, I centralized queer Hmong Americans' lived realities, embodied experiences, and critical imaginations to envision queer, anti-essentialist, and empowering formations of spirituality and cosmology that unsettle the discourse of hyperheterosexuality rooted in Hmong cultural and racial difference.

Hyperheterosexuality—and its consequent arm of forcing the invisibility of racially minoritized queerness—oversimplifies and overdetermines queer Hmong American subjectivities as lost subjects of history and victims of their homophobic native culture. That is, the oppressive binary of being an American queer or being a Hmong refugee performs the ideological work of unraveling the intersectionality of queer Hmong American identities. This undoing of intersectional queer and ethnic identities arranges Hmong and refugee subjectivities into clearly delineated compositions. Hyperheterosexuality as an ideological formation also possesses material consequences for queer Hmong Americans because it forces them to become invisible through an uncritical labeling of a minoritized culture as illiberal against a supposedly emancipated dominant society without attending to the micropolitics of violence against queer people that is not neatly contained within this binary. Neither the notion of freedom anchored in sexual and queer liberalism nor Hmong's dominant frameworks of spirituality and cosmology present feasible avenues for queer Hmong to materialize as intelligible cultural and political subjects. Queer Hmong American critical imaginations thus reorganize this materiality by disengaging from essentialist articulations of culture and entering into a domain where culture can operate sinuously with the fluctuating crescendos of race, class, gender, and sexuality.

The recognition of queer Hmong Americans as subjects of historiography discursively constructed through Hmong as lost refugees from a "primitive, agrarian society" registers their critical imaginations as direct challenges to their forced invisibility. In this vein, queer Hmong American critical imaginations disrupt simple constructions of Hmong gender and sexual representations to articulate a more nuanced formation of subjectivity rooted in ambiguity, fluidity, and contradiction that dislodges queer liberalism and cultural essentialism. Queer Hmong American lived experiences and experiential knowledge should compel the development of a queer and feminist theory that critically reimagines spirituality and cosmology as "subversive counter-usage" forms of political subjectivity.[65] Deaths of queers have consequences for us all, and so do the deaths of the many refugees in the United States' present imperial wars. The story of Xiong and Yang lingers in our memories and continues to serve as a call for us as advocates to "raise the dead" and craft a more flexible and socially just world for refugees and queer youth of color everywhere.[66]

CHAPTER 4

Vernacular Activism

RACE-RADICAL POLITICS
OF SAME-SEX MARRIAGE

Before same-sex marriage was legalized by the United States Supreme Court's 2015 landmark decision *Obergefell v. Hodges*, contentious ballot initiatives were being waged across multiple states to address its legal status. During the 2012 elections, Minnesota voters were presented with a ballot referendum called Amendment 1, colloquially known as the "marriage amendment," to change the state constitution to redefine marriage as solely a legal union between one man and one woman.[1] Minnesotans for Marriage was the organization that advocated the passage of Amendment 1. The organization Minnesotans United for All Families was established at that time to defeat the ballot referendum, while seeking to ultimately legalize same-sex marriage in Minnesota.[2] A queer Hmong American grassroots collective named MidWest Solidarity Movement (MWSM) emerged at the same time to defeat Amendment 1 and a concurrent voter ID ballot referendum, which, if passed, would have legally required voters to possess a valid identification card in order to vote. Three queer Hmong American activists founded MWSM, and the collective situated its activism within the larger mainstream movement to legalize same-sex marriage in the United States, as well as within the context of Hmong American activism against racial injustices that had been afflicting the community since at least the mid-1990s.[3]

The official vision of MWSM was to "build power through reclaiming narratives and redefining identities and organizing for cultural change and racial justice."[4] Queer Cambodian, Lao, and Vietnamese American activists subsequently participated in its organizing efforts as well, transforming MWSM into an entirely queer Southeast Asian American collective.[5] MWSM members and volunteers phone banked alongside Minnesotans United volunteers to strategically target Hmong American voters. MWSM cofounder Pao, a Thai-born twenty-six-year-old who identified as a cisgender queer man, stated to me that he estimated MWSM members and volunteers talked to nearly one thousand Hmong voters about Amendment 1 and same-sex marriage more broadly throughout 2012.[6] "I'm happy that the marriage amendment went on the ballot," proclaimed Pao. "I'm happy that it happened, because it forced tag nrho peb cov Hmoob [all us Hmong] queers to face that reality and to talk to our communities about queer and gay marriage. So that's what I loved about it."[7] MWSM members and volunteers also participated in a larger Twin Cities grassroots campaign called Vote No Twice, which highlighted the intersectional activism of organizers who understood that the constitutional amendments requiring voters to possess identification cards and restricting marriage to a legal union solely between one man and one woman were conjoined policies that harmed communities of color.[8]

MWSM's activism offered a critical Hmong American perspective on organizing that accounts for their marginalized social position within the United States' racial and sexual social order. Pao and other activists engaged in a race-radical form of activism that I term *vernacular activism*—which is a political approach that employs Hmong's hyperheterosexual status as non–model minority Asian Americans to facilitate new inquiries concerning social justice organizing and activism against racism, homophobia, and other forms of social injustice.[9] A vernacular activism draws from Hmong American epistemologies and lived experiences of gender and sexuality to respond to the failures of liberal multiculturalism and queer liberalism to bestow freedom on people of color and queer people in the United States. As the feminist scholar Aniruddha Dutta demonstrates, the vernacular form of sexuality complicates and exposes the ineffectiveness and exclusionary logics of official and global discourses on lesbian and gay identities, which constitute the formalized, institutionalized, and nonvernacular formulations of rights. A vernacular mode of knowing and performing also "displaces, expands, and reshapes" society through the knowledge and "contradictory possibilities" found within the subject positions of marginalized communities.[10] Vernacular in a linguistics sense refers to the everyday speech acts and forms of language common to a particular community. These speech acts and language forms are stigmatized as inferior to elitist "standardized languages" that have been designated as national languages formalized through official science and literature. Deployed metaphorically, a vernacular may comprise any form of cultural product or practice that is germane to minoritized, marginalized, and non-elite modes of existence beyond formalized or universalized cultural forms. A Hmong vernacular activism — by extension — utilizes Hmong language, epistemologies, practices, and aesthetics of hyperheterosexuality to enact a politics of social justice beyond the version of same-sex marriage emblematic of queer liberalism anchored in hetero- and homonormativities.

Drawing from my experiences at phone banks with MWSM members and volunteers, analysis of MWSM's photo campaign, participant observation from protests at the Minnesota state capitol in the aftermath of the defeat of Amendment 1, and interviews with queer Hmong Americans, I theorize how racially minoritized gender and sexuality are imperative to understanding Hmong American organizing for social justice in the United States. Through a vernacular activism that considers the status of Hmong American racial and sexual marginality, MWSM reframes freedom for Hmong Americans and communities of color away from queer liberal discourses of discrimination, equality, and rights by imagining and enacting vernacular forms of sociality that enact life making beyond hyperheterosexuality. MWSM's activism and queer Hmong American experiences of marriage critique queer liberal politics to reveal how nonvernacular, universalizing discourses that reproduce hetero- and homonormativities subjugate racially minoritized communities.

UNIVERSALIZING ACTIVISM FOR SAME-SEX MARRIAGE

In May 2011, the Minnesota legislature passed a bill to place Amendment 1 on the ballot in the November 2012 election. Immediately afterward, the LGBTQ organizations OutFront Minnesota and Project 515 joined forces to form Minnesotans United for All Families to defeat Amendment 1. Minnesotans United sought the help of David Fleischer, a veteran organizer who had been involved with national organizations fighting against ballot referendums to ban same-sex marriage in other states.[11] The Minnesota Family Council, the Minnesota Catholic Conference, and the National Organization for Marriage all allied to form the larger organization Minnesotans for Marriage, the leading anti-same-sex-marriage organization advocating for Amendment 1. Frank Schubert of the National Organization for Marriage — notorious for leading efforts in other states to ban same-sex marriage, including the successful passing of California's Proposition 8 in 2008 — was a central figure in the Minnesota Amendment 1 battle.[12] The reliance on individuals who had worked on this issue nationally did not make

Minnesota particularly unique in the conversation and discourse on same-sex marriage occurring across the nation from at least 1998 to 2015. However, the involvement of Hmong Americans *did* make queer politics unique in Minnesota, as Hmong Americans worked to craft a vernacular activist framework defeating Amendment 1. Minnesotans ultimately rejected both Amendment 1 and the voter ID ballot referendums on November 6, 2012; 52.56 percent of Minnesotans voted no on Amendment 1, compared to 47.44 percent who voted yes.[13] In rejecting Amendment 1, Minnesota became the first state in history—after thirty other states had passed constitutional amendments prior to *Obergefell v. Hodges* banning same-sex marriage—to defeat a ballot referendum seeking to define marriage solely as a legal union between one man and one woman.[14] Minnesota subsequently legalized same-sex marriage in May 2013 through the state legislature, when it secured enough Senate and House seats during the 2012 election cycle to do so.

The campaign to defeat Amendment 1 was well underway by early 2012. Thousands of Minnesotans United canvassers were dispatched to engage in conversations with millions of voters across the state. In a video released on its website, Minnesotans United claimed its official "special tactic" was simply talking, stating that voters were 67 percent more likely to vote against Amendment 1 when they engaged in conversations with canvassers about this issue.[15] Minnesotans United also provided "talking point" scripts to canvassers regarding African American, Latino, Asian American, and Native American communities during door-knocking and phone-banking sessions. The talking points were essentially identical for all communities of color. The only distinction made for why same-sex marriage should matter to a particular community of color was for Indigenous communities and included references to Two-Spirit people.[16] All of Minnesotans United's scripts included one illustrative text that read: "This amendment singles out a group of people and excludes them from fundamental freedoms." To underscore this point, another talking point also stated, "None of us would want to be told it is illegal to marry the persons we love" and "Reflecting on our core values helps move the conversation forward." The talking points universalized the outreach to these communities by centralizing queer liberalism's vocabulary of love. The scholar Myrl Beam has demonstrated that this pivot toward the rhetoric of love sought to universalize marriage as a common desire yet in reality entrenched whiteness, capitalism, and nationalism.[17]

The universalizing language and outreach tactics homogenized all communities of color and treated them as a monolith, despite the documents purporting to be unique talking points for the four distinct groups of Indigenous and communities of color. For example, the subpoints under the talking point "None of us would want to be told it is illegal to marry the persons we love" included the following text for all communities of color:

- Marriage is about **love, commitment, and responsibility**.[18] Same-sex couples want to marry for similar reasons as anyone else—to make a lifetime promise of love and commitment, as well as to protect their families.
- Our communities value family—and fairness—and defeating this amendment would preserve fairness for all families. None of us would want to be told it is illegal to marry, and create a family, with the person we love. None of us would want to be told what our family should look like.[19]

Scholars have critiqued the mainstream lesbian and gay movement for universalizing the notion that legalizing same-sex marriage would mean equality and emancipation for all LGBTQ people. Naming legal marriage as a universal commitment to love elides other possibilities of intimacy that are not, and cannot be, neatly folded into neoliberal or privatized regimes of monogamous legal marriage. While Minnesotans United's talking points stated that nobody wants to be told it is illegal to marry and create a family with the person they love, the legislative bills highlighting the illegality of polygamy and so-called underage marriages (chapter 2) purported to be rampant among Hmong Americans contradict this neoliberal, universalizing marriage regime that is part and parcel of queer liberal nomenclature. Universalist discourses of marriage enable racist violence and social control by juxtaposing the "illegality," "criminality," and "immorality" of certain formulations of intimacy and conjugality commonly attributed to people of color and immigrants against articulations of same-sex love that encompass homonormative politics on the fight to legalize same-sex marriage.

Hmong American organizing was even more imperative against the backdrop of the universalizing logics of mainstream lesbian and gay activism more broadly, and the whiteness of Minnesotans United in particular. Minnesotans United's expenditures and financial disbursements revealed its lack of engagement with communities of color in the quest to defeat Amendment 1 and the subsequent mission to legalize same-sex marriage in Minnesota. Minnesotans United fundraised more than $12 million in the course of eighteen months to defeat Amendment 1. Nearly $8 million of the budget was expended for advertising and "Vote no" message delivery, direct voter contact, and youth organizing. Minnesotans

United factored in only a meager $231,000 to be used for "communities of color organizing."[20] This is all the more troubling when we consider that 80 percent of its budget was used for advertising and promotion, which included minimal appearances of people of color, if at all.

Interestingly, $218,000 was also to be used for "faith organizing."[21] While it was difficult to pinpoint the specifics of "faith organizing" in Minnesotans United's archives, it is worth noting that the funding amount was comparable to that allocated for all "communities of color organizing." Concomitantly, it was also challenging to examine the archives to understand what constituted funding for "communities of color organizing" aside from the fact that Minnesotans United hired African American, Latino, Native American, and Asian American community organizers to work in the organization. Of these four groups, only the Latino and Asian American community organizers stayed with Minnesotans United from the beginning until the end of the election, while all the Native American and both African American organizers resigned several months into their position or before Election Day. Minnesotans United hired a Korean American adoptee as its Asian American organizer and later hired two additional Hmong American organizers—including MWSM cofounder Pao—to assist the Asian American community organizer in her outreach efforts to larger Asian American communities. The hiring of the two Hmong American organizers was necessary because the majority of Asian Americans living in the Twin Cities are Hmong. Pao told me, "[The Asian American organizer] came in with very little Asian American organizing background. She had not organized with Asian Americans before. Her idea of organizing, she blatantly told me, was, 'I thought about going to conferences where there are a lot of Asians and just [doing outreach] there.' I was thinking, that is not the way to do organizing at all!"[22]

Minnesotans United operated as a nonprofit organization in its short lifespan, often reproducing the long-standing structures of neoliberalism and whiteness inherent in the nonprofit industrial complex. Scholars have documented the rise in large-scale nonprofit organizations since at least the 1960s and examined their complicity in the proliferation of state surveillance of public discourse, leftist social movements, and radical politics.[23] This rise in the nonprofit industrial complex is simultaneously a gesture toward the neoliberalization of lesbian and gay social movements and, as Beam calls it, the "nonprofitization of queer politics."[24] The upwardly mobile version of social justice organizing within nonprofit organizations is problematic and ineffective, because it operates within a trickle-down economy of freedom where a few concentrated elite lesbian and gay individuals sit at the top of the social order.[25] The most elite members of lesbian and gay organizations at the forefront of the legalization of same-sex marriage were wealthy white men and women, who were detached from the material realities of poor, homeless, undocumented, queer people of color. Research on diversity work within queer activism and organizations illustrates that even though "diversity" initiatives are actively promoted, whiteness is retained through the ways people of color are marginalized and tokenized for the consumption of white activists and employees.[26] Whiteness pervades lesbian and gay organizing precisely because of the continued deployment of neoliberal corporate social configurations and modalities of organizing for rights within mainstream lesbian and gay social movements. Minnesotans United's hiring of organizers for the communities of color constituent groups did very little to bring forth racial justice within the mainstream queer organization, ultimately reproducing tokenism of people of color and exposing the futility of queer liberalism.

In constructing marriage as a homonormative practice, mainstream lesbian and gay organizations and activism have implicitly rejected the "deviant" hyperheterosexual formations that have come to constitute Hmong gender and sexuality, marriage, and culture since Hmong's arrival in the United States in the mid-1970s. The language of queer liberalism is notably anti-queer and aligns more closely with the violent structures of the heteronormative society that rejected queerness in the first place. Thus, while scholars and activists have deployed the notion of "queer" as a radical concept for enacting social change, as evident throughout the second half of the twentieth century and with the advent of queer studies in the 1990s, mainstream enactment of queerness seeks to acquire "rights" that signal assimilation into dominant society. Mainstream queer politics, then, flattens radicalism by delineating the boundaries of acceptable sexual practices and people deemed "other," most conspicuously racialized subjects with supposedly aberrant politics and practices of gender and sexuality, including Hmong. Additionally, racial justice is homogenized, marking all communities of color as a monolith in their representational and outreach politics. Minnesotans United nullified intersectional radical queerness and race radicalism when such intersectionalities mattered most in the high-stakes context of Amendment 1.

RECASTING RACIALIZED SEXUALITIES FOR SOCIAL JUSTICE

I joined MWSM during the Amendment 1 battle because of my connections and relationships with its founders. I also volunteered for the Organizing for America campaign in 2012 to reelect President Barack Obama. Organizers and volunteers at Organizing for America also phone banked to convince Minnesotans to vote against the Amendment 1 and voter ID ballots. I also attended two prominent and contentious rallies with MWSM members at the Minnesota state capitol in May 2013, when the Minnesota legislature legalized same-sex marriage. My position as an activist-scholar participating in antiracist and queer organizing at the time enabled me to observe closely the strategies of Hmong Americans at the Minnesotans United and Organizing for America offices. Shifts in scholarship in sexuality studies, particularly ethnographic studies of sexuality, from studying cultural differences of homosexuality to studies concerning globalization, neoliberalism, and activism in the United States, facilitated my interest in thinking more deeply about Hmong American gender and sexual politics, especially what they have to offer to the domain of queer theorizing, organizing, and justice.[27] As an activist-scholar committed to social justice, I felt a sense of responsibility to collaborate with MWSM members and their volunteers to brainstorm and enact a praxis of language that could be used to recast the universalizing language deployed by mainstream queer organizations such as Minnesotans United to one more attuned to the vernacular experiences of minoritized communities. Thus, articulating how queer Hmong Americans both critiqued the universalizing logics of mainstream queer activism and initiated a sustained engagement with their own communities reveals that a radical queer Hmong American vernacular activism was crucial in the quest to defeat Amendment 1 and ultimately legalize same-sex marriage for the entire state of Minnesota.

On August 5, 2012, I phone banked for Minnesotans United at its St. Paul office to sway voters against the Amendment 1 and voter ID ballot referendums. Pao also organized targeted Hmong American voter phone banks every Sunday to talk only to Hmong Americans. He told me, "Basically on Sunday, we would have all Hmong American people run the phone banks. And we would have Hmong American volunteers call Hmong people all day."[28] Pao introduced a few of us volunteers to a Minnesotans United phone script, and after the first-time phone bankers finished asking clarifying questions, we immediately started phone banking. I was an experienced phone banker and was excited to begin. I called about forty people in the three hours that I was there. Most voters spoke English, but there were also many who were non-English speakers and either supported Amendment 1 or did not know anything about it at all. The talking points on Minnesotans United's script included using language of individual liberty, the freedom to choose a partner, and notions of free love and invoked ideas about discrimination based on sexual orientation. Some of the voters I talked to even knew a lesbian or gay person, sometimes a direct relative. That made it easier to connect with them when appealing to lesbian and gay people's humanity and right to choose whom to love. While not all the individuals I spoke to changed their minds on the phone, they understood that individual freedom was important. Overall, it was easy to engage with English speakers in conversations utilizing the language and frameworks that invoked liberal freedom, freewill love, the notion of choice, and discrimination, which have since come to define the rhetoric of civil rights and liberalism in the United States.

However, the Minnesotans United phone-banking script did not resonate with non-English-speaking Hmong. I observed one volunteer struggling to articulate these talking points in the Hmong language over the phone. I admired her efforts and thought she was much better at translating these concepts into Hmong than I was. I continued to call voters after ruminating more about the script. In one conversation, I argued that lesbian and gay couples should have the right (*muaj cai*) to marry. The Hmong elderly woman on the phone was immediately confused about how two people of the same sex can marry at all, let alone have the "right" to marry. I invoked the notion of individual choice (*muaj cai xaiv tus yus xav yuav*), to marry whom one chooses. However, she was unable to comprehend that lesbian and gay people can "choose" whom to marry when for her marriage could not be solely contained within the framework of choice. In her imagination, marriage between lesbian and gay couples did not register within the paradigm of individual liberty, because she had not reached the register that such groups had "rights" at all. More importantly, marriage for her was not about rights or choices, but about Hmong's concepts of kin and community building. For the elderly woman, and perhaps for many Hmong, marriage was less about *cai* and more about how to create a life (*ua neej*). Moreover, invoking the language of discrimination in terms of withholding the right to marry from lesbian and gay couples did not have the affective or moral appeal that I had hoped it would. In fact, I struggled to translate terms such as *equality* from English into Hmong, as there is no equivalent lexicon from which to draw. From the perspective of the elderly woman I talked to, it may have been difficult to empathize with lesbian and gay couples because she was so far removed from the everyday experiences of queer individuals, coupled with her understanding of marriage not as a system of choices in the marketplace but as a structure of life making. The liberal talking points in the Minnesotans United script were not registering for non-English speakers. More tragically, I myself as a bilingual Hmong and English-speaking scholar was unable to translate and convey effectively the rhetoric of "equality," "freedom," "choice," and "discrimination" to this particular constituent group. I realized that my framework of needing to translate these concepts from English into Hmong was the problem in and of itself.

My next phone call required a new strategy. What if I did not mention lesbians and gays at all? What effect would that have? I pondered the ways that Amendment 1 limited marriage not just for queer folks but for a host of other people. Amendment 1 would define marriage as a legal union solely between one man and one woman, thus leaving no room for any nonmonogamous and nonnormative intimacies. Such a narrow configuration of marriage would exclude not only same-sex monogamous marriages but also Hmong American heterosexual plural marriages, common-law and so-called underage marriages, queer nonmonogamous marriages, or any marriages not situated within a heteronormative legal framework of family, love, and kinship. Appealing to how this amendment would cause a larger harm, and more specifically an injury to Hmong Americans, could be my best rhetorical maneuver. That is, while Amendment 1 did not formally target Hmong nonnormative kinship and intimate practices that are subsumed under hyperheterosexuality, it nonetheless promoted a de facto system of surveillance and prohibition that sought to narrowly define the purviews of intimacy. Amendment 1 represented another instantiation of white bourgeois supremacy that sought to curb and define the boundaries of belonging for all kinds of minoritized subjects. Constitutionally defining the terms of marriage as between one man and one woman would enable the state to stigmatize, at best, and criminalize, at worst, those outside of that formation, while selectively assimilating certain willing immigrants and lesbian and gay people into a respectable national body politic and culture. The state's potential intrusion into Hmong marriage practices and its forced assimilation of Hmong into white heteronormativity were issues that could resonate with Hmong Americans in opposing Amendment 1.[29]

My next phone call was again to an elderly woman. I said to her: "Nyob zoo. Kuv lub npe hu ua Koob Pheej os. Kuv hu noog koj hais tias koj puas tau hnov txog lawv txoj cai uas hais txog kev sib yuav? Tsis tau los? Tsis ua li cas." (Hello, my name is Kong Pheng. I am calling to ask if you know about the marriage amendment? Oh no? I see.) With that, I continued to inform her how the state wanted to define marriage within the constitution to be strictly between one man and one woman. I mentioned that the amendment would hurt Hmong Americans because it meant they would be prohibited from practicing de facto "marriages" under age sixteen and plural common-law marriages. In fact, it would not only prohibit but also open the door to criminalize those practicing nonmonogamous or nonnormative relationships within Hmong American society. She knew Hmong American individuals who were in loving plural common-law marriages and did not want to infringe on that kinship formation, which she understood as loving and ethical. She saw plural marriage not as a system of "choices" undertaken by the various parties, but as a mode of existence in which Hmong were creating a life (*ua lub neej Hmoob*). Ultimately, she said she would vote against Amendment 1 because she did not want the government to infringe on Hmong lives. At this point, I was certain that she did not know this amendment had anything to do with same-sex marriage. She was unaware that there were previous amendments put forth in other states, including North Carolina, Florida, and neighboring Wisconsin, to constitutionally define marriage as solely a legal union between one man and one woman.

By not mentioning lesbian and gay marriages, I was able to present Amendment 1 as a tool designed by the state to control nonmonogamous and nonnormative marriages germane to Hmong Americans.[30] I phone banked again on October 23, 2012, at the Organizing for America headquarters, where I simultaneously talked to voters about both the Amendment 1 and voter ID ballots. I continued to use my strategy, and, much to my amazement, Hmong Americans were receptive to voting against Amendment 1. To be sure, some Hmong Americans supported Amendment 1 precisely because they opposed same-sex marriage, while some opposed Amendment 1 because they supported lesbians and gays. Nonetheless, this rhetorical maneuver enabled another, often overlooked dimension of queerness and its intersection with public policy and organizing to be pertinent and salient to a Hmong vernacular politics of gender and sexuality in this specific historical moment.

In another moment of enacting a vernacular politics, Pakou, a fellow phone banker, mimicked my strategy while offering up another interpretation of Hmong American speech acts. Pakou explained to me later in an interview: "It is all words, if you are polite to older Hmong American people, they care about politeness. Because if you go to Hmong parents and say, 'Yuav tsum mus vote no nawb! [You have to vote no!],' they'd be like, 'Whoa!' Like I said, we grew up very traditional, so there's a formal Hmong, and you have to know how to speak formal Hmong to older people. So you have to say, 'Oh tus niam tais, oh tus niam ntxawm, nej mus pov npav no ces, vote no [Oh grandma, oh auntie, if you all go vote, please vote no],' speak politely, explain it thoroughly to them."[31]

In this sense, Pakou's use of kinship terms with voters by referring to them as "grandma" and "auntie" draws from a Hmong-specific mode of knowledge aimed at crafting kinship with voters. Hmong's way of recognizing strangers as family reveals how kinship is not a system of choices within a neoliberal marketplace, but rather a technique of community building aimed at cultivating a collective well-being. Pakou utilized the formal semantics of the Hmong language and exercised familiar structures of kinship in this political moment not only to educate elders about same-sex marriage but also to secure their political vote. The strategic maneuvering of semantics does not employ certain "in your face" activist strategies that are often associated with mainstream politics. In fact, Pakou's enactment of a vernacular politics does not appear to be "politics" at all in the electoral or organizing sense. Rather, Pakou cemented relationships with voters by drawing them into a wider network of kinship that is aimed at relationship building, community education, and life making.

It seems Pakou's version of vernacular politics and speech prioritized the semantics and affective elements of kin making, whereas the version that I enacted in my phone calls relied on deploying Hmong's hyperheterosexual status as a relevant analogy. Pakou engaged with formal politics by "going around in circles" through formal speech acts and talking to Hmong Americans through a personal vernacular activist approach. While I framed Amendment 1 as an injury to Hmong's kinship practices, Pakou went beyond deploying hyperheterosexuality to craft a system of life making and community building that could allow for political engagement among Hmong Americans. Pakou's knowledge of framing voters as kin revealed that it was not the issue at hand that mattered to Hmong Americans. Rather, it was *how* she engaged voters through a Hmong-specific language of kinship that drew them into her political cause. Pakou was simultaneously deploying my analogy of the criminalization of hyperheterosexuality as an appeal to Hmong's political morality as much as enacting a politics of refusal of the same analogy by broadening her framework of intimacy, which might allow voters to engage her in all sorts of political issues in the future. Thus, both the semantics of speech through reframing kinship as community building and life making and the content of analogy were crucial to securing Hmong votes in the fight against Amendment 1.

My argument here is that reframing the conversation around same-sex marriage through another angle provides the flexibility to think about state-control apparatuses that affect not just queer people but racially minoritized groups as well. Working with Hmong American activists in MWSM to phone bank and educate Hmong Americans, I observed that while the limited vocabularies of liberal freedom, individual choice, and discrimination within queer liberalism may be useful in certain contexts, it is the rethinking of freedom through a new way of relating to one another that may present a different dynamic to social justice (and social justice organizing) for a marginalized community like Hmong. Ultimately, recasting the conversations with Hmong Americans as not solely a race to secure a vote but also a process of kinship formation within the long duration of Hmong refugee life-making in the United States demonstrates how a Hmong vernacular politics can inform new modes of engaging minoritized, underserved, and underrepresented constituents within the democratic process.

A vernacular politics can be compared to a queer of color critique that unsettles the national discourses in which same-sex marriage is predicated on the use of what the queer theorist Chandan Reddy notes are new "epistemological frames."[32] Proponents of same-sex marriage must account for the material conditions of a variety of people who continue to resist the structural violence that operates as an impediment to freedom, including non-English-speaking immigrants and refugees and any other polity whose kinship and intimate practices may also be subjected to state stigmatization, surveillance, and criminalization. In other words, a queer of color critique enlivens the *bodies* and *speech* of marginalized groups in order to refurnish the epistemological frames used to narrate sexual heterogeneities—moving these narratives away from universalizing frameworks of rights, equality, and freedom and into the domain of the vernacular speech acts and semantic practices of minoritized subjects.[33] This speech formation at first seems counterintuitive to discourses on same-sex marriage, as it does not necessarily posit the same-sex couple as the central subject of the conversation. However, if we extend the conversation beyond one of universalizing rights, it becomes apparent that other nonnormative conjugalities and intimacies are very much as relevant to the debates on freedom, liberty, and democracy as are the monogamous same-sex couple and their marriage.[34] Thus, my framing of queerness in the phone banks is not disingenuous to the cause of queer justice, because it broadens the scope of "queer" to enact a form of freedom for both queer and racialized subjects—particularly Hmong Americans. Undertaking new epistemological frames around same-sex marriage as not a system of choice but a form of life making enables a rethinking of the discourses of queer liberalism by extending and complicating their vocabularies through Hmong American speech acts, cultural forms, and kinship practices—thus enacting a Hmong American vernacular activism.[35]

Members of MWSM released four photographs during the summer of 2012 as part of their campaign against Amendment 1. A total of six different individuals appeared in the four photos. MWSM's photo campaign highlighted how Hmong's presumed hyperheterosexuality—and, in fact, embodied cultural forms beyond the ideology—informed a queer Hmong American vernacular activism in the campaign to defeat Amendment 1. I do not suggest that MWSM was merely coloring in elements of diversity around the activism against Amendment 1. Instead, I foreground how the photos and the larger activism of MWSM enacted a vernacular activist approach to radical queer politics among Hmong Americans that fundamentally shifted the discourses and visuality of mainstream queer politics. MWSM's activities were in line with José Esteban Muñoz's notion of disidentification in that MWSM simultaneously participated in the mainstream same-sex marriage movement while changing the message from within.[36] Disidentification in this instance is about "expos[ing] the encoded message's universalizing and exclusionary machinations and recircuit[ing] its workings to account for, include, and empower minority identities and identifications . . . ; it proceeds to use this code as raw material for representing a disempowered politics or positionality that has been rendered unthinkable by the dominant culture."[37] MWSM used a unique Hmong American vernacular activist approach to ensure the defeat of Amendment 1, while not fully employing the same rhetoric of queer liberal inclusion that Minnesotans United did. Moreover, by aligning itself with the legal and political atmosphere of the Amendment 1 battle, MWSM critiqued and resisted the limited and violent forms of monogamous conjugality emblematic of respectability politics, while embracing and taking up the American democratic arena as a site to reenvision radical queerness through complicating Hmong American gender and sexual politics anchored in Hmong's unique refugee histories and ways of knowing. MWSM's photo campaign was posted and distributed on social media, including Facebook, Tumblr, and Twitter. According to MWSM cofounder Linda Her, the primary audience for the photographs was Hmong Americans themselves, so that they could be informed about the stakes of the Amendment 1 battle. Since Minnesotans United barely spoke to queers of color or even immigrant and refugee communities, let alone Hmong Americans, MWSM directly engaged its own communities in this pressing issue through an act of vernacular activism.

MWSM's bold and strategic use of photography is especially illuminating, as it decided to deploy representational photographs instead of abstracted figurations. The images become all the more powerful when we consider that there were few visual archives about Hmong American queerness to draw from. The photographs invite viewers to immediately acknowledge Hmong Americanness and queerness simultaneously, even before diving into the accompanying text. Viewers see a photograph of an image, or of a scene, before they can vocalize its aesthetics. Sight is one primary mechanism of cognition that "speaks" to a viewer at the moment of the visual encounter. MWSM's embodiment of two different localities and political messages directs the spectator to a queer reading of Hmong American history and politics through the images by using them to speak to its audience—through the vernacular activist politics of speech and visuality.

MWSM was a grassroots collective that moved swiftly on the ground, so for it to create a photo campaign that somehow permanently captured its activism in time was innovative. The images are crucial because they beg the viewer to read them without necessarily knowing the backdrop of MWSM's activism, establishing a double movement that imagines a Hmong American visuality of queerness while enacting a form of political outreach. In this case, MWSM's photographs further complicate the notion that there is no existence for queer Hmong Americans under the rubric of hyperheterosexuality, forcing the viewer to contemplate the deeper message that exists between the lines and beyond the immediate image. This visual representation prompts the viewer to analyze and contend with the mismatch between epistemology and visuality. That is, the knowledge that viewers have about Hmong American history and culture may not align with the discourses of queerness circulating across the battles for same-sex marriage.

The four photographs depict several individuals dressed in traditional Hmong clothing, either singly or as a couple, accompanied by the header "Hmong American LGBTQIA: Vote 'NO' on Marriage Amendment 11.06.12." The contrasting elements of the photographic subjects wearing Hmong traditional garments against backdrops of contemporary social landscapes provide viewers the opportunity to imagine two concurrent geographies. The first photo is pertinent to this simultaneity of place and portrays two men sitting in front of a river, with a city skyline behind them. The city in the background clearly connotes the United States. The two men are tightly pressed against each other and holding hands. An aesthetic serenity washes over the photo, as sunlight drenches their faces. The caption below them reads, "From the mountains of Southeast Asia to the cities of America, don't persecute our love." The photograph evokes a sense of migratory travel between two geographical time zones, namely, from Southeast

Asia to America. The aesthetic and strategic pairing, together with the text, induces histories of Hmong refugee displacement and subsequent resettlement in the United States. Establishing this visual setting enabled MWSM to bring forth histories of Hmong persecution at the hands of various colonial and imperial powers, while drawing attention to the ongoing human rights abuses that Hmong continue to experience in the communist Lao state.

The communist Lao government began persecuting Hmong for their collaboration with the US government after the end of the secret war. The Congress of World Hmong People (CWHP) has been one of the organizations at the forefront of documenting Hmong persecution in Southeast Asia at the hands of the communist Lao state. Its mission recognizes that "violence and human rights violations continue to be the root cause of the Hmong political unbalance, gender inequality, poverty, illegal political suppressions and oppressions in Laos."[38] The CWHP and the Unrepresented Nations and Peoples Organization released a statement declaring that "the human rights violation[s] in [Laos] continue to be of great concern" and condemning "the Lao Government for using starvation tactics and rural development programme[s] to hide the human rights violations committed by the military in the region."[39] In this vein, MWSM's photo of the two men (re)imagines the temporal elements of the refugees' travel, and the refugees' ultimate fate of displacement, aligned with the persecution of Hmong in the aftermath of the United States' secret war in Laos. Furthermore, the refugee resettlement process was one mechanism that fractured Hmong intimacies and sociality, as nonmonogamous intimate relations were legally delegitimized and families were separated across the United States. The ongoing violence that Hmong continue to experience within the communist Lao state and as refugees in the United States resurfaces through MWSM's visual imagery to reveal that the refugee is not a settled subject in the aftermath of the secret war. The photographs are not immediately read as refugee "persecution." However, by relating refugee migration to persecuting refugees and persecuting queers, MWSM creates the condition of Hmong Americans both as refugees and as queer.

The second photograph depicts Linda Her of MWSM, a queer lesbian spoken-word artist, holding a *qeej* (reed instrument) with the Cathedral of Saint Paul behind her. My reading of the image suggests that Her is blurring the lines of gender and sexuality by wearing traditional men's clothing and holding the *qeej* to disidentify with hyperheterosexuality. It would only make sense to dive deeper into the meaning of the *qeej* to fully appreciate Her's disidentificatory practice. The *qeej* is historically played by men during funerals to guide the souls of the deceased back to their place of birth to retrieve their amniotic sac, with the ultimate goal to *thawj thiab*, or be reborn. The *qeej* has also been played in happier or secular times, such as during New Year celebrations. Many legends and stories about the origin of the *qeej* have been documented, most notably by the education studies scholar Yer J. Thao and the ethnomusicologist Catherine Falk.[40] However, the historian Gayle Morrison recounts a fascinating legend told to her by a master *qeej* player named Nhia Dang Kue from Stockton, California. In the legend narrated by *qeej* master Kue, Sinsay (Xeem Xais), a great and powerful ancient warrior, conquered seven kingdoms, for which his prize was to marry a beautiful woman from each of the conquered kingdoms. During a festival at the time of his seventh conquer, Sinsay and all his wives were present, although not one knew that Sinsay had taken other wives besides herself. The wives were all outraged when they discovered that they were not Sinsay's only wife. The God-King appeared and resolved this quandary by issuing a challenge: if all the wives could assemble an instrument with seven parts with which words could flow, then they all would be equally proclaimed as Sinsay's wives. The wives went off on their own, and each came back with individual parts, which, when mended together, perfectly fashioned the *qeej*. With the wives ingeniously beating this challenge, the God-King ultimately declared all the women to be Sinsay's equal wives.[41]

The *qeej* is the ultimate symbol of the Hmong people. To the viewer of the MWSM photo, this symbolism visually dictates Hmong as the keepers of the *qeej* and renders Hmong Americans intelligible to those who encounter the instrument. Not only does the *qeej* symbolize Hmong Americans as a polity, but they have also historically been a nationalistic emblem of masculinity and mightiness. Thus, the *qeej*'s visuality as a form of Hmong iconicity is intimately attached to symbolisms of masculinity and, by extension, hyperheterosexuality. This physical-sexual potency offers itself as the instrument that Her creatively deployed for a queer purpose. Although historically only men played the *qeej*, women also played the instrument in some locations.[42] In the breaking of this historical tradition, Her inverts dominant Hmong epistemologies of the masculine conquerhood and gendered configurations of the *qeej*, thereby enacting a vernacular activism that becomes intelligible within the context of queer activism.

While not many Hmong stories or legends have undergone scrutiny in academic and cultural studies scholarship, I aim to problematize the masculinist origins of the *qeej* itself. The story of Sinsay shows that the women vied to be the wife of the unbeatable warrior. In some instances, plural marriages can also be normative, in the sense that it was perhaps commonplace, acceptable, or expected for a man to have multiple wives in antiquity. Yet master *qeej* player Kue's legend of Sinsay also interestingly names the women as the creators of the *qeej*. To that end, Her symbolizes this feminist viewpoint of creation that often belies the masculinist images and historical framings of the *qeej*. Her flips the legend of the *qeej* on its head by highlighting women's contributions to the formation of Hmong iconicity. An alternative reading could be that Her is Sinsay himself. If the photograph is read this way, she then becomes the conqueror of the kingdoms, who eventually married seven wives. Thus, the reading of Her's photograph becomes that of a woman (or a gender-ambiguous subject) marrying seven other women, thereby subverting Sinsay's hyperheterosexuality rooted in sexual and gendered conquerhood toward a feminist, nonmonogamous, and queer formation of Hmong heroism. Not only does this reading radically reform marriage by utilizing legend, myth, folktale, and Hmong instruments as political tools within the context of contemporary American democratic processes, but it subsumes Hmong American marriage origins, tales, and rituals into queerness, ultimately liberating and expanding the very stories that Hmong narrate about themselves regarding gender, sexuality, and the origins of their iconic objects. In sum, reading Her's image as performing a politics of refusing hyperheterosexuality of masculine conquerhood means Her's gendered ambiguity disidentifies with the masculinist iconic object as a queer object for social justice.

The remaining two images of MWSM's photo campaign are more challenging to read. The third photograph depicts a man and a woman, both dressed in Hmong men's clothing, standing together, with the caption "Standing together for equality and the human right to love/marriage." I read this photograph as an image of friendship, where the two individuals are not intimately embracing but are standing next to each other. The individuals could be friends, brothers, lovers, bisexual, queer, trans, or straight, leaving the viewer to interpret the ambivalence of their subject positions. The caption is intriguing when we consider the notion of "human rights" and "love." Thus, one might be tempted to read this photograph and its caption as an extension of Enlightenment notions of emancipation and freedom operating in the form of legal rights under queer liberalism. Furthermore, one may read this photograph and caption as universalizing the travails of queer folks through the insertion of queer Hmong Americans into this universalism. One may also deduce from the usage of "human rights" a reference to the LGBTQ establishment organization Human Rights Campaign, which advocates for queer freedom through lesbian and gay mainstream visibility and legal inclusion.[43] By doing so, the viewer may render this photo campaign as yet another instantiation in which queer Hmong Americans are seeking Western legal emancipation through the optic of representation and rights.

Scholars have critiqued this framework of "human rights" as insufficient for understanding oppression and freedom. MWSM did not strive to reify the nation and Western law in "standing up" for human rights. Rather, when considering that the whole of MWSM's campaign was a critique of homonormativity and the absence of intersectionality within white mainstream lesbian and gay activism, and that its campaign was unapologetically Hmong American, we can deduce that the notion of "human rights" was not referencing the Human Rights Campaign, but was referring to human rights abuse of refugees. As in line with the reading of the previous photograph, MWSM seeks to render intelligible a politics that engages same-sex marriage with a critical Hmong politics. Despite framing same-sex marriage in relation to Hmong American political subjectivity vis-à-vis human rights, MWSM achieves a double maneuver, subjecting human rights to a critical inquiry about whether it can be useful both for refugeehood and for sexual subjugation. Furthermore, the gesture toward "human rights" is also about whether an indispensable dimension of a critical Hmong politics is to enact a politics of consciousness-raising for Hmong Americans while reminding non-Hmong of Hmong's continued oppression in the United States and abroad.

The fourth photograph shows two women holding hands as they walk toward the St. Paul state capitol. The two persons are dressed in traditional Hmong women's attire. The caption below the photograph reads, "Turn your back on hate, walk towards love." I want to consider a possible rendering of this photograph that may inadvertently serve to legitimate a state-based version of freedom for queer people. Taking cues from the political theorist Wendy Brown, we may read the photograph as a plea to the state in redressing a "wounded" identity. That is, identities such as race, gender, or sexuality have historically been excluded from state-based protections. Appealing to the state to compensate for this historical injury only renders the state as the powerful guarantor of rights rather than questioning the state's role in producing the injury in the first place.[44] Framing freedom in this sense means that identity is perpetually situated within structures of domination that will risk future injuries. In this reading, the depiction of the subjects at the Minnesota state capitol could represent a turn toward the state in seeking belonging and protection. The positioning of the women's bodies toward the state capitol is further evidence that a literal "turning toward" the state is inevitable. To be a legible citizen means to constantly seek out redress from this structure of domination that can simultaneously confer or deny freedom and rights. This formulation of freedom is a troubling fact especially for feminist and queer activism, because it creates the paradox of denouncing patriarchy and gendered subjugation of culture while reifying another violence in the form of the state.

However, if we read the photograph and caption in what I have described as a critical Hmong politics, an act of disidentification, and a form of vernacular activism, then an alternative message emerges. It is true that Hmong Americans have historically sought legitimation within the state. As stateless people, Hmong had a precarious relationship with Chinese, French, and American empires throughout the nineteenth and twentieth centuries. A queer reading of the state does not suggest that the photograph depicts a politics of injury within state-based protections, although it certainly also does not foreclose that possibility. Rather, it contextualizes Hmong's historical participation within the state that has enabled them to be both legible and illegible to dominant structures of power. That is, to make certain that Hmong can maintain their political sovereignty, or rather their autonomy, Hmong have maneuvered varying strategies to outsmart the state in asserting their political aspirations while remaining "close enough" within its purview.[45] If we consider that Hmong as stateless subjects have always engaged the state differently from those of state-situated polities, we can "queer" this reading not by denouncing queer Hmong Americans as accepting the state as a guarantor of rights. Rather, Hmong American vernacular activism in this instance means centering the relationality and strategies by which refugees and queers can simultaneously disidentify with the democratic processes within the state to fashion racial and queer self-making outside of it.

The photographs are also affective. The captions of all four photographs contain the word *love*. Philosophers have theorized love for centuries. Some scholars have also criticized love as inherently patriarchal and heteronormative, particularly as deployed by mainstream lesbian and gay organizations in the context of queer liberalism. However, queer theorists such as Teresa de Lauretis, Eve Kosofsky Sedgwick, and Lauren Berlant have reclaimed love as a political concept. Love is that thing that makes us long for new possibilities in the midst of imperfection. Berlant writes, "Love is one of the few situations where we desire to have patience for what isn't working, and affective binding that allows us to iron things out, or to be elastic, or to try a new incoherence. This is the main upside of making love a properly political concept."[46] In essence, loosening the parameters of love enables a reimagining of what a livable world would mean for those whose lives are never guaranteed. MWSM's conceptualization of love, as a properly political concept, means a journeying into a domain where the recognition of one's desire to thrive in precarious life conditions withstands the multitude of state and interpersonal violences. Love as politics means that social relations must be contingent on what is never guaranteed. It is a laborious process to carve out radical visions within the discomforts of always having to do better. MWSM's visions of love in the photographs situated this political concept in four different social relations, all of which direct our attention to its messiness and multiplicity: singular, coupled, friendships, and/or ambiguous unions. For MWSM, love is relational, political, transformational, and it is not always white, heterosexual, or coupled. In fact, MWSM's version of love differs from the love pivot that was used by Minnesotans United to gesture toward assimilation, capitalism, nationalism, and whiteness. The photographs—both explicitly and implicitly—move queer kinship away from the nuclear white gay family and into a realm where multiple and enigmatic social relations are possible. Thus, from the hidden meanings of plural relations in Her's depiction of Sinsay to an ambiguous pairing of two gender-nonconforming friends, the photographs reveal that Hmong epistemologies of sociality, intimacy, and love extend beyond the homonormative lesbian and gay subjects in mainstream queer politics—and indeed beyond the misuse of culture in propagating the ideology of hyperheterosexuality.

RALLYING AT THE CAPITOL

Five MWSM members and I were present at the state capitol when the Minnesota legislature was on the brink of legalizing same-sex marriage in 2013. To my surprise, members from the Hmong American Alliance Church were also present to protest the legalization of same-sex marriage. Inside the state capitol, an elderly Hmong American man held a bright pink sign with stick figures of a man and a woman while endlessly chanting the phrase "Mej cov mi tub mi nyuas sawv dlaws yuav moog dlaab teb" (All of you children will go to hell). We were frightened and shocked. We avoided this man while moving along the thousands of protesters inside the cramped capitol and ultimately stumbled outside, where we encountered more Hmong American Alliance Church members holding the pink signs. A protester from the church cautiously moved toward our group, and asked, "Nej yog cov uas nyiam cov neeg nkes los nej yog cov uas tsis nyiam lawv?" (Are you all people who like gays or people who do not like gays?) I affirmatively proclaimed, "Peb yog cov uas nyiam gay!" (We are the people who like gays!) She exhibited a sense of curiosity about our stance and asked us whether we were comfortable with changing Hmong culture and families in light of the legalization of same-sex marriage. I confirmed that we were. She sustained a long conversation with Pao, asking, "Yog hais tias poj niam yuav poj niam, es leej twg yuav los ua tus coj hauv tsev neeg? Koj puas kam cia poj niam los ua tus coj?" (If a woman married another woman, who will become the leader of the household? Are you willing to let the woman become the leader of the household?) Pao insisted that women can "lead" a household, but he also argued that there "does not need to be a leader in a household." I interjected with the argument that we were willing to revolutionize our conceptualization of family so that women and queer people can be empowered within Hmong American communities without gendered hierarchies.

It struck me that the woman's question highlighted the concerns of anti-same-sex-marriage Hmong Americans and their anxieties over the transformation of culture and family, particularly the heterosexual family unit. Her inquiry "Who will become the leader of the household?" functioned as a sincere gesture toward learning and curiosity about change rather than operating as a condemnation of queerness. Additionally, her question "Are you willing to let the woman become the leader of the household?" can be interpreted as not just concerning the women in a same-sex marriage becoming the "leader of the household." In fact, her inquiry may also suggest apprehensions about women becoming the leader of the household within a heterosexual marriage and family unit. Her anxieties concerning gender and its connection to the heterosexual family unit may not be about being anti-same-sex marriage at all, but be more so about the transformation and deconstruction of gender as a whole and its relationship to power. Furthermore, her inquiries reveal how reticence is integral to the harmony of the family beyond the context of same-sex marriage, as women becoming leaders of the household may potentially disrupt the normative order of things within the heterosexual familial unit. Indeed, subverting gender hierarchies entails a fracturing of the face-value harmony that has become compulsive within heteronormativity. In the environment of the battle for the legalization of same-sex marriage, Pao and I answered her questions about the changing norms of women in Hmong America in a way that, hopefully, became empowering for her as a Hmong American Christian woman. By engaging with our own communities during this political moment, we reframed gender for Hmong Americans in a way that raised their consciousness about women's political empowerment while also rallying for support of same-sex marriage.

These instances of elder Hmong Americans rallying against the legalization of same-sex marriage saw moments where "culture" was usurped for various interpretations within religio-cultural-legal contexts. Hmong Americans have reconstructed notions of culture and family that remix gender, sexuality, and, in this case, religion to articulate a politics of anti-same-sex marriage and anti-queerness within the context of the Hmong American Alliance Church. In Pao's conversation with the protester, his insistence that there "does not need to be a leader in a household" puzzled her but nonetheless forced her to rethink her position of anti-same-sex marriage. Pao demonstrated a vernacular activism by insisting on the particularities of culture that were relevant to the protester's concerns about heterosexual family politics in a way that opened new doors for Hmong American women to be empowered. I reinforced the notion that culture and family are and will always be dynamic and transforming, arguing that the church and Christianity itself were forms of change within Hmong communities in French colonial and post-migration periods of Hmong history. The battle to legalize same-sex marriage meant Hmong Americans were able to engage each other over their interpretations of gender and sexuality and its ramifications for life making and community building, ultimately reimagining it in ways that were conducive to a race-radical queer politics. When minoritized subjects engaged each other within social movements to remake kinship, new forms of activism and vocabularies emerged to complicate universalizing discourses of freedom and choice under liberalism. More importantly, existing orthodoxies of Hmong as fixed cultural subjects became dislodged. Immediately after our conversation, the protester abandoned her pink sign and headed home.[47] MWSM's version of social justice thus engaged with its own Hmong community in order to foster education, relationship building, and life making in ways that deconstructed dominant narratives of Hmong as possessing stagnant cultures and illiberal outlooks on gender, sexuality, and queerness. More importantly, MWSM's vernacular activism broadened the repertoire of queer radicalism and democratic engagement by expanding Hmong American speech acts and embodiment beyond the liberal terminology of choices and rights.

BEYOND SAME-SEX MARRIAGE

From the time lesbian and gay activists began to push more forcefully for the legalization of same-sex marriage in the early 1990s to when the United States Supreme Court finally legalized same-sex marriage through *Obergefell v. Hodges* in 2015, scholars have critiqued same-sex marriage because of its complicity in the increasing ties between the state, the market, and lesbian and gay rights. Undeniably, the desire to be included in this institution has engendered more "capitalist exploitation, racial domination, and gender subordination in a domestic as well as global context" for a variety of minoritarian subjects.[48] Minnesotans United's utilization of the universalistic language of love and freedom made visible the detachment of mainstream lesbian and gay social movements from the material and lived experiences of queer people of color. My interviews with queer Hmong Americans demonstrated that not all of them believed in the rhetoric of freedom and rights that will be actualized in the aftermath of the legalization of same-sex marriage. Furthermore, they revealed to me the limits of legalizing same-sex marriage as a means of changing social perspectives among Hmong Americans. Because queer Hmong American subjectivities and livelihoods are contingent on and intimately connected to, rather than independent and detached from, their Hmong ways of knowing and living, the purported freedoms promised by state benevolence fall short in their deliverance of recognition, inclusion, and empowerment.

Queer Hmong Americans have written about queer marriage, asking provocative existential questions concerning their ongoing invisibility and precarity within existing kinship structures. In MWSM's "Raising UP" narratives project, an initiative that collected queer Hmong Americans' personal stories, Em Thao, a twenty-six-year-old lesbian residing in California, writes, "How do you perform a [traditional Hmong American wedding] ceremony with two women or two men? Who's going to be the one to pay [the dowry]? What about children? We all know that Hmong American parents are not very open-minded when it comes to adoption, how will they treat their grandchildren? What will these children learn from their community? I am getting to that stage [in life] and I am afraid that I don't know any of these answers."[49] I asked queer Hmong Americans whether the legalization of same-sex marriage in the United States will lead to Hmong Americans accepting lesbian and gay people in both minor and major scales of change. Phong, a thirty-year-old who identified as a non-cisgender straight man, did not believe the legalization of same-sex marriage would change Hmong Americans in any profound way, stating, "I don't think so. I don't think anyone who is not exposed to nonheterosexual couples, they're gonna say it's just a white thing. Miskas ua rau Miskas xwb [White people marrying white people]. That's what I think, I could be wrong."[50]

Since Hmong Americans utilize both traditional and legal systems of marriage in order to be recognized as "married," sometimes one system more than the other, the legalization of one system may not necessarily produce freedom for the subject. Whereas law has normalizing powers, spiritual acceptance is also a force that renders belonging for queer Hmong Americans (chapter 3). Tou Bee, a twenty-nine-year-old gay man, shared with me how he distinguished traditional Hmong American marriage and legal marriage: "A Mis Kas [white Western] wedding is not the official way to do it. So [Hmong American elders] could not give a shit about the legality of it. But if it was a Hmong wedding where two queers marry, it would be an issue for them, because it becomes 'real' for them."[51] From Tou Bee's perspective, rendering traditional marriage as queer would be an affront to a legitimate system of conjugality for some elders, whereas the legal marriage may not immediately represent a change relevant to Hmong American social and spiritual life. Tou Bee's claim mirrors Phong's stance that systematic change relies not on the legalization of same-sex marriage but rather on a more holistic transformation of Hmong American perspectives about queer sexuality, kinship, and politics through revising their traditional procedures of officiating marriages. In the context of the legalization of same-sex marriage in the United States, Tou Bee's and Phong's claims do not necessarily situate Hmong marriage forms outside of legal marriage. Rather, their knowledge shows that the legalization of same-sex marriage, while not all-encompassing, does indeed have effects on Hmong Americans, as they now have the power to enter into legal marriages, which could open the door for queer intimacies to emerge out of the shadows in their ethnic communities.

In my conversations and interviews, queer Hmong Americans often refer back to how they would marry (or have married) a partner of the same sex using traditional procedures of marriage. Some instances also demonstrate how legal marriage may not have had an effect on queer Hmong Americans' decisions to marry, as Leng, a twenty-year-old trans man stated to me: "I feel like even if it's legalized or not legalized, I would've gotten married regardless. Because, I don't know, I'm not really huge with politics and stuff, I just don't really care about it. But now that it's legalized, I guess it makes it okay to get married."[52] What Leng referred to is how Hmong Americans already have such systems in place to circumvent legal marriage. The indifference to legal marriage seems much like an afterthought and aftereffect of Hmong American traditional marriages. Since marriages may not have been contingent on the legal for many Hmong Americans, queer Hmong Americans first sought this avenue of marriage long before the legalization of same-sex marriage in Minnesota.

My conversation with Phong revealed that he and his wife had entered into a traditional marriage five years before the initiation of Amendment 1 in 2012 and before the legalization of same-sex marriage in Minnesota in 2015. He heard rumors from his wife's family that they would not condone a queer relationship, but they also received mixed messages that their relatives and clan leaders were willing to perform a wedding and recognize their union as a "marriage" under certain circumstances. Phong stated, "They weren't okay with it, but then I was hearing messages from my wife's tus coj noj coj ua [clan leader]. He would confront us, saying we're terrible people because we're in a queer relationship together, but then he would say things like, just bring the money, you know, bring the money."[53] In this instance, "just bring the money" meant that if Phong was able to provide a dowry for his wife, then the clan leader was willing to execute a wedding ceremony and permit their relationship to be recognized as a "marriage" among the larger clan, although he also seemingly disapproved of the relationship as queer. In short, the clan leader understood the exchange of a dowry to be a fundamental element of a traditional marriage that "proved" their queer love, one that might legitimate queerness if the individuals participated in it.

Phong legally married his wife after Minnesota legalized same-sex marriage in 2013. After all the years in which his wife's clan leaders concurrently supported and denounced their union, it became a legal marriage. "Fast forward to once same-sex marriage passed, we planned this mixture between a white wedding and a Hmong wedding. So, we dressed up, we asked our family to dress up. My wife got a white dress. We found a pastor, a Hmong pastor. And then she wed us. And I asked her not to make any Christian [references]—we're not Christians, so I asked her to keep all that out."[54] Phong and his wife also organized a reception after the wedding ceremony, where a large feast took place. There, Phong's family took note of all the gifts that were given to them by family members. His wife received a gold necklace and one thousand dollars from her own father, and Phong and his father provided a five-thousand-dollar dowry to his wife's father, with the promise that they would arrange the funeral for the daughter upon her death, in accordance with Hmong practices of transferring her spirits to Phong's household. The dowry was critical in this moment because it functioned as the symbolic gesture cementing his queer marriage as a form of Hmong life-making. Phong's wife's clan leader advised him to "bring the money" as a mode of formalizing a queer moment, challenging the understanding that the hyperheterosexual act of exchanging a dowry represented the oppression ("selling") of Hmong women. In addition, the promise of providing Phong's wife with spiritual belonging further legitimized their union as a "marriage." While Phong disclosed to me that the gifting of the dowry to his wife's father was done "under the table," the wedding and feast were nonetheless public and well attended by family and friends, including an elderly grandfather from his wife's side of the family, who congratulated them on their new union. Phong's critical imagination of queer kinship and the manifestation of this imagination into reality underscore the argument that negotiating the nuances of the so-called bride price in the context of a queer marriage ultimately garnered the acceptance and legitimation of their union as a "marriage" by their family members. Read in this way, the dowry—when deployed for their purpose and on their own terms—was empowering to Phong, his wife, and their larger network of kin.

Although legalizing same-sex marriage will undoubtedly provide legal sanctions for same-sex couples and may bring a sense of inclusion to individuals such as Phong, some queer Hmong Americans still do not necessarily see that the legalization of same-sex marriage will profoundly change the cultural politics or attitudes about queer sexuality within Hmong American communities. This is something that was important to my interviewees in our conversations. Moua Kong, a twenty-eight-year-old gay man, stated, "I don't believe in what marriage really is, because it aligns with the hetero community in what they believe and what they see, but when they see that queers can commit to each other, then I think they will be more accepting of it. But that doesn't really answer the question of, are they really truly accepting of it?"[55] Pushing Moua Kong to speak further on this claim, however, uncovered that he believed Hmong's marriage systems could accommodate same-sex marriages beyond the legal, which would otherwise produce a different set of alterities for imagining belonging beyond the mainstream legalization of same-sex marriage. He stated, "I think it's complicated, but when your family is accepting of it—obviously I'm not going to do a Hmong wedding if my family is not accepting of it—but I mean, if I were to do a Hmong wedding myself, and my parents were accepting of it, I think they would accommodate it no matter what. And I think it's great that we have the same-sex marriage passed, because it opens their eyes, it opens their eyes that we live in this life." Consciously aware that the law *may* provide opportunities for Hmong American communities to "see" queerness, queer Hmong Americans can perhaps begin to craft their own versions of marriage that reflect alternative forms of belonging in creating a life (*ua neej*). Indeed, Moua Kong's articulation of his family's acceptance of his queer identity is anchored not in the notion of "choice" but rather through a vernacular framework of queerness as a form of Hmong American life-making.

Hyperheterosexuality was opened up for reinterpretation and rearticulation in the political campaign to defeat the ballot referendum Amendment 1. Queer Hmong Americans' disidentification with hyperheterosexuality during the battle against Amendment 1 and subsequent engagement of it in the aftermath of the legalization of same-sex marriage prove that queer political identities, sexualities, and modes of existence can emerge in vernacular forms. Queer Hmong Americans disrupt state operations of marriage that propagate liberal understandings of freedom and rights, while concomitantly derailing the stasis of culture and tradition that presupposes racial and ethnic minority politics in the United States. As seen through MWSM's vernacular activist approaches of fighting to defeat Amendment 1 and in the narratives of queer Hmong Americans through oral interviews, a vernacular activism is a set of disidentificatory practices, of speech and mobility, of ideas and bodies, that situate Hmong American political practice within intersectional, intergenerational, and intercultural arrangements of freedom. Queer Hmong Americans understand the limits of law and tradition to provide freedom and belonging within their families, clans, and nations. However, their engagements with marriage during the same-sex marriage battles in Minnesota provide meaningful ways to analyze how it is that "culture" and law are dialectical systems of belonging and nonbelonging. The narratives that Hmong gender and sexual practices and politics do not provide flexibility for queerness or queer marriage due to their construction as hyper*heterosexual* and the claim that law is the ultimate guarantor of queer freedom under the current phase of liberal multiculturalism and sexual and queer liberalism do not adequately capture the complex Hmong American disidentification practices and acts of refusal that are enacted and negotiated in their everyday lives. Queer Hmong American vernacular activism, speech acts, material realities, embodied practices, and politics of refusal completely surpass and undo these discourses.

While the legalization of same-sex marriage in 2015 presents the illusion that queer people have achieved full rights, continuing legislation in states and municipalities across the Unites States targeting transgender healthcare and participation in sports, banning drag shows, and censoring literature on gender and sex evidences the violence that many continue to experience in the current phase of sexual and queer liberalism. Those whose embodiments are deemed homonormative continue to reap the rewards of same-sex marriage through assimilation and capital, while those whose modes of existence constructed as deviant are continually targeted for surveillance, criminalization, and destruction. The activism and ongoing creative gesturing of transgender individuals, refugees, immigrants, and women and queers of color can teach us valuable lessons about how to continue reimagining freedom even as we continue to witness the state-sanctioned backlash against queer and trans visibility. Vernacular activism reveals that the organizing germane to queer Hmong Americans does not delineate between a binarized "vernacular activism" and the "universalizing activisms" of mainstream queer social movements. Hmong American vernacular activism in fact very much affirmed the idea of marriage, and even advocated for legalizing same-sex marriage. The ways Hmong Americans engaged with the legalization of same-sex marriage constitute disidentificatory practices that situate queer Hmong American political practices within more capacious arrangements of marriage and, in some instances, through the refusal *and* co-optation of the ideology of hyperheterosexuality. This formation follows the critiques of same-sex marriage that have been articulated by critical ethnic and queer studies scholars, although it does not necessarily exist within an oppositional framework for the wholesale rejection of legal same-sex marriage.

My phone-banking conversations with elders, MWSM's activism and photo campaign, and queer Hmong American narratives and their critical imaginations disidentify with same-sex marriage and invigorate it with alternative potencies that refuse the misuse of their culture to buttress the ideology of hyperheterosexuality as a form of native homophobia. The implications of vernacular activism for minoritized and marginalized groups mean that there does not necessarily need to be an antagonistic position related to same-sex marriage for a group to experience empowerment, if they are afforded flexibility and complete freedom to critically reimagine it for their own purposes. The intersection of US-based democratic processes such as voter mobilization, coupled with Hmong American vernacular activism, enabled a queer and race-radical politics to emerge that reorients Hmong American community building and life making beyond racialized scripts of culture, queer invisibility, and assimilation. Therefore, queer Hmong American vernacular activism and the consideration of racially minoritized sexuality through Hmong American speech acts, modes of knowledge, embodied practices, and critical imaginations recast social justice organizing toward more creative forms of queer world-making.

Epilogue

MANY WORDS FOR QUEER

On March 7, 2021, singer-songwriter, performer, and beat producer Schoua Na Yang, known artistically as S U N A H, debuted their project *No Word for Queer* at the Cedar Commissions' Tenth Annual Showcase of Brave New Work by Emerging Minnesota Artists. *No Word for Queer* was accomplished in collaboration with Bunny Lee (guitar), Cheng Len Yang (songwriter), and Lisa Khang (songwriter) and was described as "a journey searching for language to humanize Hmong LGBTQ+ folx."[1] S U N A H fused hip-hop, electronic dance, groovy tones, and chill vibes together to create a project that wrestles with the ongoing invisibility of queer Hmong Americans. Ultimately, the eleven-track musical project *No Word for Queer* was an artistic production that sought to critically imagine affirming language to capture queer Hmong American identities and experiences. S U N A H's project also addressed gender-based violence against queer and trans people.[2] Such a production, for S U N A H, is a process of challenging the logics of hyperheterosexuality that work to render invisible racialized queerness. S U N A H imagined *No Word for Queer* as a method of manifesting inspiration, of enacting a critical imagination through a vernacular activist framework: "I look at this project in a music form right now as the first phase of creating inspiration, getting people curious about actually what that can look like in hopes that maybe one day we could create actual positive labels for Hmong LGBTQ folks."[3]

Queering the Hmong Diaspora has demonstrated how dominant understandings of "Hmong gender and sexuality," "Hmong marriage," and "Hmong culture" as hyperheterosexual enact profound ideological and symbolic violence on Hmong Americans through the selective distortion of their gendered and sexual politics and practices that further entrench their nonbelonging, particularly for queer Hmong Americans. In turn, queer Hmong Americans have used their critical imaginations to experiment with spirituality and cosmology and performed a vernacular activism to reimagine kinship as political life-making in ways that are radically antiracist, feminist, and queer. S U N A H's *No Word for Queer* addresses the continuing assumption embedded in prevailing understandings of hyperheterosexuality, namely, that in the Hmong language the absence of nomenclature to name queerness renders it as nonexistent and operates as a form of queer oppression. This postulation further fuels the charge of homophobia among Hmong as it is contrasted with the politics of gender and sexual identitarianisms emblematic of the contemporary phase of queer liberalism. In my interview with S U N A H, they stated, "I have always pondered in the back of my head for a really long time, we don't have language for LGBTQ folks, specifically Hmong folks. So, our connection to being queer and trans is this term *kathoey*, which is not even our Hmong language anyway. It's a borrowed word [from the Thai language], and it's used in a derogatory way. For me, I think for a real long time that wasn't something I connected with."[4] Gloria Anzaldúa also recognized how her own Spanish language was oppressive: "Talking back to my mother, *hablar pa' 'trás, repelar. Hocicona, repelona, chismosa*, having a big mouth, questioning, carrying tales are all signs of being *mal criada*. In my culture they are all words that are derogatory if applied to women—I've never heard them applied to men."[5]

Yet S U N A H complicates this dominant framing by positioning *No Word for Queer* as a process to attain alignment within their own community: "*No Word for Queer* is not the magic pill to solve everything, but it's in phases. I feel, this is phase one to bring awareness to what other LGBTQ folks are thinking. Our culture has harmed us in so many ways that we divorce our culture, and we go find support in other communities. And yes, that's great . . . [but] I didn't want to do that."[6] S U N A H is enacting a politics of refusal by framing *No Word for Queer* as a phase, rather than a finite project that seeks to create a "better" or "more accurate" form of culture. The discourse of hyperheterosexuality, and the sexual and queer liberalism that has come to define dominant lesbian and gay rights, renders dualistic the experiences of queer people as either oppressed or free. The violent contradictions within liberalism provide no pathway to freedom for racially minoritized queer subjects, and there is little space within their own internal communities to enable their flourishing. Spoken word and music afford racially minoritized queer subjects like Hmong an alternative medium for envisioning subjectivity anew. This creative gesture has no starting or end point—as it is a phase—which fundamentally mirrors the long-winded process of subject formation. s u n a h admitting that their political project is not meant to be the totalizing force of delivering visibility, freedom, or empowerment to queer Hmong Americans means that they leave the door open for their community to imagine life making as an open-ended process rooted in a politics of continuous community engagement.

To accomplish their goal, s u n a h solicited ideas from other queer Hmong Americans by posting prompts on various social media outlets. The prompts included "What are your stories dealing with the Hmong language?" and "If you could dream of a positive and empowering word for your identities, what would that be?" s u n a h's communal approach decolonizes language by allowing community members to critically imagine possible scenarios, language, and words that may not yet exist. Thus, *No Word for Queer* recognizes the importance of language and its connection to sexuality and identity, particularly outside the English-language context. s u n a h's consciousness mirrors Anzaldúa's theorizations of language's centrality to cultural identity and subjectivity itself. For Anzaldúa, language is the mechanism with which to convey "the realities and values" true to ourselves.[7] The dominant white supremacist society deems native languages that do not have terminology to name sexuality as premodern and backward. In this vein, the English language comes to dominate the ways identities are named or made legible. Yet how does one reclaim language in ways that are empowering to one's sense of self as Hmong American while challenging the hegemony of English identitarianisms?

s u n a h at first wanted "pronouns," in the ways we understand them in the English language. They stated,

> When I was trying to think about language, I kept thinking it needs to be like the English language. We have "she," "her," "they," "them" pronouns. But then I realized that the Hmong language is not like the English language. Our language is poetic in some ways, I feel in that sense there's room for creativity. I had to do a little bit of decolonizing too. When I did that, I felt there was more room to be creative, to allow people to identify as what they feel powerful to. I would say that was one of my favorite processes in making this project.[8]

Because dominant narratives of hyperheterosexuality in media and law position Hmong culture and language as deficient, it was tempting to stray toward

English as a means of "naming" identity. It is easy to fall into the trap of the English language as the primary mechanism for emerging as a legible cultural and political subject. Yet English-language identitarianism simultaneously marks the impossible emergence of a racialized Hmong American queer subject-position precisely through the failure of its narrative act. s u n a h decolonized this paradigm by tapping into the creative potential of the Hmong language even though words may not always perfectly capture identity. Their repudiation of assimilating into English-language identitarianisms defines the project as a politics of refusal. In order to take pride in oneself, one must also take pride in one's language, even if it is imperfect.

s u n a h's solicitation of terminology and concepts from queer Hmong Americans through a community forum on social media generated a host of creative feedback. Ideas that were collectively generated include *zaj sawv* (awakening dragon or emerging rainbow), *yam ntxwv hnub qub* (attitude of the stars), *keej* (possessing talent or skills), *tub zoo nkauj* (pretty boy), *ntxhais zoo nraug* (handsome girl), *hauv paus cua* (root of the wind), and *npauj npaim* (butterfly).[9] In fact, these concepts mirror a similar situation that one interviewee, Crimson, a twenty-one-year-old queer and gender-nonconforming individual, had pointed out to me: "A great friend of mine, we were discussing [terminology for the word *queer*], and we were thinking, what about *yaj yuam* [peacock]?"[10] The campiness of such terminology is a strategic play on the Hmong language by utilizing alliteration, for example, in *npauj npaim* and *yaj yuam*. Queer Hmong American critical imaginations enabled the flourishing of a multiplicity of concepts that can displace the myth of hyperheterosexuality and its inherent invisibility of queer people. s u n a h realized that dominant understandings of "pronouns" or even a singular, all-encompassing word such as *queer* would not capture the complexity of Hmong American queerness. Instead, these concepts do not emerge in the mainstream, but rather they operate as vernacular terminology among a small and marginalized population to affirm their existence amid the backdrop of continual erasure. Thus, the terminology and concepts are not legible or even conceivable to non-queer Hmong Americans or non-Hmong queer people. Anzaldúa aptly describes this creative process as a way of communicating with ourselves through a secret language.[11]

No Word for Queer consists of eleven tracks, with "Peb txoj sia muaj nuj nqis" (Our lives have value / Our lives matter) being the song that best reflects the essence of the project. s u n a h utilized the concepts from the community forum as the lyrics for "Peb txoj sia muaj nuj nqis." The song is lyrically about two people who are in love and who are needing to reveal that their love and their lives matter. The song begins by highlighting elements of beauty found in the world, of gorgeous and plentiful land, crystal-clear aqua oceans, and sun-filled skies. Yet the love between the individuals is much larger. Their love, equally as beautiful, is not as obvious to the eye:

Teb chaws zoo nkauj [A beautiful land]
Ntiaj teb muaj ntau [plentiful land]
Hiav txwv ntsuab xiab [crystal-clear aqua oceans]
Tshav ntuj sov siab [sun-filled skies warming our livers]
Tiam sis yog hais txog kuv thiab koj [But regarding us]
Yeej tsis muaj dabtsi yuav piv tau [nothing can compare]
Txoj kev hlub txhua leej [to our love]

. . . .

Koj yog hauv paus cua [You are the root of the wind]
Kuv yog yam ntxwv hnub qub [and I am the attitude of the stars]
Vim koj yog zaj sawv [Because you are an awakening dragon / emerging rainbow]
Es kuv yog npauj npaim [And I am a butterfly]
Tuaj qhia rau ntiaj teb paub hais tias [Yearning to tell the world]
Koj yog ntxhais zoo nraug [You are a handsome girl]
Kuv yog tub zoo nkauj [I am a beautiful boy]
Peb txoj sia muaj nuj nqis [Our lives matter][12]

"Peb txoj sia muaj nuj nqis" proffers a secret language to express queerness outside the hegemony of English-language legibility. s u n a h's contention that the Hmong language is poetic enables creative articulations of queerness. They named queers as *hauv paus cua* (the root of the wind) as a means of highlighting queerness as the origin of subjectivity. Furthermore, possessing *yam ntxwv hnub qub* (attitude of the stars) denotes the campiness of Hmong American experiences, particularly of queer love, which is full of exuberance, sparkles, and fabulousness. In essence, s u n a h envisioned a process where a cacophony of voices can be heard and multiple ideas can coalesce into one melody. The concepts and metaphors that were generated in the community dominate the music and lyrics of "Peb txoj sia muaj nuj nqis" and capture the radical antiracist, feminist, and queer potential of *No Word for Queer*. s u n a h's decision to construct a song out of the community-generated concepts positions the song (and their entire project) as one rooted in community building.

The critical imaginations enacted by queer Hmong Americans to deconstruct hyperheterosexuality and breathe life into queerness yielded a multiplicity of ideas. *No Word for Queer* highlighted s u n a h's creativity in collaborating with their community to resist the forced invisibility under the myth of hyperheterosexuality. The results from s u n a h's community forums were surprising, as they did not produce any form of linguistic equivalence to the English-language identity terms *gay*, *lesbian*, or *transgender*. Coining such metaphysical formations as *hauv paus cua* or *yam ntxwv hnub qub* marks queerness as a conceptual mode of life transcending identity and elevates it into the realm of the fantastic. That is, queerness is the root of the wind and possessing an attitude befitting of the stars, both elements of divinity that mark queer individuals not as marginal but as central to the functioning of the universe itself. In fact, the project marks a shift away from English-based identitarianisms and moves queer Hmong American subjectivity into a post-identity framework. Identity is not stagnated as permanent. The desire for legibility is thrown out the window. This creativity further suggests that Hmong possess a "cultural tradition that d[oes] not mark and stigmatize homosexual behaviors or think of sexuality as a central core of a person's identity" in the sense of identity marking in the so-called West.[13] Thus, the charge of homophobia—and, by extension, hyperheterosexuality itself—that has come to racially define Hmong in America becomes untenable when the complex layers of Hmong American subjecthood, and queer Hmong American subjecthood more precisely, are deconstructed and peeled back. In a world where racially minoritized subjects are perpetually marked for death or death-in-waiting, *No Word for Queer* shows that Hmong life-making matters, as s u n a h declared: "I am not dead yet. I say that because Hmong folks who are queer and trans can never imagine that you can live this long because of the pain, suffering, and the rejection. The rejection takes lives away. I didn't think I could live this long. I plan to live long."[14] In essence, s u n a h's entire project *No Word for Queer*, and in particular the track "Peb txoj sia muaj nuj nqis," reveals that within the Hmong language, there are in fact *many* words for queer.

s u n a h's *No Word for Queer* demonstrates the ways Hmong American cultural productions have addressed the myriad questions about gender and sexuality—and, in fact, Hmong's very place—in America. This book has revealed that the intersections of Asian American racialization, gender, and sexuality are quite complicated, and they become even more muddied when a group like Hmong refugees/Americans are genuinely considered. Gender and sexuality have been crucial optics with which to marginalize, criminalize, and exoticize minoritized communities—and, in the case of *Queering the Hmong Diaspora*, Hmong—and their cultures and histories as premodern and illiberal, particularly in the contemporary era of sexual and queer liberalism, where gender and sexual freedom is supposedly at its greatest height in the United States. However, queer Hmong Americans have resisted both dominant narratives and Hmong ethnonationalist narratives about gender and sexuality that have continually marked them as invisible. Their critical imaginations force us to reflect, How does queerness complicate and challenge ideological and material formations of Asian American gender and sexuality broadly, and Hmong's assumed hyperheterosexuality specifically? What radical antiracist, feminist, and queer potentials for freedom emerge when Hmong American histories and experiences are seriously considered within Asian American studies and feminist and queer theorizing and organizing? A project like s u n a h's *No Word for Queer* is an ethical rumination on how Hmong American experiences and cultural productions reveal the critical imaginations, vernacular activist practices, and creative potentialities that lie beyond the myth of hyperheterosexuality.

Notes

INTRODUCTION.

Constructing Hyperheterosexual Subjects

1. Sarah Rosser, "Anti-Hmong Comments Set Off a Law School," *Inside Higher Ed*, February 25, 2007, https://www.insidehighered.com/news/2007/02/26/anti -hmong-comments-set-law-school; Scott Jaschik, "What the Professor Said," *Inside Higher Ed*, March 6, 2007, https://www.insidehighered.com/news/2007/03/07 /what-professor-said; Jason Shepard, "Prof Pays Price for Causing Offense," *Isthmus*, March 8, 2007, http://isthmus.com/news/news/prof-pays-price-for-causing -offense.

2. Pat Schneider, "Hmong Wonder: How Could Law Professor Make Such Remarks?," *Free Republic*, February 28, 2007, http://www.freerepublic.com/focus/f-news /1792974/posts.

3. Mai Zong Vue, *Hmong in Wisconsin* (Madison: Wisconsin Historical Society Press, 2020), 46.

4. Pedro Oliveira Jr., "Kaplan Revisits Hmong Issues," *Badger Herald*, December 6, 2007, https://badgerherald.com/news/2007/12/06/kaplan-revisits-hmon; Anita Weier, "UW Law Prof Who Irked Hmong Speaks Up," *Cap Times*, December 6, 2007, https://captimes.com/news/local/education/university/uw-law-prof-who -irked-hmong-speaks-up/article_30ca2ab5-a220-5d10-b077-e93ae9ce7cf8.html.

5. Dia Cha, Leena Her, Pao Lee Vue, Ly Thong Chong Jalao, Louisa Schein, Chia Youyee Vang, Ma Vang, and Yang Sao Xiong, "Perspectives: Knowledge, Authority, and Hmong Invisibility," *Diverse: Issues in Higher Education*, March 12, 2008, http://diverseeducation.com/article/10828.

6. On representations of sexual violence, see Beth L. Goldstein, "Resolving Sexual Assault: Hmong and the American Legal System," in *The Hmong in Transition*, ed. Glenn L. Hendricks, Bruce T. Downing, and Amos S. Deinard (Staten Island, NY:

Center for Migration Studies of New York; Minneapolis: Southeast Asian Refugee Studies of the University of Minnesota, 1986), 135–143. On the dowry / bride price, see William H. Meredith and George P. Rowe, "Changes in Lao Hmong Marital Attitudes After Immigrating to the United States," *Journal of Comparative Family Studies* 17, no. 1 (1986): 117–126; Kao N. Vang, "Hmong Marriage Customs: A Current Assessment," in *The Hmong in the West: Observations and Reports*, ed. Bruce T. Downing and Douglas P. Olney (Minneapolis: Center for Urban and Regional Affairs, University of Minnesota, 1982), 29–47; Thi Huong Nguyen, Pauline Oosterhoff, and Joanna White, "Aspirations and Realities of Love, Marriage and Education Among Hmong Women," *Culture, Health and Sexuality* 13, no. S2 (2011): S201–S215; Mai Neng Moua, *The Bride Price: A Hmong Wedding Story* (Minneapolis: Minnesota Historical Society Press, 2017). On bride kidnapping, see George M. Scott, "To Catch or Not to Catch a Thief: A Case of Bride Theft Among the Lao Hmong Refugees in Southern California," *Ethnic Groups* 7 (1987): 137–151; Deirdre Evans-Pritchard and Alison Dundes Renteln, "The Interpretation and Distortion of Culture: A Hmong 'Marriage by Capture' Case in Fresno, California," *Southern California Interdisciplinary Law Journal* 4, no. 1 (1994): 1–48; Choua Ly, "The Conflict Between Law and Culture: The Case of the Hmong in America," *Wisconsin Law Review* 2001: 478–481; Jennifer Ann Yang, "Marriage by Capture in the Hmong Culture: The Legal Issue of Cultural Rights Versus Women's Rights," *Law and Society Review at the University of California, Santa Barbara* 3 (2004): 39–50; Lea Mwanbene, "Hmong 'Marriage by Capture' in the United States of America and *Ukuthwala* in South Africa: Unfolding Discussions," *Comparative and International Law Journal of Southern Africa* 53, no. 3 (2020): 1–25. On polygamy, see Pa Der Vang, "Violence Against Women and Hmong Religious Belief," in *Religion and Men's Violence Against Women*, ed. Andy J. Johnson (New York: Springer, 2015), 383–398; Robert G. Cooper, *The Hmong: A Guide to Traditional Lifestyles* (Bangkok: Artasia Press, 1995), 26–30. On cousin marriage, see Yih-Fu Ruey, "The Magpie Miao of Southern Szechuan," in *Social Structure in Southeast Asia*, ed. George Peter Murdock (Chicago: Quadrangle Books, 1960), 143–155; Lindy Li Mark, "Patrilateral Cross-Cousin Marriage Among the Magpie Miao: Preferential or Prescriptive," *American Anthropologist* 69, no. 1 (1967): 57. On teenage and underage marriage, see Ray Hutchison and Miles McNall, "Early Marriage in a Hmong Cohort," *Journal of Marriage and Family* 56, no. 3 (1994): 579–590; Bic Ngo, "Contesting 'Culture': The Perspective of Hmong American Female Students on Early Marriage," *Anthropology and Education Quarterly* 33, no. 2 (2002): 163–188; Peter Kunstadter, "Hmong Marriage Patterns in Thailand in Relation to Social Change," in *Hmong/Miao in Asia*, ed. Nicholas Tapp, Jean Michaud, Christian Culas, and Gary Yia Lee (Chiang Mai, Thailand: Silkworm Books, 2004), 375–420;

Serge Lee, Zha Blong Xiong, and Francis K. O. Yuen, "Explaining Early Marriage in the Hmong American Community," in *Teenage Pregnancy and Parenthood: Global Perspectives, Issues and Interventions*, ed. Helen S. Holgate, Roy Evans, and Francis K. O. Yuen (New York: Routledge, 2006), 26–27; Pa Der Vang and Matthew Bogenschutz, "Teenage Marriage, and the Socioeconomic Status of Hmong Women," *International Migration* 52, no. 3 (2014): 144–159; Pa Der Vang, "Teenage Marriage Among Hmong American Women," *Journal of Human Behavior in the Social Environment* 24, no. 2 (2014): 138–155. On queer sexualities and identities, see Pahoua K. Yang, "A Phenomenological Study of the Coming Out Experiences of Gay and Lesbian Hmong" (PhD diss., University of Minnesota, 2008); Walter T. Boulden, "Gay Hmong: A Multifaceted Clash of Cultures," *Journal of Gay and Lesbian Social Services* 21, no. 2 (2009): 134–150.

7. Patricia Hill Collins, *Black Feminist Thought: Knowledge, Consciousness, and the Politics of Empowerment*, 2nd ed. (New York: Routledge, 2002), 129.

8. Linda Williams, "Type and Stereotype: Chicano Images in Film," in *Latin Looks: Images of Latinas and Latinos in the U.S. Media*, ed. Clara E. Rodriguez (New York: Routledge, 1997), 214–220; Deborah R. Vargas, "Representations of Latina/o Sexuality in Popular Culture," in *Latina/o Sexualities: Proving Powers, Passions, Practices, and Policies*, ed. Marysol Asencio (New Brunswick, NJ: Rutgers University Press, 2010), 117–136; Jillian M. Báez, *In Search of Belonging: Latinas, Media, and Citizenship* (Urbana: University of Illinois Press, 2018).

9. Patricia Hill Collins, *Black Sexual Politics: African Americans, Gender, and the New Racism* (New York: Routledge, 2004), 63–64; Mireille Miller-Young, *A Taste for Brown Sugar: Black Women in Pornography* (Durham, NC: Duke University Press, 2014), 4.

10. Celine Parreñas Shimizu, *The Hypersexuality of Race: Performing Asian/American Women on Screen and Scene* (Durham, NC: Duke University Press, 2007), 6.

11. Sucheng Chan, "The Exclusion of Chinese Women," in *Entry Denied: Exclusion and the Chinese Community in America, 1882–1943*, ed. Sucheng Chan (Philadelphia: Temple University Press, 1991), 94–146; George Anthony Peffer, *If They Don't Bring Their Women Here: Chinese Female Immigration Before Exclusion* (Urbana: University of Illinois Press, 1999); Eithne Luibhéid, *Entry Denied: Controlling Sexuality at the Border* (Minneapolis: University of Minnesota Press, 2002), 31–54.

12. Renee E. Tajima, "Lotus Blossoms Don't Bleed: Images of Asian Women," in *Making Waves: An Anthology of Writing By and About Asian American Women*, ed. Asian Women United of California (Boston: Beacon Press, 1989), 308–317.

13. As Stuart Hall succinctly puts it, ideologies are not merely "free-floating" ideas in people's heads, but rather manifest into physical violence. For example, Hall shows how the "ideological construction of black people as a 'problem population'"

corresponds to, and "mutually reinforce[s]," police violence within Black communities. Stuart Hall, "The Whites of Their Eyes: Racist Ideologies and the Media," in *Silver Linings: Some Strategies for the Eighties*, ed. George Bridges and Rosalind Brunt (London: Lawrence and Wishart, 1981), 33.

14. Erin Khuê Ninh, "Without Enhancements: Sexual Violence in the Everyday Lives of Asian American Women," in *Asian American Feminisms and Women of Color Politics*, ed. Lynn Fujiwara and Shireen Roshanravan (Seattle: University of Washington Press, 2018), 69–81; Shamita Das Dasgupta, ed., *Body Evidence: Intimate Violence Against South Asian Women in America* (New Brunswick, NJ: Rutgers University Press, 2007); Mo Yee Lee and Phyllis F. M. Law, "Perception of Sexual Violence Against Women in Asian American Communities," *Journal of Ethnic and Cultural Diversity in Social Work* 10, no. 2 (2001): 3–25. In 2021, the murder of eight people at two spa parlors in Atlanta, six of whom were Asian women, by a twenty-one-year-old white man demonstrates the interlocking dimensions of racial and gendered violence. In particular, the perpetrator's targeting of Asian women working in spa parlors (a metaphor for Asian sex work) illustrates how images of Asian women as hypersexualized sex workers are configured in dominant discourse.

15. David L. Eng, *Racial Castration: Managing Masculinity in Asian America* (Durham, NC: Duke University Press, 2001).

16. Kelly Stamper Balistreri, Kara Joyner, and Grace Kao, "Relationship Involvement Among Young Adults: Are Asian American Men an Exceptional Case?," *Population Research and Policy Review* 34, no. 5 (2015): 709–732; Grace Kao, Kelly Stamper Balistreri, and Kara Joyner, "Asian American Men in Romantic Dating Markets," *Contexts* 17, no. 4 (2018): 48–53.

17. C. Winter Han, *Geisha of a Different Kind: Race and Sexuality in Gaysian America* (New York: New York University Press, 2015), 93–94. White gay men Grindr users also filter out other queer men of color, including Black and Latino men. Oftentimes, these Grindr users justify such phrases as a "personal preference" to suggest that sexual attraction is a matter of self-evident taste rather than a form of systemic dehumanization based on racist ideas about sexuality. The problem had become so pervasive that Grindr finally eliminated the "ethnicity filter" in 2020, during the height of the #BlackLivesMatter movement, as a form of "solidarity" with Black communities. C. Winter Han, *Racial Erotics: Gay Men of Color, Sexual Racism, and the Politics of Desire* (Seattle: University of Washington Press, 2021).

18. Celine Parreñas Shimizu, *Straitjacket Sexualities: Unbinding Asian American Manhoods in the Movies* (Stanford, CA: Stanford University Press, 2012); Nguyen Tan Hoang, *A View from the Bottom: Asian American Masculinity and Sexual Representation* (Durham, NC: Duke University Press, 2014).

19. Cynthia Wu, *Sticky Rice: A Politics of Intraracial Desire* (Philadelphia: Temple University Press, 2018).

20. Jane Ward, *The Tragedy of Heterosexuality* (New York: New York University Press, 2020), 29.

21. Mai Na M. Lee, "The Thousand-Year Myth: Construction and Characterization of Hmong," *Hmong Studies Journal* 2, no. 2 (1998): 6.

22. Christian Culas and Jean Michaud, "A Contribution to the Study of Hmong (Miao) Migrations and History," *Bijdragen tot de Taal-, Land- en Volkenkunde* 153, no. 2 (1997): 212–213; Vwj Zoov Tsheej, with Yaj Ntxoo Yias and Txiv Plig Nyiav Pov, *Haiv Hmoob liv xwm* [Hmong history] (Quezon City, Philippines: Patrimoine Culturel Hmong, 1997).

23. Mai Na M. Lee, *Dreams of the Hmong Kingdom: The Quest for Legitimation in French Indochina, 1850–1960* (Madison: University of Wisconsin Press, 2015), 104–120.

24. Dao Yang, *Hmong at the Turning Point* (Minneapolis: WorldBridge Associates, 1993), 37; Lee, "The Thousand-Year Myth," 10.

25. Chia Youyee Vang, *Fly Until You Die: An Oral History of Hmong Pilots in the Vietnam War* (New York: Oxford University Press, 2019).

26. Evyn Lê Espiritu Gandhi, "Indigenous Soldiering: CHamoru, Māori, and Hmong Narratives of the Trans-Pacific Vietnam War," *Critical Ethnic Studies* 7, no. 2 (2021), https://manifold.umn.edu/read/ces0702-08/section/4273299b-143e-41b7-b129 -d905f6d3ce6e.

27. Chia Youyee Vang, *Hmong America: Reconstructing Community in Diaspora* (Urban: University of Illinois Press, 2010), 23–24.

28. Lisa Blackstone, dir., *Minnesota Remembers Vietnam: America's Secret War* (St. Paul, MN: Twin Cities PBS, 2017), DVD.

29. Ma Vang, *History on the Run: Secrecy, Fugitivity, and Hmong Refugee Epistemologies* (Durham, NC: Duke University Press, 2021), 80.

30. Alfred W. McCoy, "America's Secret War in Laos, 1955–75," in *A Companion to the Vietnam War*, ed. Marilyn B. Young and Robert Buzzanco (Malden, MA: Blackwell Publishing, 2002), 303.

31. Vang, *History on the Run*, 77–78.

32. Yang Sao Xiong, *Immigrant Agency: Hmong American Movements and the Politics of Racialized Incorporation* (New Brunswick, NJ: Rutgers University Press, 2022), 47–50.

33. Simeon Man, *Soldiering Through Empire: Race and the Making of the Decolonizing Pacific* (Berkeley: University of California Press, 2018).

34. Vang, *History on the Run*, 39.

35. Espiritu Gandhi, "Indigenous Soldiering."

36. Vang, *Hmong America*, 38.

37. Glenn L. Hendricks, Bruce T. Downing, and Amos S. Deinard, eds., *The Hmong in Transition* (Staten Island, NY: Center for Migration Studies of New York; Minneapolis: Southeast Asian Refugee Studies of the University of Minnesota, 1986), 180.

38. Mark E. Pfeifer, John Sullivan, Kou Yang, and Wayne Yang, "Hmong Population and Demographic Trends in the 2010 Census and 2010 American Community Survey," in *The State of the Hmong American Community: 2013*, ed. Mark E. Pfeifer and Bruce K. Thao (Washington, DC: Hmong National Development, 2013), 9; Mark E. Pfeifer, "Hmong Population Trends in the 2020 U.S. Census," *Hmong Studies Journal* 26, no. 1 (2024): 2–5.

39. Vang, *Hmong America*, 48–59.

40. Talal Asad, "Two European Images of Non-European Rule," in *Anthropology and the Colonial Encounter*, ed. Talal Asad (London: Ithaca Press, 1973), 103–104.

41. Franz Boas, *The Mind of Primitive Man* (New York: Macmillan, 1911); Franz Boas, *Anthropology and Modern Life* (New York: W. W. Norton, 1928); James Clifford, *The Predicament of Culture: Twentieth-Century Ethnography, Literature, and Art* (Cambridge, MA: Harvard University Press, 1988); Renato Rosaldo, *Culture and Truth: The Remaking of Social Analysis* (Boston: Beacon Press, 1989); Lila Abu-Lughod, "Writing Against Culture," in *Recapturing Anthropology*, ed. Richard Fox (Santa Fe, NM: School of American Research Press, 1991), 137–162; Michel-Rolph Trouillot, *Global Transformations: Anthropology and the Modern World* (New York: Palgrave Macmillan, 2003); Kamala Visweswaran, "Race and the Culture of Anthropology," *American Anthropologist* 100, no. 1 (1998): 70–83; Lee Baker, *From Savage to Negro: Anthropology and the Construction of Race* (Berkeley: University of California Press, 1998); Lee Baker, *Anthropology and the Racial Politics of Culture* (Durham, NC: Duke University Press, 2010).

42. Trouillot, *Global Transformations*, 100–103.

43. Abu-Lughod, "Writing Against Culture," 143–147; Visweswaran, "Race and the Culture of Anthropology," 77–79; Baker, *From Savage to Negro*; Baker, *Anthropology and the Racial Politics of Culture*.

44. Nicholas Tapp, *The Impossibility of Self: An Essay on the Hmong Diaspora* (Berlin: Lit Verlag, 2010), 67–76.

45. William Robert Geddes, *Migrants of the Mountains: The Cultural Ecology of the Blue Miao (Hmong Njua) of Northern Thailand* (Oxford, UK: Clarendon Press, 1976), vi, vii, 57–61, 79–85.

46. Robert G. Cooper, *Resource Scarcity and the Hmong Response: Patterns of Settlement and Economy in Transition* (Singapore: Singapore University Press, 1984), 136; Robert G. Cooper, "Sexual Inequality Among the Hmong," in *Highlanders of*

Thailand, ed. John McKinnon and Wanat Bhruksasri (New York: Oxford University Press, 1983), 173–186.

47. Cooper, *Resource Scarcity and the Hmong Response*, 138.

48. Cooper, *Resource Scarcity and the Hmong Response*, 137.

49. Gary Yia Lee, "Hmong Postwar Identity Production: Heritage Maintenance and Cultural Reinterpretation," in *Cultural Heritage in Postwar Recovery*, ed. Nicholas Stanley-Price (Rome: ICCROM, 2007), 55; italics added.

50. Kou Yang, "Hmong Diaspora of the Post-War Period," *Asian and Pacific Migration Journal* 12, no. 3 (2003): 295–296.

51. Tapp, *The Impossibility of Self*, 131–147; Lee, "Hmong Postwar Identity Production"; Prasit Leepreecha, "Hmong Across Borders or Borders Across Hmong? Social and Political Influences upon Hmong People," *Hmong Studies Journal* 15, no. 2 (2014): 1–12; Sangmi Lee, *Reclaiming Diasporic Identity: Transnational Continuity and National Fragmentation in the Hmong Diaspora* (Urbana: University of Illinois Press, 2024).

52. Gary Yia Lee, "Nostalgia and Cultural Re-creation: The Case of the Hmong Diaspora," *Crossroads: An Interdisciplinary Journal of Southeast Asian Studies* 19, no. 2 (2008): 125–154.

53. Lee, "Hmong Postwar Identity Production," 56–57; Louisa Schein, "Homeland Beauty: Transnational Longing and Hmong American Video," *Journal of Asian Studies* 63, no. 2 (2004): 433–463.

54. Jodi Melamed, *Represent and Destroy: Rationalizing Violence in the New Racial Capitalism* (Minneapolis: University of Minnesota Press, 2011), 91–94.

55. Akhil Gupta and James Ferguson, "Beyond 'Culture': Space, Identity, and the Politics of Difference," *Cultural Anthropology* 7, no. 1 (1992): 6–8; Rosaldo, *Culture and Truth*, 198–203. Rosaldo in his early anthropological fieldwork demonstrated how culture and space are dialectical, famously showing that Ilongots in the Philippines were "precultural" Negritos who were physically separated from "postcultural" lowlanders and that "uncultured" Ilongots were precariously situated in between.

56. Kamala Visweswaran, *Un/common Cultures: Racism and the Rearticulation of Cultural Difference* (Durham, NC: Duke University Press, 2010).

57. Melamed, *Represent and Destroy*, 26–36.

58. Jeremy Hein, "From Migrant to Minority: Hmong Refugees and the Social Construction of Identity in the United States," *Sociological Inquiry* 64, no. 3 (1994): 290–294.

59. Jennifer Lee and Min Zhou, *The Asian American Achievement Paradox* (New York: Russell Sage Foundation, 2015), 21–23; Melamed, *Represent and Destroy*, 38.

60. K. Anthony Appiah and Amy Gutmann, *Color Conscious: The Political Morality of Race* (Princeton, NJ: Princeton University Press, 1996), 89.

61. Christin DePouw, "When Culture Implies Deficit: Placing Race at the Center of Hmong American Education," *Race Ethnicity and Education* 15, no. 2 (2012): 223–239; Ngo, "Contesting 'Culture.'"

62. Stuart Hall, "Cultural Identity and Diaspora," in *Identity: Community, Culture, Difference*, ed. Jonathan Rutherford (London: Lawrence and Wishart, 1990), 224.

63. Nicholas Tapp, "The Reformation of Culture: Hmong Refugees from Laos," *Journal of Refugee Studies* 1, no. 1 (1988): 20–37; Kong Pheng Pha, "Colorblindness as Anti-Asian Racism in the Midwest," *American Studies* 62, no. 3 (2023): 119–142.

64. Leo R. Chavez, *Covering Immigration: Popular Images and the Politics of the Nation* (Berkeley: University of California Press, 2001), 84–90; Yen Lê Espiritu, Lan Duong, Ma Vang, Victor Bascara, Khatharya Um, Lila Sharif, and Nigel Hatton, *Departures: An Introduction to Critical Refugee Studies* (Berkeley: University of California Press, 2022), 77–88.

65. Margot Hornblower, "Hmongtana," *Washington Post*, July 4, 1980.

66. "Laos Hill People Try Yet Again in California Valley," Special to the *New York Times*, July 17, 1983.

67. Cathy J. Cohen, "Punks, Bulldaggers, and Welfare Queens: The Radical Potential of Queer Politics?," *GLQ* 3, no. 4 (1997): 437–465.

68. Michel Foucault, *The History of Sexuality* (New York: Vintage, 1978), 147.

69. Foucault, *The History of Sexuality*, 140.

70. Glen Coulthard, *Red Skin, White Masks: Rejecting the Colonial Politics of Recognition* (Minneapolis: University of Minnesota Press, 2014); Audra Simpson, *Mohawk Interruptus: Political Life Across the Borders of Settler States* (Durham, NC: Duke University Press, 2014); Jodi Byrd, *The Transit of Empire: Indigenous Critiques of Colonialism* (Minneapolis: University of Minnesota Press, 2011); Rebecca Tsosie, "The Politics of Inclusion: Indigenous Peoples and U.S. Citizenship," *UCLA Law Review* 63 (2016): 1692–1751; Samantha Balaton-Chrimes and Victoria Stead, "Recognition, Power and Coloniality," *Postcolonial Studies* 20, no. 1 (2017): 1–17.

71. Simpson, *Mohawk Interruptus*, 20.

72. Simpson, *Mohawk Interruptus*, 20.

CHAPTER 1. Stories of Commotion

1. Kimberlé Crenshaw, "Mapping the Margins: Intersectionality, Identity Politics, and Violence Against Women of Color," *Stanford Law Review* 46, no. 6 (1991): 1241–1299.

2. Leti Volpp, "Blaming Culture for Bad Behavior," *Yale Journal of Law and the Humanities* 12, no. 1 (2000): 89.

3. Hall, "The Whites of Their Eyes," 32.

4. "Man Helping Woman Find Job Gets 7-Year Prison Term for Rape," *Pioneer Press* (St. Paul, MN), January 16, 1991; "St. Paul Man Gets Seven-Year Term for Rape," *Star Tribune* (Minneapolis), January 16, 1991.

5. Leti Volpp, "Framing Cultural Difference: Immigrant Women and Discourses of Tradition," *differences: A Journal of Feminist Cultural Studies* 22, no. 1 (2011): 96–97.

6. Jacques Lemoine has written about the ways Hmong in the Southeast Asian context deal with rape. Lemoine writes at length: "When a girl complains of rape, it is . . . surprising and unpleasant. Her parents, however, backed by their lineage local leaders seek an arrangement with the family of the 'rapist,' including marriage or social punishment in form of monetary compensation. Marriage is a pressing issue if the girl happens to be pregnant. The stigma of having been raped or being an unmarried mother is strong enough for both parties to find a decent resolution to this situation." Jacques Lemoine, "Gender-Based Violence Among the (H)mong," *Hmong Studies Journal* 13, no. 1 (2012): 3.

7. Lemoine, "Gender-Based Violence Among the (H)mong," 4.

8. State of Minnesota v. New Chue Her, No. C4-93-860, 510 N.W.2d 218 (Minn. Ct. App. Jan. 4, 1994). The survivor in the case was identified only in the court records as L.Y.

9. *Her*, 510 N.W.2d 218.

10. *Her*, 510 N.W.2d 218.

11. William E. Martin and Peter N. Thompson, "Judicial Tolerance and Racial Bias in the Minnesota Justice System," *Hamline Law Review* 25, no. 2 (2002): 258.

12. *Her*, 510 N.W.2d 218.

13. *Her*, 510 N.W.2d 218.

14. Leti Volpp, "Disappearing Acts: On Gendered Violence, Pathological Cultures, and Civil Society," *PMLA* 121, no. 5 (2006): 1636.

15. *Her*, 510 N.W.2d 218.

16. The Hmong word *mos* can be translated into English as "rape" or "wrestle," depending on the context. For example, "Muab nws mos" is translated as "They raped her," whereas "Nkawv sib mos" is translated as "They wrestled each other." However, additional language is needed to further cement the context to ensure the accurate translation of *mos* as either "rape" or "wrestle." For example, "Neeg phem muab nws txhom mus, ces lawv muab nws mos" is translated as "Bad people kidnapped her and then they raped her," whereas "Nkawv ua si thiab nkawv sib mos sab tas" is translated as "They playfully wrestled each other and became really fatigued."

17. *Her*, 510 N.W.2d 218. The professions of these two cultural experts were not specified in the court documents or in subsequent media reporting.

18. Stuart Hall, "Gramsci's Relevance for the Study of Race and Ethnicity," *Journal of Communication Inquiry* 10, no. 5 (1986): 26–27.

19. Leti Volpp, "(Mis)Identifying Culture: Asian Women and the Cultural Defense," *Harvard Women's Law Journal* 57 (1994): 94. Other scholars have debated the politics of the cultural defense. See Malek-Mithra Sheybani, "Cultural Defense: One Person's Culture Is Another's Crime," *Loyola of Los Angeles International and Comparative Law Review* 9, no. 3 (1987): 751–783; Nancy S. Kim, "The Cultural Defense and the Problem of Cultural Preemption: A Framework for Analysis," *New Mexico Law Review* 27, no. 1 (1997): 101–139; Alison Dundes Renteln, "The Use and Abuse of the Cultural Defense," *Canadian Journal of Law and Society* 20, no. 1 (2005): 47–67; Sarah Song, *Justice, Gender, and the Politics of Multiculturalism* (Cambridge: Cambridge University Press, 2007), 107–108.

20. Chandan Reddy, *Freedom with Violence: Race, Sexuality, and the US State* (Durham, NC: Duke University Press, 2011), 150–156.

21. *Her*, 510 N.W.2d 218.

22. "New Trial Denied," *Pioneer Press*, March 5, 1993.

23. State of Minnesota v. King Buachee Lee, No. C9-91-560, 494 N.W.2D 475 (Minn. Sup. Ct. Dec. 31, 1992).

24. The fact that the husbands also believed that the women engaged in an "affair" with Lee, while revealing the complexity of gender and sexual relations in the everyday lives of Hmong more generally, was not admissible in court. Ultimately, the fact that one survivor was abused by her husband after she divulged her rape to him and her family was not presented as evidence for the defense at trial. Lee's appeal argued that this information would have benefited him at trial because it was evidence that the ordeal between him and the woman was indeed an "affair."

25. Virginia Rybin, "Bid to Use 'Curse Water' at Trial Denied," *Pioneer Press*, November 22, 1990.

26. Conrad deFiebre, "Cultural Issues Surface in Rape Trial—Hmong Man Guilty of 3 Counts," *Star Tribune*, December 16, 1990.

27. Quoted in deFiebre, "Cultural Issues Surface in Rape Trial." It is also noteworthy that Donnelly is the author of an anthropological study of Hmong women in Washington state. In a critique of Donnelly's study, Leena Her argues that Donnelly misrepresents Hmong women's experiences of gender subjugation. Leena Her, "Rewriting Hmong Women in Western Texts," in *Claiming Place: On the Agency of Hmong Women*, ed. Chia Youyee Vang, Faith Nibbs, and Ma Vang (Minneapolis: University of Minnesota Press, 2016), 3–27.

28. Virginia Rybin, "Appeals Court Overturns Conviction of Maplewood Man in 2 Rape Cases," *Pioneer Press*, February 4, 1992.

29. State of Minnesota v. King Buachee Lee, No. C9-91-560, 480 N.W.2d 668 (Minn. Ct. App., Feb. 4, 1992).

30. Quoted in deFiebre, "Cultural Issues Surface in Rape Trial."

31. Volpp, "Blaming Culture for Bad Behavior."

32. Volpp discusses the ways feminism and justice for women elide questions of multiculturalism and racial justice. Leti Volpp, "Feminism Versus Multiculturalism," *Columbia Law Review* 101, no. 5 (2001): 1181–1218.

33. *Lee*, 480 N.W.2d 668.

34. Virginia Rybin, "Minnesota High Court Reinstates Man's Sexual Conduct Convictions," *Pioneer Press*, December 31, 1992.

35. Quoted in Wendy Tai, "High Court Affirms Convictions in 1990 Hmong Rape Case," *Star Tribune*, December 31, 1992.

36. For a discussion on Hmong "subject-in-becoming," see Vang, *History on the Run*, 102–110.

37. Leti Volpp, "Engendering Culture: Citizenship, Identity, and Belonging," in *Citizenship, Borders, and Human Needs*, ed. Rogers M. Smith (Philadelphia, University of Pennsylvania Press, 2011), 177–191.

38. Martin and Thompson, "Judicial Tolerance and Racial Bias," 258.

39. Quoted in deFiebre, "Cultural Issues Surface in Rape Trial."

40. Kong Pheng Pha, "Testimony as Justice: An Anti-Carceral Transformative Feminist Response to Sexual Violence and Abusive International Marriages," *Frontiers: A Journal of Women Studies* 44, no. 3 (2023): 18–41.

41. Chia Youyee Vang, Faith Nibbs, and Ma Vang, "Introduction: Hmong Women, Gender, and Power," in *Claiming Place: On the Agency of Hmong Women*, ed. Chia Youyee Vang, Faith Nibbs, and Ma Vang (Minneapolis: University of Minnesota Press, 2016), ix.

42. For more on "saving" women of color from their own cultures, see Lila Abu-Lughod, "Do Muslim Women Really Need Saving? Anthropological Reflections on Cultural Relativism and Its Others," *American Anthropologist* 104, no. 3 (2002): 783–790.

43. Volpp, "(Mis)Identifying Culture," 83.

44. Louisa Schein and Bee Vang, "The Unbearable Racedness of Being Natural," *Cultural Studies* 28, no. 4 (2014): 570.

45. Louisa Schein, Va-Megn Thoj, Bee Vang, and Ly Chong Thong Jalao, "Beyond *Gran Torino*'s Guns: Hmong Cultural Warriors Performing Genders," *positions: asia critique* 20, no. 3 (2012): 763–792.

46. Louisa Schein and Va-Megn Thoj, "*Gran Torino*'s Boys and Men with Guns: Hmong Perspectives," *Hmong Studies Journal* 10 (2009): 28.

47. Lisa Duggan, *Sapphic Slashers: Sex, Violence, and American Modernity* (Durham, NC: Duke University Press, 2000), 38.

48. Robert F. Moore, "Police Warn Hmong After Rapes," *Pioneer Press*, December 19, 1997; Robert F. Moore, "Seven to Face Charges in 'Chat Line' Rape Case," *Pioneer*

Press, January 1, 1998; Lucy Quinlivan, "'Chat Line' Rape Defendant Pleads Guilty, Closing Case," *Pioneer Press*, December 15, 1998.

49. The *New York Times* article does not mention the ethnicity of the survivors or the perpetrators. While this article may not be helpful in establishing Hmong racial and sexual images, it does go into detail about the dangers of gang rapes and gangs themselves. By striving to connect "gang" to "rape," the article succeeds in creating the notion that gangs are ubiquitous and sexually dangerous. Don Terry, "Gang Rape of Three Girls Leaves Fresno Shaken, and Questioning," *New York Times*, May 1, 1998; Associated Press, "Indictment Charges 23 Hmong with Series of Rapes," *Los Angeles Times*, October 21, 1999.

50. Brian Melley, "Seven Hmong Gang Members Convicted in Rape Case," Associated Press, July 13, 2000.

51. Associated Press, "Trial Begins in Hmong Gang Rape Case," February 2, 2000.

52. Terry Collins, "Minneapolis Man Arrested in Rape Crackdown; He Was One of 23 Hmong Men and Boys Suspected of Forcing Girls into Prostitution," *Star Tribune*, October 21, 1999; Associated Press, "23 Charged in California Sex Case," *Pioneer Press*, October 21, 1999.

53. Associated Press, "23 Charged in California Sex Case."

54. Paul Gustafson, "Reported Gang Leader Pleads Guilty to 3 Counts of Rape, 1 Other Charge," *Star Tribune*, July 3, 1998.

55. Paul Gustafson, "Authorities Crack Down on Asian Gang Accused of Raping Hmong Girls," *Star Tribune*, June 7, 1998. See additional articles also discussing the case: Robert F. Moore, "Adult, 4 Teens Suspected of Raping Girls as Gang Initiation," *Pioneer Press*, April 15, 1998; Leslie Brooks Suzukamo, "Alleged Gang Leader Gets 11-Year Sentence in Girls' Rapes," *Pioneer Press*, August 15, 1998.

56. Associated Press, "Reputed Detroit Gang Member Charged with Kidnapping St. Paul Girls," November 19, 1999.

57. Nancy Ngo, "First Suspect Charged in Gang Rape Pleads Guilty," *Pioneer Press*, March 11, 2000.

58. Ngo, "First Suspect Charged."

59. Mara Gottfried, "Rape Charges Allege Gang Rite," *Pioneer Press*, February 25, 2009.

60. Emily Gurnon, "9 Jailed in Rape of St. Paul Teen," *Pioneer Press*, March 24, 2012; Marino Eccher, "Man Gets 25 Years in Rape of Girl Who Trusted Him—Sentence Is the Most Severe So Far in Case," *Pioneer Press*, March 28, 2013.

61. State of Minnesota v. Mang Yang, No. A13-1125, N.W.2d (Minn. Ct. App. 2014).

62. Gurnon, "9 Jailed in Rape of St. Paul Teen."

63. Lisa Marie Cacho, *Social Death: Racialized Rightlessness and the Criminalization of the Unprotected* (New York: New York University Press, 2012), 63.

64. Cacho, *Social Death*, 43.

65. Cacho, *Social Death*, 44.

66. Cacho, *Social Death*, 47.

67. Sergio Delgado Moya, "An Archive of Violence: The Obscene Visuality of Sensationalism," *Critical Times* 3, no. 2 (2020): 203.

68. Jack Kresnak and Mei-Ling Hopgood, "Wisconsin Teens Tell of Rape Ordeal," *Pioneer Press*, October 13, 1999.

69. Conrad deFiebre, "Hmong Community Leader Is Sentenced to 17 Years for Rapes," *Star Tribune*, March 14, 1991.

70. Quinlivan, "'Chat Line' Rape Defendant Pleads Guilty."

71. Pam Louwagie and Dan Browning, "Shamed into Silence," 4 pts., *Star Tribune*, October 9–10, 2005.

72. Louwagie and Browning, "Shamed into Silence," pt. 1.

73. Louwagie and Browning, "Shamed into Silence," pt. 2.

74. Louwagie and Browning, "Shamed into Silence," pt. 3.

75. Louwagie and Browning, "Shamed into Silence," pt. 4.

76. Lynnae Nelson, "Letter of the Day: Culture Affects Hmong Attitudes Towards Girls," *Star Tribune*, October 12, 2005.

77. For example, survivor and artist Chanel Miller has extensively documented the equally violent "shame and blame" she experienced through the judicial system as she sought justice for herself after Brock Turner assaulted her on the Stanford University campus. Chanel Miller, *Know My Name: A Memoir* (New York: Viking, 2019).

78. Louwagie and Browning, "Shamed into Silence," pt. 4.

79. Cacho, *Social Death*, 84. Straka was a well-known police officer and detective in the St. Paul police department. In his long career, he was notorious for operating the often-racist Federal Bureau of Investigation's Twin Cities Safe Streets Violent Gang Task Force and for being an "expert" on Asian gangs in the Twin Cities and across the United States. See his original article, Richard Straka, "The Violence of Hmong Gangs and the Crime of Rape," *FBI Law Enforcement Bulletin* 72, no. 2 (2003): 12–16.

80. Straka, "The Violence of Hmong Gangs," 16.

81. Bic Ngo, "Beyond 'Culture Clash': Understandings of Immigrant Experiences," *Theory into Practice* 47, no. 1 (2008): 4–6.

CHAPTER 2. Legislating Conjugalities

1. I refer to common-law marriages in this chapter as "traditional marriages." While "common-law marriage" is the correct legal definition of what many consider

a "traditional marriage," it further implies that the marriage is not legitimate or legally "valid." Hmong do in fact consider their traditional marriages to be valid and akin to civil, legal marriages. Thus, what are referred to as their "common-law marriages" are valid "traditional marriages" in accordance with Hmong religious traditions. I do not use "cultural marriages," as it implies that they are somehow essentially different from civil, legal marriages.

2. In fact, many other polities have been included or excluded in marriage and its social, cultural, and legal benefits within the United States. Before the American Civil War, slaves were prohibited from legal marriage. Interracial marriage was also outlawed prior to the 1967 Supreme Court case *Loving v. Virginia*. Lesbian and gay couples have historically been excluded from the institution of marriage as well, up until the 2015 legalization of marriage for same-sex couples through the Supreme Court case *Obergefell v. Hodges*. The heterogeneity of marriages, including child marriages, plural marriages, same-sex marriages, and interracial marriages, among others, has been contested for the past three centuries.

3. I use the two forms interchangeably throughout this chapter, but with a slight preference for "marriage bills" because that is how most of the individuals whom I interviewed for the chapter referred to it.

4. Ma Vang, "The Refugee Soldier: A Critique of Recognition and Citizenship in the Hmong Veterans' Naturalization Act of 1997," *positions: asia critique* 20, no. 3 (2012): 697; Vang, *History on the Run*, 93–115.

5. Tera W. Hunter, *Bound in Wedlock: Slave and Free Black Marriage in the Nineteenth Century* (Cambridge, MA: Harvard University Press, 2017), 254–258.

6. Hunter, *Bound in Wedlock*, 235.

7. Amy L. Brandzel, *Against Citizenship: The Violence of the Normative* (Urbana: University of Illinois Press, 2016), 77.

8. Rebecca L. Davis, *More Perfect Unions: The American Search for Marital Bliss* (Cambridge, MA: Harvard University Press, 2010), 9.

9. Davis, *More Perfect Unions*, 9.

10. Ironically, Americans accepted the marrying of children up until the late nineteenth century, and contemporary "child marriages" persist today. See Nicholas L. Syrett, "Statutory Marriage Ages and the Gendered Construction of Adulthood in the Nineteenth Century," in *Age in America: The Colonial Era to the Present*, ed. Corinne T. Field and Nicholas L. Syrett (New York: New York University Press, 2015), 103–123; Nicholas L. Syrett, "The Contested Meanings of Child Marriage in the Turn-of-the-Century United States," in *Children and Youth During the Gilded Age and Progressive Era*, ed. James Marten (New York: New York University Press, 2014), 145–165; Nicholas L. Syrett, *American Child Bride: A History of Minors and Marriage in the United States* (Chapel Hill: University of North Carolina, 2016).

11. Andrew J. Dawkins (retired Minnesota state representative), interview with the author, November 23, 2019.

12. *Journal of the House of Representatives, Seventy-Seventh Session of the Legislature, State of Minnesota, 1991*, vol. 1, 162.

13. Blong Yang, "The Hmong Marriage Bill Action Alert," *Hmong Times*, February 12, 2004.

14. Howard Winant, *The World Is a Ghetto: Race and Democracy Since World War II* (New York: Basic Books, 2002), 1–2.

15. Winant, *The World Is a Ghetto*, 169–176.

16. Foucault, *The History of Sexuality*, 133–159.

17. Scholars have critiqued racial liberalism and the reproduction of racism through inclusion. See Kimberlé Crenshaw, "Race, Reform, and Retrenchment: Transformation and Legitimation in Antidiscrimination Law," *Harvard Law Review* 101, no. 7 (1988): 1331–1387; Derrick A. Bell Jr., "The Unintended Lessons in *Brown v. Board of Education*," *New York Law School Law Review* 49, no. 4 (2004): 1053–1067; Jodi Melamed, "The Spirit of Neoliberalism: From Racial Liberalism to Neoliberal Multiculturalism," *Social Text* 24, no. 4 (2006): 1–24; Charles Mills, "Racial Liberalism," *PMLA* 122, no. 5 (2008): 1380–1397; Daniel Martinez-HoSang, "The Triumph of Racial Liberalism, the Demise of Racial Justice," in *Race and American Political Development*, ed. Joseph Lowndes, Julie Novkov, and Dorian T. Warren (New York: Routledge, 2008), 288–311; Robin Marie Averbeck, *Liberalism Is Not Enough: Race and Poverty in Postwar Political Thought* (Chapel Hill: University of North Carolina Press, 2018).

18. H.F. 91, Minnesota House of Representatives, 77th Legislature (1991).

19. Dawkins, interview.

20. Dawkins, interview.

21. Another difference is that the wedding ceremony could be considered a religious ceremony. The actual wedding ceremony may precede or succeed the signing of the marriage certificate by an officiator at the district court. Some individuals may have been civilly and legally married many months or years before an actual Hmong American wedding ceremony. Hence, the division between civil and legal marriage, and then the commemoration of that marriage through a wedding ceremony, serves as the clear distinction.

22. Dawkins, interview.

23. Minnesota Senate, *Hearing on S.F. 107 Before Senate Judiciary Committee Hearing*, 77th Legislature, February 6, 1991 (statement of James Coben).

24. Coben also rehashes his ideologies by positioning state intervention into Hmong kinship matters such as marriage, divorce, and domestic violence as a "bridge" to facilitate and alleviate Hmong failed assimilation. James Coben, "Building a

Bridge: Lessons Learned from Family Mediation Training for the Hmong Community of Minnesota," *Family Court Review* 40, no. 3 (2002): 338–349.

25. Minnesota Senate, *Hearing on S.F. 107* (statement of Choua Lee).

26. Dawkins, interview.

27. Minnesota House of Representatives, *Session Weekly* 8, no. 20 (May 24, 1991): 26.

28. Dawkins, interview.

29. Vang, *Hmong America*, 76.

30. Yang Lor, "Hmong Political Involvement in St. Paul, Minnesota and Fresno, California," *Hmong Studies Journal* 10 (2009): 1–53.

31. Mee Moua (former Minnesota state senator), interview with the author, February 19, 2021.

32. Taeko Yoshikawa, "From a Refugee Camp to the Minnesota State Senate: A Case Study of a Hmong American Woman's Challenge," *Hmong Studies Journal* 7 (2006): 1–23.

33. Moua, interview.

34. Patricia J. Williams, *The Alchemy of Race and Rights: Diary of a Law Professor* (Cambridge, MA: Harvard University Press, 1991), 149.

35. Moua, interview.

36. Marriage Solemnization Provisions Modification, S.F. 3368, 82nd Legislature (2001–2002).

37. Moua, interview.

38. Moua, interview.

39. Mee Moua, "Hmong Marriage Bill Before Senate," *Asian Pages*, March 15, 2002.

40. Cy Thao (former Minnesota state representative), interview with the author, April 14, 2020.

41. Thao, interview.

42. Hmong Marriage Solemnization Form Provided, H.F. 707, 83rd Legislature (2003–2004).

43. Moua, interview.

44. Minnesota House of Representatives, *Session Weekly* 20, no. 12 (March 28, 2003): 16.

45. Minnesota House, *Hearing on H.F. 707 Before Committee on Civil Law*, 83rd Legislature, March 25, 2003 (statement of Cy Thao).

46. Thao, interview.

47. Minnesota House, *Hearing on H.F. 707* (statement of Sher Lee).

48. Minnesota House, *Hearing on H.F. 707* (statement of Ai Vang).

49. In their archived testimonies, these women identified themselves as "concerned private citizens" who were opposed to the bill. While their instructional or organizational affiliations cannot be substantiated, it is important to include their

statements as part of the only known testimonies from private Hmong American women who were opposed to the bill.

50. Minnesota House, *Hearing on H.F. 707* (statement of Ka Vang).
51. Minnesota House, *Hearing on H.F. 707* (statement of Pacyinz Lyfoung).
52. Minnesota House, *Hearing on H.F. 707* (statement of Out Vang).
53. For discussion on the sexual contract, see Carole Pateman, *The Sexual Contract* (Stanford, CA: Stanford University Press, 1988).
54. Minnesota House, *Hearing on H.F. 707* (statement of Dick Borrell).
55. I had planned to interview Ilean Her for this book; however, she passed away due to complications from COVID-19 in 2021. With that setback, I acknowledge that my analysis is only partially complete, as with any analysis in any book. I rely on the testimonies given by Her, and I try my best to contextualize them in good faith, given that I am missing Her's direct reflections that could have resulted from a personal interview.
56. Minnesota Senate, *Hearing on S.F. 827 Before Committee on Judiciary*, 83rd Legislature, April 8, 2003 (statement of Ilean Her).
57. Minnesota Senate, *Hearing on S.F. 827* (statement of Thomas M. Neuville).
58. Minnesota Senate, *Hearing on S.F. 827* (statement of Mee Moua).
59. Marriage Solemnization Provisions Modifications, S.F. 2403, 84th Legislative Session (2006).
60. Blong Yang, "The Hmong Marriage Bill" (unpublished opinion, 2006).
61. Blong Yang (attorney), interview with the author, June 14, 2021.
62. Yang, interview.
63. In another example, Katharine Charley and Anika Liversage have illuminated similar marriages among Pakistani and Turkish Muslim migrants living in the United Kingdom. They show that Muslim migrants enact formal and informal (or de facto) forms of polygamy using both religious and state-sanctioned institutions. Migrants then can use travel to and from Europe and Pakistan as a way to enter polygamous marriages, which occur through a religious *and* state-sanctioned marriage, or two state-sanctioned marriages within two different nation-states, which they call de jure "technical" polygamy. In certain situations, Muslims would rather follow religious law, and they circumvent state laws in ways that will permit them to follow religious laws. Thus, English laws are not the sole determinants of intimate relations, as is also the case with US law. Thus, de facto marriages elude de jure marriages, constituting "polygamy," but not in the legal sense within the parameters of a singular nation-state. Katharine Charsley and Anika Liversage, "Transforming Polygamy: Migration, Transnationalism and Multiple Marriages Among Muslim Minorities," *Global Networks* 13, no. 1 (2013): 60–78.

64. Minnesota Senate, *Hearing on S.F. 2403 Before Judiciary Subcommittee on Family Law*, 84th Legislature, March 3, 2006 (statement of Wesley J. Skoglund).

65. Minnesota Senate, *Hearing on S.F. 2403* (statement of Thomas M. Neuville).

66. Minnesota Senate, *Hearing on S.F. 2403* (statement of Ilean Her).

67. Minnesota Senate, *Hearing on S.F. 2403* (statement of Wesley J. Skoglund).

68. Child brides in the Global South and among people of color living in the United States have been understood only through narratives of victimization that furnish dominant understandings about those particular cultures among white liberal feminism. Feminist legal scholars have demonstrated how the metanarratives of victimization work to secure distorted representations of gender and cultural essentialisms of cultures and peoples of the Global South. Ratna Kapur, "The Tragedy of Victimization Rhetoric: Resurrecting the 'Native' Subject in International/ Post-Colonial Feminist Legal Politics," *Harvard Human Rights Journal* 15 (2002): 1–38; Chandra Talpade Mohanty, "Under Western Eyes: Feminist Scholarship and Colonial Discourses," *boundary 2* 12, no. 3 / 13, no. 1 (1984): 333–358; Uma Narayan, "Essence of Culture and Sense of History: A Feminist Critique of Cultural Essentialism," *Hypatia* 13, no. 2 (1998): 86–106; Uma Narayan, "Undoing the 'Package Picture' of Cultures," *Signs: Journal of Women in Culture and Society* 25, no. 4 (2000): 1083–1086.

69. On the "saving" of women from their cultures, see Abu-Lughod, "Do Muslim Women Really Need Saving?," 783–790. Abu-Lughod expands on her arguments further in a book: Lila Abu-Lughod, *Do Muslim Women Need Saving?* (Cambridge, MA: Harvard University Press, 2013).

70. Toni Randolph, "Hmong Legislators Say Cultural Marriage Bill Is Unnecessary," *Minnesota Public Radio News*, March 20, 2006.

71. Moua, interview.

72. Minnesota House of Representatives, *Session Weekly* 23, no. 6 (April 7, 2006): 9.

73. Minnesota House, *Hearing on H.F. 3674 Before Civil Law and Elections Committee*, 84th Legislature, April 3, 2006 (statement of Michael Paymar).

74. Volpp, "Engendering Culture," 185–186.

75. For example, the US television show *Married by America* demonstrates the contraction of a marriage organized by the American public. Volpp shows how such "arranged marriages" on *Married by America* are deemed acceptable by the West, despite the fallacy of marriage as a private decision agreed on by the couple. This contradiction forces a closer examination of "arranged marriages" and their place in American culture, particularly the racialized dimensions of how some "arranged marriages" are more acceptable than others. Volpp, "Engendering Culture," 181–182.

76. Volpp, "Engendering Culture," 186.

77. Volpp, "Engendering Culture," 191.

78. Minnesota House, *Hearing on H.F. 3674 Before Committee on Public Safety Policy and Finance*, 84th Legislature, April 6, 2006 (statement of Ilean Her).

79. Minnesota House, *Hearing on H.F. 3674* (statement of Rob Eastlund).

80. Minnesota House, *Hearing on H.F. 3674* (statement of Cy Thao).

81. Minnesota House, *Hearing on H.F. 3674* (statement of Sia Lo).

82. Thao, interview.

83. Uma Narayan, *Dislocating Cultures: Identities, Traditions, and Third-World Feminism* (New York: Routledge, 1997), 142.

84. Narayan, *Dislocating Cultures*, 145.

85. Moua, interview.

86. Moua was pregnant with her daughter at the time and had a conference call with the chair of the Senate Judiciary Committee to table the bill (Moua, interview). At the final hearing on April 6, 2006, Thao requested that the committee downright table the marriage bills until Hmong Americans themselves had deliberated about how to move forward. It remains unclear whether further conversations took place within the legislature or within community forums, and thus the marriage bills essentially halted altogether (Thao, interview).

CHAPTER 3. **Queering Spirituality**

1. Among the stories in the "Lost in America" report published by the *Fresno Bee* were other cases of Hmong American teenagers who had died by suicide because of differences resulting from their desire to be American and the desires of their refugee parents to maintain their Hmong culture. These cases include Hue Vue, who killed himself because of his failure to live up to the expectations of a Hmong American son; Richard A. Vang, who shot himself because of his failures in school; Gerry Vang, who hung himself rather than go to juvenile hall for car theft and property crimes; Gozouapa Her, who drank cyanide because her father had been against everything she has done all her life; and Mai Kor Vang, who, after finding out she was pregnant, also poisoned herself with cyanide, fearing she would bring shame to her family. Anne Dudley Ellis, introduction to "Lost in America," special report, *Fresno Bee*, August 11, 2002.

2. Anne Dudley Ellis, "Embracing the Forbidden," in "Lost in America," special report, *Fresno Bee*, August 11, 2002.

3. Ellis, introduction to "Lost in America."

4. Ellis, introduction to "Lost in America."

5. Xiong's and Yang's deaths have been transformed into origin stories that impact the subjectivities of queer Hmong Americans in profound ways. MidWest Solidarity Movement (MWSM), a collective of queer Hmong American activists

and organizers who participated in various community-based projects and social activism (which I analyze in chapter 4), initiated the "Raising Our Narratives" survey project to collect coming-out stories and life narratives of queer Hmong Americans across the United States in 2013–2014. The queer Hmong Americans in MWSM's project were asked to recount stories they had heard about LGBTQ Hmong growing up. The testimonies of queer Hmong Americans link back to Xiong and Yang in significant ways. For example, a nineteen-year-old bisexual woman from California named Emo Miao Girl wrote, "I have not heard about any queer Hmong growing up. However, my curiosity began to peak, and I began to Google about Hmong queers and Hmong LGBTQ to see if there was anything out there. Sadly, the first story that I stumbled upon was about the couple that had committed suicide many years ago. It makes me extremely sad when I read tragic stories like this." Xyooj Xub, an eighteen-year-old gay/queer male residing in Minnesota, wrote, "I've heard of queer Hmong American youth being thrown out of their homes, disowned by their families, rejected by peers, or were told not to reveal their sexual identity to others in the family and community. In the worst-case scenario, death occurs. The most prominent story I can recall was reading about the young lesbian couple, Pa Nhia Xiong and Yee Yang, who committed suicide together in their despair of knowing their love would not be accepted by their families or community." Jackie, a twenty-two-year-old lesbian from California, wrote, "Like every Hmong American lesbian with internet access, I Googled 'Hmong lesbian' and came across the Hmong double lesbian suicide pact. It broke my heart to know that it was the best answer they could come up with. The girls could not overcome the 'now moment' and resorted to suicide." Xiong's and Yang's suicides are important origin points for these queer Hmong Americans in the discovery of queerness. Their narratives expose the painful cultural memories that are transmitted in the present. Lives that are concurrently remembered and repeated within a particular group's history eventually come to constitute that group's cultural, social, and political consciousness. In this case, Xiong and Yang resonate throughout queer Hmong Americans' coming-of-age narratives by referring them back to the hardships that come with negotiating queer sexuality and their native "culture." While Xiong's and Yang's deaths were acts that were deeply personal, the stories that have circulated about them in subsequent years have become political. Emo Miao Girl, "Raising UP the Hmong American Bisexual Narrative," MidWest Solidarity Movement blog, July 6, 2013, https://mwsmovement.com/2013/07/06 /raising-up-the-hmong-american-bisexual-narrative; Xyooj Xub, "Raising UP Xyooj Xub's Struggle and Acceptance Narrative," MidWest Solidarity Movement blog, October 18, 2013, https://mwsmovement.com/2013/10/18/xyooj-xubs-struggle -for-love-and-acceptance-narrative; Jackie, "Raising UP Jackie's Realization and

Navigation Narrative," MidWest Solidarity Movement blog, December 6, 2013, https://mwsmovement
.com/2013/12/06/raising-up-jackies-realization-navigation-narrative.

6. For critiques of queer liberalism, see Lisa Duggan, *The Twilight of Equality? Neoliberalism, Cultural Politics, and the Attack on Democracy* (Boston: Beacon Press, 2003); Jasbir Puar, *Terrorist Assemblages: Homonationalism in Queer Times* (Durham, NC: Duke University Press, 2007); Chandan Reddy, "Time for Rights? *Loving*, Gay Marriage, and the Limits of Legal Justice," *Fordham Law Review* 76, no. 6 (2008): 2849–2872; David L. Eng, *The Feeling of Kinship: Queer Liberalism and the Racialization of Intimacy* (Durham, NC: Duke University Press, 2010); Dean Spade, *Normal Life: Administrative Violence, Critical Trans Politics, and the Limits of Law* (Brooklyn, NY: South End Press, 2011); Roderick A. Ferguson, *One-Dimensional Queer* (Cambridge, UK: Polity Press, 2019).

7. Duggan, *The Twilight of Equality?*

8. Sara Ahmed, *Queer Phenomenology: Orientations, Objects, Others* (Durham, NC: Duke University Press, 2006), 6–9.

9. Mai See Thao, "Bittersweet Migrations: Type II Diabetes and Healing in the Hmong Diaspora" (PhD diss., University of Minnesota, 2018), 26.

10. Ahmed, *Queer Phenomenology*, 119.

11. Sigmund Freud, "Mourning and Melancholia," in *The Standard Edition of the Complete Psychological Works of Sigmund Freud*, trans. and ed. James Strachey (London: Hogarth Press, 1957), 14:250.

12. David L. Eng and David Kazanjian, "Introduction: Mourning Remains," in *Loss: The Politics of Mourning*, ed. David L. Eng and David Kazanjian (Berkeley: University of California Press, 2003), 2.

13. Thao, "Bittersweet Migrations," 26–27, 96–98.

14. Vang, *History on the Run*, 33–38.

15. Thao, "Bittersweet Migrations," 26.

16. Roderick A. Ferguson, *Aberrations in Black: Toward a Queer of Color Critique* (Minneapolis: University of Minnesota Press, 2004), 90–91.

17. Jen-peng Liu and Naifei Ding, "Reticent Poetics, Queer Politics," *Inter-Asia Cultural Studies* 6, no. 1 (2005): 33.

18. Suzanna Danuta Walters also dissects the politics of tolerance as it relates to gay equality. See Suzanna Danuta Walters, *The Tolerance Trap: How God, Genes, and Good Intentions Are Sabotaging Gay Equality* (New York: New York University Press, 2017), 1–16.

19. Liu and Ding, "Reticent Poetics, Queer Politics," 49. Liu and Ding analyze Xioulan Du's 1996 novel *The Unfilial Daughter* to show how the pressures of needing to maintain peace and upholding the tradition of harmony within a Taiwanese

household become too unbearable for the lesbian daughter, Zhan Qingqing, leading her to take her own life. In this sense, the need to appear "proper" in terms of social class and sexual propriety by "tolerating" queerness through not acknowledging Zhan Qingqing's queerness is the reticent force and aesthetic-moral value deployed to contain nonnormative sexuality.

20. David A. B. Murray, introduction to *Homophobias: Lusting and Loathing Across Time and Space*, ed. David A. B. Murray (Durham, NC: Duke University Press, 2009), 3.

21. Eric Stanley, *Atmospheres of Violence: Structuring Antagonism and the Trans/Queer Ungovernable* (Durham, NC: Duke University Press, 2021), 98.

22. Kong Pheng Pha, "Finding Queer Hmong America: Gender, Sexuality, Culture, and Happiness Among Hmong LGBTQ," in *Claiming Place: On the Agency of Hmong Women*, ed. Chia Youyee Vang, Faith Nibbs, and Ma Vang (Minneapolis: University of Minnesota Press, 2016), 303–326.

23. Bic Ngo, "The Importance of Family for a Gay Hmong American Man: Complicating Discourses of 'Coming Out,'" *Hmong Studies Journal* 13, no. 1 (2012): 1–27.

24. Ngo, "The Importance of Family," 12.

25. Liu and Ding, "Reticent Poetics, Queer Politics," 49.

26. Liu and Ding, "Reticent Poetics, Queer Politics," 49.

27. Ngo, "The Importance of Family," 16.

28. Liu and Ding, "Reticent Poetics, Queer Politics," 36.

29. Soul release, or *tso plig*, is the secondary ceremonial rite usually conducted a year after an individual's death to "release" the soul from the grave and allow the soul to travel to the domain of the upper realm, or *ntuj*, in order to reincarnate. Vincent K. Her, "Hmong Cosmology: Proposed Model, Preliminary Insights," *Hmong Studies Journal* 6 (2005): 1–25.

30. Ellis, "Embracing the Forbidden."

31. Her, "Hmong Cosmology," 8.

32. Her, "Hmong Cosmology," 7.

33. Kao Kalia Yang, *The Latehomecomer: A Hmong Family Memoir* (St. Paul, MN: Coffee House Press, 2005), 14.

34. Her, "Hmong Cosmology," 7.

35. Liu and Ding offer a similar critique of the relegation of queerness to the realm of ghosts: "Reticent and indirect speech and ritual acts reinforce the restraining power of such a field and postulate a 'like' heart for all players within that game field. This then is how a reigning order (a force-field) might be preserved through the circulation of reticent forces of self(other)-discipline and self(other)-preservation: those bodies occupying the liminal sites of this force-field immediately

become shades or ghosts, deprived of the resources for life or action." Liu and Ding, "Reticent Poetics, Queer Politics," 35.

36. Stanley, *Atmospheres of Violence*, 24.
37. Khoua, interview with the author, January 5, 2017. In all the interviews referenced in this chapter and chapter 4, I gave the participants complete freedom to select their pseudonyms and descriptive identities.
38. Keng, interview with the author, December 30, 2016.
39. Keng, interview.
40. Pakou, interview with the author, January 16, 2017.
41. Mai Tooj, interview with the author, January 26, 2017.
42. Gloria Anzaldúa, "Creativity and Switching Modes of Consciousness," in *The Gloria Anzaldúa Reader*, ed. AnaLouise Keating (Durham, NC: Duke University Press, 2009), 106.
43. Anzaldúa, "Creativity and Switching Modes of Consciousness," 104.
44. Gloria Anzaldúa, *Light in the Dark / Luz En Lo Oscuro: Rewriting Identity, Spirituality, Reality*, ed. AnaLouise Keating (Durham, NC: Duke University Press, 2015), 34.
45. José Esteban Muñoz, *Cruising Utopia: The Then and There of Queer Futurity* (New York: New York University Press, 2009), 185.
46. Anzaldúa, *Light in the Dark*, 35.
47. Anzaldúa, *Light in the Dark*, 36; Muñoz, *Cruising Utopia*, 19.
48. Anzaldúa, *Light in the Dark*, 36.
49. Anzaldúa, *Light in the Dark*, 43.
50. Anzaldúa makes this contradictory and ambiguous form of subjectivity and consciousness clear through her articulation of the new mestiza consciousness that processes contradictory information and sensation and develops a "tolerance for ambiguity." Gloria Anzaldúa, *Borderlands / La Frontera: The New Mestiza*, 4th ed. (San Francisco: Aunt Lute Books, 2012), 101.
51. Pa Houa, interview with the author, February 21, 2017.
52. Pa Houa, interview.
53. Pa Houa, interview.
54. Nhia uses the word *plig* here to mean "soul," but it can also mean "spirit," as used later in the chapter.
55. Nhia, interview with the author, March 7, 2017.
56. Anzaldúa, *Borderlands / La Frontera*, 104.
57. Siv Yis, interview with the author, June 24, 2021.
58. Jacques Lemoine, "The (H)mong Shamans' Power of Healing: Sharing the Esoteric Knowledge of a Great Mong Shaman," *Hmong Studies Journal* 12 (2011): 21.

59. Siv Yis, interview.

60. Siv Yis, interview.

61. Siv Yis, interview.

62. Lemoine, "The (H)mong Shamans' Power of Healing," 22.

63. Siv Yis, interview.

64. Vang, *History on the Run*, 3.

65. Liu and Ding, "Reticent Poetics, Queer Politics," 33.

66. In reading Randall Kenan's novel *A Visitation of Spirits*, about the suicide of a Black gay teenager named Horace in North Carolina, Sharon Patricia Holland argues for the reorganization of subjects of focus within African American studies, feminist studies, and queer studies. Holland illuminates how Horace's suicide has "spoken" to the living in enabling a rethinking of traditional objects within the canons of these particular disciplines. Precisely, Holland does this through placing Black gay subjects and their deaths at the heart of a queer African Americanist critique of death. Sharon Patricia Holland, *Raising the Dead: Readings of Death and (Black) Subjectivity* (Durham, NC: Duke University Press, 2000), 118–123.

CHAPTER 4. Vernacular Activism

1. I use the formal name Amendment 1 when referring to the ballot referendum throughout.

2. I use the phrase "same-sex marriage" rather than "marriage equality." "Same-sex marriage" more accurately depicts the legalities of a marriage between a same-sex couple, whereas "marriage equality" is the rhetorical phrase used by leftist activists to equate it with monogamous heterosexual marriage, namely, through the word *equality*. I also use the phrase "the legalization of same-sex marriage" rather than "achieving marriage equality."

3. For example, Helen Zia and Erika Lee have both documented how Hmong Americans resisted the caricaturing of their communities by the Twin Cities radio station KQRS when a talk show host made racist comments about Hmong Americans as racially primitive people with regard to kinship systems. Helen Zia, *Asian American Dreams: The Emergence of an American People* (New York: Farrar, Straus and Giroux, 2000), 257–263, 278–280; Erika Lee, *The Making of Asian America: A History* (New York: Simon and Schuster, 2015), 350–353.

4. MidWest Solidarity Movement, "About MWSMovement," accessed January 1, 2013, https://mwsmovement.com/about.

5. Kong Pheng Pha, "'Minnesota Is Open to Everything': Queer Hmong and the

Politics of Community Formation in the Diaspora," *Minnesota History* 66, no. 6 (2019): 255–263.

6. Pao, interview with the author, January 2017.

7. Pao, interview.

8. Tim Pugmire, "'Vote No Twice' a Grass-Roots Push to Reject Amendments on Ballot," *Minnesota Public Radio News*, October 29, 2012.

9. Kong Pheng Pha, "The Politics of Vernacular Activism: Hmong Americans Organizing for Social Justice in Minnesota," *Amerasia Journal* 45, no. 2 (2019): 207–221.

10. Aniruddha Dutta, "An Epistemology of Collusion: *Hijras, Kothis* and the Historical (Dis)continuity of Gender/Sexual Identities in Eastern India," *Gender and History* 24, no. 3 (2012): 839–842; Aniruddha Dutta, "Claiming Citizenship, Contesting Civility: The Institutional LGBT Movement and the Regulation of Gender/Sexual Dissidence in West Bengal, India," *Jindal Global Law Review* 4, no. 1 (2012): 135, 141.

11. Beth Bibus, "Battleground State: Minnesota," in *Gay, Lesbian, Bisexual, and Transgender Civil Rights: A Public Policy Agenda for Uniting a Divided America*, ed. Wallace Swan (Boca Raton, FL: CRC Press, 2015), 101.

12. Bibus, "Battleground State," 101.

13. The data reveals that a total of 2,950,780 Minnesotans voted during the 2012 elections, with 1,399,916 voting yes and 1,510,434 voting no on Amendment 1. There were 40,430 votes that were labeled as blanks. Minnesota Secretary of State, "Constitutional Amendment 1: Recognition of Marriage Solely Between One Man and One Woman," 2012, https://electionresults.sos.state.mn.us/Results/Amendment ResultsStatewide/1.

14. Sasha Aslanian and Eric Ringham, "'Eighteen Months to History: How the Minnesota Marriage Amendment Was Defeated—Money, Passion, Allies," *Minnesota Public Radio News*, November 9, 2012.

15. Minnesotans United for All Families, "Special Tactics Video from Minnesotans United," September 14, 2012, Jean-Nickolaus Tretter Collection in Gay, Lesbian, Bisexual, and Transgender Studies, University of Minnesota.

16. Minnesotans United for All Families, "Native American Talking Points," 2012, Tretter Collection.

17. Myrl Beam, "What's Love Got to Do with It? Queer Politics and the 'Love Pivot,'" in *Queer Activism After Marriage Equality*, ed. Joseph Nicholas DeFilippis, Michael W. Yarbrough, and Angela Jones (London: Routledge, 2018), 59. Renata Grossi also analyzes the deploying of romantic love in the debate over legalizing same-sex marriage in the Australian context. Renata Grossi, "The Meaning of Love

in the Debate for Legal Recognition of Same-Sex Marriage in Australia," *International Journal of Law in Context* 8, no. 4 (2012): 487–505.

18. Emphasis in original.

19. Minnesotans United for All Families, "Native American Talking Points."

20. Aslanian and Ringham, "Eighteen Months to History"; OutFront Minnesota, "Budget Memo—OutFront," September 18, 2012, Tretter Collection.

21. OutFront Minnesota, "Budget Memo."

22. Pao, interview.

23. Dylan Rodriguez, "The Political Logic of the Non-Profit Industrial Complex," in *The Revolution Will Not Be Funded: Beyond the Non-Profit Industrial Complex*, ed. INCITE! Women of Color Against Violence (Cambridge, MA: South End Press, 2007).

24. Myrl Beam, *Gay, Inc.: The Nonprofitization of Queer Politics* (Minneapolis: University of Minnesota Press, 2018).

25. Rickke Mananzala and Dean Spade, "The Nonprofit Industrial Complex and Trans Resistance," *Sexuality Research and Social Policy* 5, no. 1 (2008): 53–71; Spade, *Normal Life*, 29–33.

26. Jane Ward, "White Normativity: The Cultural Dimensions of Whiteness in a Racially Diverse LGBT Organization," *Sociological Perspectives* 51, no. 3 (2008): 563–586; Jane Ward, *Respectably Queer: Diversity in LGBT Activist Organizations* (Nashville: Vanderbilt University Press, 2008); Beam, *Gay, Inc.*

27. Martin F. Manalansan IV, *Global Divas: Filipino Gay Men in the Diaspora* (Durham, NC: Duke University Press, 2003); Tom Boellstorff, "Queer Studies in the House of Anthropology," *Annual Review of Anthropology* 36, no. 17 (2007): 20–27; Michelle Walks, "'We're Here and We're Queer!': An Introduction to Studies in Queer Anthropology," *Anthropologica* 56, no. 1 (2014): 14–25.

28. Pao, interview.

29. Brian Bix, "State of the Union: The States' Interest in the Marital Status of Their Citizens," *University of Miami Law Review* 55, no. 1 (2000): 26–29.

30. Cohen, "Punks, Bulldaggers, and Welfare Queens," 440–441.

31. Pakou, interview with the author, January 16, 2017.

32. Reddy, *Freedom with Violence*, 185.

33. Reddy, *Freedom with Violence*, 205–218.

34. Reddy, *Freedom with Violence*, 221.

35. Other studies of Hmong American politics and activism have made similar conclusions about how Hmong Americans have enacted new frames to redefine the terms of their liberation in accordance with their interests. Nengher N. Vang, "Unlawful or Not? Reassessing the Value and Impact of Hmong American Transnational Politics," *Amerasia Journal* 44, no. 2 (2018): 43–64; Yang Sao Xiong, "The

Dynamics of Discursive Opportunities in the Hmong Campaign for Inclusion in California," *Amerasia Journal* 44, no. 2 (2018): 65–87.

36. José Esteban Muñoz, *Disidentifications: Queers of Color and the Performance of Politics* (Minneapolis: University of Minnesota Press, 1999), 11–12.

37. Muñoz, *Disidentifications*, 31.

38. Congress of World Hmong People, "Organization and Mission," accessed January 1, 2016, http://www.cwhp.net/mission.html.

39. Unrepresented Nations and Peoples Organization, "UNPO XII's General Assembly Adopts Resolution on Hmong," July 23, 2015, http://unpo.org/article/18406.

40. Yer J. Thao, "Culture and Knowledge of the Sacred Instrument *Qeej* in the Mong-American Community," *Asian Folklore Studies* 65, no. 2 (2006): 262; Catherine Falk, "The Dragon Taught Us: Hmong Stories About the Origin of the Free Reed Pipes *Qeej*," *Asian Music* 35, no. 1 (2003–2004): 17–56; Catherine Falk, "The Private and Public Lives of the Hmong *Qeej* or Miao *Lusheng*," in *The Hmong of Australia: Culture and Diaspora*, ed. Nicholas Tapp and Gary Yia Lee (Canberra: Pandanus Books, 2004), 123.

41. Gayle Morrison, "The Hmong *Qeej*: Speaking to the Spirit World," *Hmong Studies Journal* 2 (1998): 3–5.

42. Louisa Schein, *Minority Rules: The Miao and the Feminine in China's Cultural Politics* (Durham, NC: Duke University Press, 2000), 60.

43. Julie Mertus, "The Rejection of Human Rights Framing: The Case of LGBT Advocacy in the US," *Human Rights Quarterly* 29, no. 4 (2007): 1036–1064.

44. Wendy Brown, *States of Injury: Power and Freedom in Late Modernity* (Princeton, NJ: Princeton University Press, 1995), 54–57.

45. Mai Na M. Lee also discusses Hmong's political participation with states. Lee, *Dreams of the Hmong Kingdom*.

46. Lauren Berlant, "A Properly Political Concept of Love: Three Approaches in Ten Pages," *Cultural Anthropology* 26, no. 4 (2011): 685–686.

47. Here, I am suggesting that a Hmong American–centered conversation about freedom must occur concomitantly, as Hmong Americans are speaking back to and against the state in articulating their ideas about freedom.

48. Eng, *The Feeling of Kinship*, 29.

49. Em Thao, "Raising UP Emily's What's After Acceptance Narrative," MidWest Solidarity Movement blog, April 24, 2014, https://mwsmovement.com/2014/04/24/raising-up-emilys-whats-after-acceptance-narrative.

50. Phong, interview with the author, December 27, 2016.

51. Tou Bee, interview with the author, December 5, 2016.

52. Leng, interview with the author, December 7, 2016.

53. Phong, interview.

54. Phong, interview.
55. Moua Kong, interview with the author, December 20, 2016.

EPILOGUE. Many Words for Queer

1. Cedar Commissions, "The Tenth Annual Showcase of Brave New Work by Emerging Minnesota Artists Commissioned by the Cedar Cultural Center with Funding from the Jerome Foundation" (Minneapolis: Cedar Cultural Center, 2021), 7.
2. Marla Khan-Schwartz, "There's 'No Word for Queer' in the Hmong Language. Musician and Spoken Word Artist SUNAH Crafts New, Positive Phrases in Hmong to Identify Members of the LGBTQ Community," *Sahan Journal*, May 12, 2022, https://sahanjournal.com/immigration/sunah-hmong-lgbtq-queer-language-the-cedar
-commission.
3. Cedar Cultural Center, "Cedar Commissions Spotlight—S U N A H," Cedar Commissions News, February 27, 2021, https://www.thecedar.org/news-articles/2021/2/24/cedar-commissions-spotlight-s-u-n-a-h.
4. S U N A H (Schoua Na Yang), interview with the author, September 12, 2021.
5. Anzaldúa, *Borderlands / La Frontera*, 76.
6. S U N A H, interview with the author.
7. Anzaldúa, *Borderlands / La Frontera*, 77.
8. S U N A H, interview.
9. Khan-Schwartz, "There's 'No Word for Queer.'"
10. Crimson, interview with the author, March 21, 2022.
11. Anzaldúa, *Borderlands / La Frontera*, 77.
12. Cedar Cultural Center, "S U N A H 'No Word for Queer'—2021 Cedar Commissions (Full Performance)," posted April 9, 2021, performance video, 33:30–38:45, https://www.youtube.com/watch?v=iQCmGx5SNmY. All lyric translations are mine.
13. Han, *Geisha of a Different Kind*, 76.
14. Quoted in Khan-Schwartz, "There's 'No Word for Queer.'"

Bibliography

Abu-Lughod, Lila. *Do Muslim Women Need Saving?* Cambridge, MA: Harvard University Press, 2013.

Abu-Lughod, Lila. "Do Muslim Women Really Need Saving? Anthropological Reflections on Cultural Relativism and Its Others." *American Anthropologist* 104, no. 3 (2002): 783–790.

Abu-Lughod, Lila. "Writing Against Culture." In *Recapturing Anthropology*, edited by Richard Fox, 137–162. Santa Fe, NM: School of American Research Press, 1991.

Ahmed, Sara. *Queer Phenomenology: Orientations, Objects, Others.* Durham, NC: Duke University Press, 2006.

Anzaldúa, Gloria. *Borderlands / La Frontera: The New Mestiza.* 4th ed. San Francisco: Aunt Lute Books, 2012.

Anzaldúa, Gloria. "Creativity and Switching Modes of Consciousness." In *The Gloria Anzaldúa Reader*, edited by AnaLouise Keating, 103–110. Durham, NC: Duke University Press, 2009.

Anzaldúa, Gloria. *Light in the Dark / Luz en lo Oscuro: Rewriting Identity, Spirituality, Reality.* Edited by AnaLouise Keating. Durham, NC: Duke University Press, 2015.

Appiah, K. Anthony, and Amy Gutmann. *Color Conscious: The Political Morality of Race.* Princeton, NJ: Princeton University Press, 1996.

Asad, Talal. "Two European Images of Non-European Rule." In *Anthropology and the Colonial Encounter*, edited by Talal Asad, 103–118. London: Ithaca Press, 1973.

Averbeck, Robin Marie. *Liberalism Is Not Enough: Race and Poverty in Postwar Political Thought.* Chapel Hill: University of North Carolina Press, 2018.

Báez, Jillian M. *In Search of Belonging: Latinas, Media, and Citizenship.* Urbana: University of Illinois Press, 2018.

Baker, Lee. *Anthropology and the Racial Politics of Culture*. Durham, NC: Duke University Press, 2010.

Baker, Lee. *From Savage to Negro: Anthropology and the Construction of Race*. Berkeley: University of California Press, 1998.

Balaton-Chrimes, Samantha, and Victoria Stead. "Recognition, Power and Coloniality." *Postcolonial Studies* 20, no. 1 (2017): 1–17.

Balistreri, Kelly Stamper, Kara Joyner, and Grace Kao. "Relationship Involvement Among Young Adults: Are Asian American Men an Exceptional Case?" *Population Research and Policy Review* 34, no. 5 (2015): 709–732.

Beam, Myrl. *Gay, Inc.: The Nonprofitization of Queer Politics*. Minneapolis: University of Minnesota Press, 2018.

Beam, Myrl. "What's Love Got to Do with It? Queer Politics and the 'Love Pivot.'" In *Queer Activism After Marriage Equality*, edited by Joseph Nicholas DeFilippis, Michael W. Yarbrough, and Angela Jones, 53–60. London: Routledge, 2018.

Bell, Derrick A., Jr. "The Unintended Lessons in *Brown v. Board of Education*." *New York Law School Law Review* 49, no. 4 (2004): 1053–1067.

Berlant, Lauren. "A Properly Political Concept of Love: Three Approaches in Ten Pages." *Cultural Anthropology* 26, no. 4 (2011): 683–691.

Bibus, Beth. "Battleground State: Minnesota." In *Gay, Lesbian, Bisexual, and Transgender Civil Rights: A Public Policy Agenda for Uniting a Divided America*, edited by Wallace Swan, 83–116. Boca Raton, FL: CRC Press, 2015.

Bix, Brian. "State of the Union: The States' Interest in the Marital Status of Their Citizens." *University of Miami Law Review* 55, no. 1 (2000): 1–30.

Blackstone, Lisa, dir. *Minnesota Remembers Vietnam: America's Secret War*. St. Paul, MN: Twin Cities PBS, 2017. DVD.

Boas, Franz. *Anthropology and Modern Life*. New York: W. W. Norton, 1928.

Boas, Franz. *The Mind of Primitive Man*. New York: Macmillan, 1911.

Boellstorff, Tom. "Queer Studies in the House of Anthropology." *Annual Review of Anthropology* 36, no. 17 (2007): 17–35.

Boulden, Walter T. "Gay Hmong: A Multifaceted Clash of Cultures." *Journal of Gay and Lesbian Social Services* 21, no. 2 (2009): 134–150.

Brandzel, Amy L. *Against Citizenship: The Violence of the Normative*. Urbana: University of Illinois Press, 2016.

Brown, Wendy. *States of Injury: Power and Freedom in Late Modernity*. Princeton, NJ: Princeton University Press, 1995.

Byrd, Jodi. *The Transit of Empire: Indigenous Critiques of Colonialism*. Minneapolis: University of Minnesota Press, 2011.

Cacho, Lisa Marie. *Social Death: Racialized Rightlessness and the Criminalization of the Unprotected*. New York: New York University Press, 2012.

Chan, Sucheng. "The Exclusion of Chinese Women." In *Entry Denied: Exclusion and the Chinese Community in America, 1882-1943*, edited by Sucheng Chan, 94-146. Philadelphia: Temple University Press, 1991.

Charsley, Katharine, and Anika Liversage. "Transforming Polygamy: Migration, Transnationalism and Multiple Marriages Among Muslim Minorities." *Global Networks* 13, no. 1 (2013): 60-78.

Chavez, Leo R. *Covering Immigration: Popular Images and the Politics of the Nation.* Berkeley: University of California Press, 2001.

Clifford, James. *The Predicament of Culture: Twentieth-Century Ethnography, Literature, and Art*. Cambridge, MA: Harvard University Press, 1988.

Coben, James. "Building a Bridge: Lessons Learned from Family Mediation Training for the Hmong Community of Minnesota." *Family Court Review* 40, no. 3 (2002): 338-349.

Cohen, Cathy J. "Punks, Bulldaggers, and Welfare Queens: The Radical Potential of Queer Politics?" *GLQ* 3, no. 4 (1997): 437-465.

Collins, Patricia Hill. *Black Feminist Thought: Knowledge, Consciousness, and the Politics of Empowerment*. 2nd ed. New York: Routledge, 2002.

Collins, Patricia Hill. *Black Sexual Politics: African Americans, Gender, and the New Racism*. New York: Routledge, 2004.

Cooper, Robert G. *The Hmong: A Guide to Traditional Lifestyles*. Bangkok: Artasia Press, 1995.

Cooper, Robert G. *Resource Scarcity and the Hmong Response: Patterns of Settlement and Economy in Transition*. Singapore: Singapore University Press, 1984.

Cooper, Robert G. "Sexual Inequality Among the Hmong." In *Highlanders of Thailand*, edited by John McKinnon and Wanat Bhruksasri, 173-186. New York: Oxford University Press, 1983.

Coulthard, Glen. *Red Skin, White Masks: Rejecting the Colonial Politics of Recognition*. Minneapolis: University of Minnesota Press, 2014.

Crenshaw, Kimberlé. "Mapping the Margins: Intersectionality, Identity Politics, and Violence Against Women of Color." *Stanford Law Review* 46, no. 6 (1991): 1241-1299.

Crenshaw, Kimberlé. "Race, Reform, and Retrenchment: Transformation and Legitimation in Antidiscrimination Law." *Harvard Law Review* 101, no. 7 (1988): 1331-1387.

Culas, Christian, and Jean Michaud. "A Contribution to the Study of Hmong (Miao) Migrations and History." *Bijdragen tot de Taal-, Land- en Volkenkunde* 153, no. 2 (1997): 211-243.

Dasgupta, Shamita Das, ed. *Body Evidence: Intimate Violence Against South Asian Women in America*. New Brunswick, NJ: Rutgers University Press, 2007.

Davis, Rebecca L. *More Perfect Unions: The American Search for Marital Bliss*. Cambridge, MA: Harvard University Press, 2010.

DePouw, Christin. "When Culture Implies Deficit: Placing Race at the Center of Hmong American Education." *Race Ethnicity and Education* 15, no. 2 (2012): 223–239.

Duggan, Lisa. *Sapphic Slashers: Sex, Violence, and American Modernity*. Durham, NC: Duke University Press, 2000.

Duggan, Lisa. *The Twilight of Equality? Neoliberalism, Cultural Politics, and the Attack on Democracy*. Boston: Beacon Press, 2003.

Dutta, Aniruddha. "Claiming Citizenship, Contesting Civility: The Institutional LGBT Movement and the Regulation of Gender/Sexual Dissidence in West Bengal, India." *Jindal Global Law Review* 4, no. 1 (2012): 110–141.

Dutta, Aniruddha. "An Epistemology of Collusion: *Hijras, Kothis* and the Historical (Dis)continuity of Gender/Sexual Identities in Eastern India." *Gender and History* 24, no. 3 (2012): 825–849.

Eng, David L. *The Feeling of Kinship: Queer Liberalism and the Racialization of Intimacy*. Durham, NC: Duke University Press, 2010.

Eng, David L. *Racial Castration: Managing Masculinity in Asian America*. Durham, NC: Duke University Press, 2001.

Eng, David L., and David Kazanjian. "Introduction: Mourning Remains." In *Loss: The Politics of Mourning*, edited by David L. Eng and David Kazanjian, 1–25. Berkeley: University of California Press, 2003.

Espiritu, Yen Lê, Lan Duong, Ma Vang, Victor Bascara, Khatharya Um, Lila Sharif, and Nigel Hatton. *Departures: An Introduction to Critical Refugee Studies*. Berkeley: University of California Press, 2022.

Espiritu Gandhi, Evyn Lê. "Indigenous Soldiering: CHamoru, Māori, and Hmong Narratives of the Trans-Pacific Vietnam War." *Critical Ethnic Studies* 7, no. 2 (2021). https://manifold.umn.edu/read/ceso702-08/section/4273299b-143e-41b7-b129-d905f6d3ce6e.

Evans-Pritchard, Deirdre, and Alison Dundes Renteln. "The Interpretation and Distortion of Culture: A Hmong 'Marriage by Capture' Case in Fresno, California." *Southern California Interdisciplinary Law Journal* 4, no. 1 (1994): 1–48.

Falk, Catherine. "The Dragon Taught Us: Hmong Stories About the Origin of the Free Reed Pipes *Qeej*." *Asian Music* 35, no. 1 (2003–2004): 17–56.

Falk, Catherine. "The Private and Public Lives of the Hmong *Qeej* or Miao *Lusheng*." In *The Hmong of Australia: Culture and Diaspora*, edited by Nicholas Tapp and Gary Yia Lee, 123–152. Canberra: Pandanus Books, 2004.

Ferguson, Roderick A. *Aberrations in Black: Toward a Queer of Color Critique*. Minneapolis: University of Minnesota Press, 2004.

Ferguson, Roderick A. *One-Dimensional Queer*. Cambridge, UK: Polity Press, 2019.

Foucault, Michel. *The History of Sexuality*. New York: Vintage, 1978.

Freud, Sigmund. "Mourning and Melancholia." In *The Standard Edition of the*

Complete Psychological Works of Sigmund Freud, translated and edited by James Strachey, 14:243–258. London: Hogarth Press, 1957.

Geddes, William Robert. *Migrants of the Mountains: The Cultural Ecology of the Blue Miao (Hmong Njua) of Northern Thailand.* Oxford, UK: Clarendon Press, 1976.

Goldstein, Beth L. "Resolving Sexual Assault: Hmong and the American Legal System." In *The Hmong in Transition*, edited by Glenn L. Hendricks, Bruce T. Downing, and Amos S. Deinard, 135–143. Staten Island, NY: Center for Migration Studies of New York; Minneapolis: Southeast Asian Refugee Studies of the University of Minnesota, 1986.

Grossi, Renata. "The Meaning of Love in the Debate for Legal Recognition of Same-Sex Marriage in Australia." *International Journal of Law in Context* 8, no. 4 (2012): 487–505.

Gupta, Akhil, and James Ferguson. "Beyond 'Culture': Space, Identity, and the Politics of Difference." *Cultural Anthropology* 7, no. 1 (1992): 6–23.

Hall, Stuart. "Cultural Identity and Diaspora." In *Identity: Community, Culture, Difference*, edited by Jonathan Rutherford, 222–237. London: Lawrence and Wishart, 1990.

Hall, Stuart. "Gramsci's Relevance for the Study of Race and Ethnicity." *Journal of Communication Inquiry* 10, no. 5 (1986): 5–27.

Hall, Stuart. "The Whites of Their Eyes: Racist Ideologies and the Media." In *Silver Linings: Some Strategies for the Eighties*, edited by George Bridges and Rosalind Brunt, 28–52. London: Lawrence and Wishart, 1981.

Han, C. Winter. *Geisha of a Different Kind: Race and Sexuality in Gaysian America.* New York: New York University Press, 2015.

Han, C. Winter. *Racial Erotics: Gay Men of Color, Sexual Racism, and the Politics of Desire.* Seattle: University of Washington Press, 2021.

Hein, Jeremy. "From Migrant to Minority: Hmong Refugees and the Social Construction of Identity in the United States." *Sociological Inquiry* 64, no. 3 (1994): 281–306.

Hendricks, Glenn L., Bruce T. Downing, and Amos S. Deinard, eds. *The Hmong in Transition.* Staten Island, NY: Center for Migration Studies of New York; Minneapolis: Southeast Asian Refugee Studies of the University of Minnesota, 1986.

Her, Leena. "Rewriting Hmong Women in Western Texts." In *Claiming Place: On the Agency of Hmong Women*, edited by Chia Youyee Vang, Faith Nibbs, and Ma Vang, 3–27. Minneapolis: University of Minnesota Press, 2016.

Her, Vincent K. "Hmong Cosmology: Proposed Model, Preliminary Insights." *Hmong Studies Journal* 6 (2005): 1–25.

Hoang, Nguyen Tan. *A View from the Bottom: Asian American Masculinity and Sexual Representation.* Durham, NC: Duke University Press, 2014.

Holland, Sharon Patricia. *Raising the Dead: Readings of Death and (Black) Subjectivity.* Durham, NC: Duke University Press, 2000.

Hunter, Tera W. *Bound in Wedlock: Slave and Free Black Marriage in the Nineteenth Century*. Cambridge, MA: Harvard University Press, 2017.

Hutchison, Ray, and Miles McNall. "Early Marriage in a Hmong Cohort." *Journal of Marriage and Family* 56, no. 3 (1994): 579–590.

Kao, Grace, Kelly Stamper Balistreri, and Kara Joyner. "Asian American Men in Romantic Dating Markets." *Contexts* 17, no. 4 (2018): 48–53.

Kapur, Ratna. "The Tragedy of Victimization Rhetoric: Resurrecting the 'Native' Subject in International/Post-Colonial Feminist Legal Politics." *Harvard Human Rights Journal* 15 (2002): 1–38.

Kim, Nancy S. "The Cultural Defense and the Problem of Cultural Preemption: A Framework for Analysis." *New Mexico Law Review* 27, no. 1 (1997): 101–139.

Kunstadter, Peter. "Hmong Marriage Patterns in Thailand in Relation to Social Change." In *Hmong/Miao in Asia*, edited by Nicholas Tapp, Jean Michaud, Christian Culas, and Gary Yia Lee, 375–420. Chiang Mai, Thailand: Silkworm Books, 2004.

Lee, Erika. *The Making of Asian America: A History*. New York: Simon and Schuster, 2015.

Lee, Gary Yia. "Hmong Postwar Identity Production: Heritage Maintenance and Cultural Reinterpretation." In *Cultural Heritage in Postwar Recovery*, edited by Nicholas Stanley-Price, 51–59. Rome: ICCROM, 2007.

Lee, Gary Yia. "Nostalgia and Cultural Re-creation: The Case of the Hmong Diaspora." *Crossroads: An Interdisciplinary Journal of Southeast Asian Studies* 19, no. 2 (2008): 125–154.

Lee, Jennifer, and Min Zhou. *The Asian American Achievement Paradox*. New York: Russell Sage Foundation, 2015.

Lee, Mai Na M. *Dreams of the Hmong Kingdom: The Quest for Legitimation in French Indochina, 1850–1960*. Madison: University of Wisconsin Press, 2015.

Lee, Mai Na M. "The Thousand-Year Myth: Construction and Characterization of Hmong." *Hmong Studies Journal* 2, no. 2 (1998): 1–23.

Lee, Mo Yee, and Phyllis F. M. Law. "Perception of Sexual Violence Against Women in Asian American Communities." *Journal of Ethnic and Cultural Diversity in Social Work* 10, no. 2 (2001): 3–25.

Lee, Sangmi. *Reclaiming Diasporic Identity: Transnational Continuity and National Fragmentation in the Hmong Diaspora*. Urbana: University of Illinois Press, 2024.

Lee, Serge, Zha Blong Xiong, and Francis K. O. Yuen. "Explaining Early Marriage in the Hmong American Community." In *Teenage Pregnancy and Parenthood: Global Perspectives, Issues and Interventions*, edited by Helen S. Holgate, Roy Evans, and Francis K. O. Yuen, 24–35. New York: Routledge, 2006.

Leepreecha, Prasit. "Hmong Across Borders or Borders Across Hmong? Social and Political Influences upon Hmong People." *Hmong Studies Journal* 15, no. 2 (2014): 1–12.

Lemoine, Jacques. "Gender-Based Violence Among the (H)mong." *Hmong Studies Journal* 13, no. 1 (2012): 1–27.

Lemoine, Jacques. "The (H)mong Shamans' Power of Healing: Sharing the Esoteric Knowledge of a Great Mong Shaman." *Hmong Studies Journal* 12 (2011): 1–36.

Liu, Jen-peng, and Naifei Ding. "Reticent Poetics, Queer Politics." *Inter-Asia Cultural Studies* 6, no. 1 (2005): 30–55.

Lor, Yang. "Hmong Political Involvement in St. Paul, Minnesota and Fresno, California." *Hmong Studies Journal* 10 (2009): 1–53.

Luibhéid, Eithne. *Entry Denied: Controlling Sexuality at the Border*. Minneapolis: University of Minnesota Press, 2002.

Ly, Choua. "The Conflict Between Law and Culture: The Case of the Hmong in America." *Wisconsin Law Review* 2001: 471–499.

Man, Simeon. *Soldiering Through Empire: Race and the Making of the Decolonizing Pacific*. Berkeley: University of California Press, 2018.

Manalansan, Martin F., IV. *Global Divas: Filipino Gay Men in the Diaspora*. Durham, NC: Duke University Press, 2003.

Mananzala, Rickke, and Dean Spade. "The Nonprofit Industrial Complex and Trans Resistance." *Sexuality Research and Social Policy* 5, no. 1 (2008): 53–71.

Mark, Lindy Li. "Patrilateral Cross-Cousin Marriage Among the Magpie Miao: Preferential or Prescriptive." *American Anthropologist* 69, no. 1 (1967): 55–62.

Martin, William E., and Peter N. Thompson. "Judicial Tolerance and Racial Bias in the Minnesota Justice System." *Hamline Law Review* 25, no. 2 (2002): 235–270.

Martinez-HoSang, Daniel. "The Triumph of Racial Liberalism, the Demise of Racial Justice." In *Race and American Political Development*, edited by Joseph Lowndes, Julie Novkov, and Dorian T. Warren, 288–311. New York: Routledge, 2008.

McCoy, Alfred W. "America's Secret War in Laos, 1955–75." In *A Companion to the Vietnam War*, edited by Marilyn B. Young and Robert Buzzanco, 283–313. Malden, MA: Blackwell Publishing, 2002.

Melamed, Jodi. *Represent and Destroy: Rationalizing Violence in the New Racial Capitalism*. Minneapolis: University of Minnesota Press, 2011.

Melamed, Jodi. "The Spirit of Neoliberalism: From Racial Liberalism to Neoliberal Multiculturalism." *Social Text* 24, no. 4 (2006): 1–24.

Meredith, William H., and George P. Rowe. "Changes in Lao Hmong Marital Attitudes After Immigrating to the United States." *Journal of Comparative Family Studies* 17, no. 1 (1986): 117–126.

Mertus, Julie. "The Rejection of Human Rights Framing: The Case of LGBT Advocacy in the US." *Human Rights Quarterly* 29, no. 4 (2007): 1036–1064.

Miller, Chanel. *Know My Name: A Memoir*. New York: Viking, 2019.

Miller-Young, Mireille. *A Taste for Brown Sugar: Black Women in Pornography.* Durham, NC: Duke University Press, 2014.

Mills, Charles. "Racial Liberalism." *PMLA* 122, no. 5 (2008): 1380–1397.

Mohanty, Chandra Talpade. "Under Western Eyes: Feminist Scholarship and Colonial Discourses." *boundary 2* 12, no. 3 / 13, no. 1 (1984): 333–358.

Morrison, Gayle. "The Hmong *Qeej*: Speaking to the Spirit World." *Hmong Studies Journal* 2 (1998): 1–17.

Moua, Mai Neng. *The Bride Price: A Hmong Wedding Story.* Minneapolis: Minnesota Historical Society Press, 2017.

Moya, Sergio Delgado. "An Archive of Violence: The Obscene Visuality of Sensationalism." *Critical Times* 3, no. 2 (2020): 200–223.

Muñoz, José Esteban. *Cruising Utopia: The Then and There of Queer Futurity.* New York: New York University Press, 2009.

Muñoz, José Esteban. *Disidentifications: Queers of Color and the Performance of Politics.* Minneapolis: University of Minnesota Press, 1999.

Murray, David A. B. Introduction to *Homophobias: Lusting and Loathing Across Time and Space*, edited by David A. B. Murray, 1–15. Durham, NC: Duke University Press, 2009.

Mwanbene, Lea. "Hmong 'Marriage by Capture' in the United States of America and *Ukuthwala* in South Africa: Unfolding Discussions." *Comparative and International Law Journal of Southern Africa* 53, no. 3 (2020): 1–25.

Narayan, Uma. *Dislocating Cultures: Identities, Traditions, and Third-World Feminism.* New York: Routledge, 1997.

Narayan, Uma. "Essence of Culture and Sense of History: A Feminist Critique of Cultural Essentialism." *Hypatia* 13, no. 2 (1998): 86–106.

Narayan, Uma. "Undoing the 'Package Picture' of Cultures." *Signs: Journal of Women in Culture and Society* 25, no. 4 (2000): 1083–1086.

Ngo, Bic. "Beyond 'Culture Clash': Understandings of Immigrant Experiences." *Theory into Practice* 47, no. 1 (2008): 4–11.

Ngo, Bic. "Contesting 'Culture': The Perspective of Hmong American Female Students on Early Marriage." *Anthropology and Education Quarterly* 33, no. 2 (2002): 163–188.

Ngo, Bic. "The Importance of Family for a Gay Hmong American Man: Complicating Discourses of 'Coming Out.'" *Hmong Studies Journal* 13, no. 1 (2012): 1–27.

Nguyen, Thi Huong, Pauline Oosterhoff, and Joanna White. "Aspirations and Realities of Love, Marriage and Education Among Hmong Women." *Culture, Health and Sexuality* 13, no. S2 (2011): S201–S215.

Ninh, erin Khuê. "Without Enhancements: Sexual Violence in the Everyday Lives of Asian American Women." In *Asian American Feminisms and Women of Color*

Politics, edited by Lynn Fujiwara and Shireen Roshanravan, 69–81. Seattle: University of Washington Press, 2018.

Pateman, Carole. *The Sexual Contract*. Stanford, CA: Stanford University Press, 1988.

Peffer, George Anthony. *If They Don't Bring Their Women Here: Chinese Female Immigration Before Exclusion*. Urbana: University of Illinois Press, 1999.

Pfeifer, Mark E. "Hmong Population Trends in the 2020 U.S. Census." *Hmong Studies Journal* 26, no. 1 (2024): 1–12.

Pfeifer, Mark E., John Sullivan, Kou Yang, and Wayne Yang. "Hmong Population and Demographic Trends in the 2010 Census and 2010 American Community Survey." In *The State of the Hmong American Community: 2013*, edited by Mark E. Pfeifer and Bruce K. Thao, 8–20. Washington, DC: Hmong National Development, 2013.

Pha, Kong Pheng. "Colorblindness as Anti-Asian Racism in the Midwest." *American Studies* 62, no. 3 (2023): 119–142.

Pha, Kong Pheng. "Finding Queer Hmong America: Gender, Sexuality, Culture, and Happiness Among Hmong LGBTQ." In *Claiming Place: On the Agency of Hmong Women*, edited by Chia Youyee Vang, Faith Nibbs, and Ma Vang, 303–326. Minneapolis: University of Minnesota Press, 2016.

Pha, Kong Pheng. "'Minnesota Is Open to Everything': Queer Hmong and the Politics of Community Formation in the Diaspora." *Minnesota History* 66, no. 6 (2019): 255–263.

Pha, Kong Pheng. "The Politics of Vernacular Activism: Hmong Americans Organizing for Social Justice in Minnesota." *Amerasia Journal* 45, no. 2 (2019): 207–221.

Pha, Kong Pheng. "Testimony as Justice: An Anti-Carceral Transformative Feminist Response to Sexual Violence and Abusive International Marriages." *Frontiers: A Journal of Women Studies* 44, no. 3 (2023): 18–41.

Puar, Jasbir. *Terrorist Assemblages: Homonationalism in Queer Times*. Durham, NC: Duke University Press, 2007.

Reddy, Chandan. *Freedom with Violence: Race, Sexuality, and the US State*. Durham, NC: Duke University Press, 2011.

Reddy, Chandan. "Time for Rights? *Loving*, Gay Marriage, and the Limits of Legal Justice." *Fordham Law Review* 76, no. 6 (2008): 2849–2872.

Renteln, Alison Dundes. "The Use and Abuse of the Cultural Defense." *Canadian Journal of Law and Society* 20, no. 1 (2005): 47–67.

Rodriguez, Dylan. "The Political Logic of the Non-Profit Industrial Complex." In *The Revolution Will Not Be Funded: Beyond the Non-Profit Industrial Complex*, edited by INCITE! Women of Color Against Violence, 21–40. Cambridge, MA: South End Press, 2007.

Rosaldo, Renato. *Culture and Truth: The Remaking of Social Analysis*. Boston: Beacon Press, 1989.

Ruey, Yih-Fu. "The Magpie Miao of Southern Szechuan." In *Social Structure in Southeast Asia*, edited by George Peter Murdock, 143–155. Chicago: Quadrangle Books, 1960.

Schein, Louisa. "Homeland Beauty: Transnational Longing and Hmong American Video." *Journal of Asian Studies* 63, no. 2 (2004): 433–463.

Schein, Louisa. *Minority Rules: The Miao and the Feminine in China's Cultural Politics.* Durham, NC: Duke University Press, 2000.

Schein, Louisa, and Va-Megn Thoj. "*Gran Torino*'s Boys and Men with Guns: Hmong Perspectives." *Hmong Studies Journal* 10 (2009): 1–52.

Schein, Louisa, Va-Megn Thoj, Bee Vang, and Ly Chong Thong Jalao. "Beyond *Gran Torino*'s Guns: Hmong Cultural Warriors Performing Genders." *positions: asia critique* 20, no. 3 (2012): 763–792.

Schein, Louisa, and Bee Vang. "The Unbearable Racedness of Being Natural." *Cultural Studies* 28, no. 4 (2014): 561–573.

Scott, George M. "To Catch or Not to Catch a Thief: A Case of Bride Theft Among the Lao Hmong Refugees in Southern California." *Ethnic Groups* 7 (1987): 137–151.

Sheybani, Malek-Mithra. "Cultural Defense: One Person's Culture Is Another's Crime." *Loyola of Los Angeles International and Comparative Law Review* 9, no. 3 (1987): 751–783.

Shimizu, Celine Parreñas. *The Hypersexuality of Race: Performing Asian/American Women on Screen and Scene.* Durham, NC: Duke University Press, 2007.

Shimizu, Celine Parreñas. *Straitjacket Sexualities: Unbinding Asian American Manhoods in the Movies.* Stanford, CA: Stanford University Press, 2012.

Simpson, Audra. *Mohawk Interruptus: Political Life Across the Borders of Settler States.* Durham, NC: Duke University Press, 2014.

Song, Sarah. *Justice, Gender, and the Politics of Multiculturalism.* Cambridge: Cambridge University Press, 2007.

Spade, Dean. *Normal Life: Administrative Violence, Critical Trans Politics, and the Limits of Law.* Brooklyn, NY: South End Press, 2011.

Stanley, Eric. *Atmospheres of Violence: Structuring Antagonism and the Trans/Queer Ungovernable.* Durham, NC: Duke University Press, 2021.

Straka, Richard. "The Violence of Hmong Gangs and the Crime of Rape." *FBI Law Enforcement Bulletin* 72, no. 2 (2003): 12–16.

Syrett, Nicholas L. *American Child Bride: A History of Minors and Marriage in the United States.* Chapel Hill: University of North Carolina Press, 2016.

Syrett, Nicholas L. "The Contested Meanings of Child Marriage in the Turn-of-the-Century United States." In *Children and Youth During the Gilded Age and Progressive Era*, edited by James Marten, 145–165. New York: New York University Press, 2014.

Syrett, Nicholas L. "Statutory Marriage Ages and the Gendered Construction of Adulthood in the Nineteenth Century." In *Age in America: The Colonial Era to the Present*, edited by Corinne T. Field and Nicholas L. Syrett, 103–123. New York: New York University Press, 2015.

Tajima, Renee E. "Lotus Blossoms Don't Bleed: Images of Asian Women." In *Making Waves: An Anthology of Writing By and About Asian American Women*, edited by Asian Women United of California, 308–317. Boston: Beacon Press, 1989.

Tapp, Nicholas. *The Impossibility of Self: An Essay on the Hmong Diaspora*. Berlin: Lit Verlag, 2010.

Tapp, Nicholas. "The Reformation of Culture: Hmong Refugees from Laos." *Journal of Refugee Studies* 1, no. 1 (1988): 20–37.

Thao, Mai See. "Bittersweet Migrations: Type II Diabetes and Healing in the Hmong Diaspora." PhD diss., University of Minnesota, 2018.

Thao, Yer J. "Culture and Knowledge of the Sacred Instrument *Qeej* in the Mong-American Community." *Asian Folklore Studies* 65, no. 2 (2006): 249–267.

Trouillot, Michel-Rolph. *Global Transformations: Anthropology and the Modern World*. New York: Palgrave Macmillan, 2003.

Tsosie, Rebecca. "The Politics of Inclusion: Indigenous Peoples and U.S. Citizenship." *UCLA Law Review* 63 (2016): 1692–1751.

Vang, Chia Youyee. *Fly Until You Die: An Oral History of Hmong Pilots in the Vietnam War*. New York: Oxford University Press, 2019.

Vang, Chia Youyee. *Hmong America: Reconstructing Community in Diaspora*. Urbana: University of Illinois Press, 2010.

Vang, Chia Youyee, Faith Nibbs, and Ma Vang. "Introduction: Hmong Women, Gender, and Power." In *Claiming Place: On the Agency of Hmong Women*, edited by Chia Youyee Vang, Faith Nibbs, and Ma Vang, vii–xxviii. Minneapolis: University of Minnesota Press, 2016.

Vang, Kao N. "Hmong Marriage Customs: A Current Assessment." In *The Hmong in the West: Observations and Reports*, edited by Bruce T. Downing and Douglas P. Olney, 29–47. Minneapolis: Center for Urban and Regional Affairs, University of Minnesota, 1982.

Vang, Ma. *History on the Run: Secrecy, Fugitivity, and Hmong Refugee Epistemologies*. Durham, NC: Duke University Press, 2021.

Vang, Ma. "The Refugee Soldier: A Critique of Recognition and Citizenship in the Hmong Veterans' Naturalization Act of 1997." *positions: asia critique* 20, no. 3 (2012): 685–712.

Vang, Nengher N. "Unlawful or Not? Reassessing the Value and Impact of Hmong American Transnational Politics." *Amerasia Journal* 44, no. 2 (2018): 43–64.

Vang, Pa Der. "Teenage Marriage Among Hmong American Women." *Journal of Human Behavior in the Social Environment* 24, no. 2 (2014): 138–155.

Vang, Pa Der. "Violence Against Women and Hmong Religious Belief." In *Religion and Men's Violence Against Women*, edited by Andy J. Johnson, 383–398. New York: Springer, 2015.

Vang, Pa Der, and Matthew Bogenschutz. "Teenage Marriage, and the Socioeconomic Status of Hmong Women." *International Migration* 52, no. 3 (2014): 144–159.

Vargas, Deborah R. "Representations of Latina/o Sexuality in Popular Culture." In *Latina/o Sexualities: Proving Powers, Passions, Practices, and Policies*, edited by Marysol Asencio, 117–136. New Brunswick, NJ: Rutgers University Press, 2010.

Visweswaran, Kamala. "Race and the Culture of Anthropology." *American Anthropologist* 100, no. 1 (1998): 70–83.

Visweswaran, Kamala. *Un/common Cultures: Racism and the Rearticulation of Cultural Difference*. Durham, NC: Duke University Press, 2010.

Volpp, Leti. "Blaming Culture for Bad Behavior." *Yale Journal of Law and the Humanities* 12, no. 1 (2000): 89–116.

Volpp, Leti. "Disappearing Acts: On Gendered Violence, Pathological Cultures, and Civil Society." *PMLA* 121, no. 5 (2006): 1631–1638.

Volpp, Leti. "Engendering Culture: Citizenship, Identity, and Belonging." In *Citizenship, Borders, and Human Needs*, edited by Rogers M. Smith, 177–191. Philadelphia: University of Pennsylvania Press, 2011.

Volpp, Leti. "Feminism Versus Multiculturalism." *Columbia Law Review* 101, no. 5 (2001): 1181–1218.

Volpp, Leti. "Framing Cultural Difference: Immigrant Women and Discourses of Tradition." *differences: A Journal of Feminist Cultural Studies* 22, no. 1 (2011): 90–110.

Volpp, Leti. "(Mis)Identifying Culture: Asian Women and the Cultural Defense." *Harvard Women's Law Journal* 57 (1994): 57–101.

Vue, Mai Zong. *Hmong in Wisconsin*. Madison: Wisconsin Historical Society Press, 2020.

Vwj, Zoov Tsheej, with Yaj Ntxoo Yias and Txiv Plig Nyiav Pov. *Haiv Hmoob liv xwm* [Hmong history]. Quezon City, Philippines: Patrimoine Culturel Hmong, 1997.

Walks, Michelle. "'We're Here and We're Queer!': An Introduction to Studies in Queer Anthropology." *Anthropologica* 56, no. 1 (2014): 14–25.

Walters, Suzanna Danuta. *The Tolerance Trap: How God, Genes, and Good Intentions Are Sabotaging Gay Equality*. New York: New York University Press, 2017.

Ward, Jane. *Respectably Queer: Diversity in LGBT Activist Organizations*. Nashville: Vanderbilt University Press, 2008.

Ward, Jane. *The Tragedy of Heterosexuality*. New York: New York University Press, 2020.

Ward, Jane. "White Normativity: The Cultural Dimensions of Whiteness in a Racially Diverse LGBT Organization." *Sociological Perspectives* 51, no. 3 (2008): 563–586.

Williams, Linda. "Type and Stereotype: Chicano Images in Film." In *Latin Looks: Images of Latinas and Latinos in the U.S. Media*, edited by Clara E. Rodriguez, 214–220. New York: Routledge, 1997.

Williams, Patricia J. *The Alchemy of Race and Rights: Diary of a Law Professor*. Cambridge, MA: Harvard University Press, 1991.

Winant, Howard. *The World Is a Ghetto: Race and Democracy Since World War II*. New York: Basic Books, 2002.

Wu, Cynthia. *Sticky Rice: A Politics of Intraracial Desire*. Philadelphia: Temple University Press, 2018.

Xiong, Yang Sao. "The Dynamics of Discursive Opportunities in the Hmong Campaign for Inclusion in California." *Amerasia Journal* 44, no. 2 (2018): 65–87.

Xiong, Yang Sao. *Immigrant Agency: Hmong American Movements and the Politics of Racialized Incorporation*. New Brunswick, NJ: Rutgers University Press, 2022.

Yang, Dao. *Hmong at the Turning Point*. Minneapolis: WorldBridge Associates, 1993.

Yang, Jennifer Ann. "Marriage by Capture in the Hmong Culture: The Legal Issue of Cultural Rights Versus Women's Rights." *Law and Society Review at the University of California, Santa Barbara* 3 (2004): 39–50.

Yang, Kao Kalia. *The Latehomecomer: A Hmong Family Memoir*. St. Paul, MN: Coffee House Press, 2005.

Yang, Kou. "Hmong Diaspora of the Post-War Period." *Asian and Pacific Migration Journal* 12, no. 3 (2003): 271–300.

Yang, Pahoua K. "A Phenomenological Study of the Coming Out Experiences of Gay and Lesbian Hmong." PhD diss., University of Minnesota, 2008.

Yoshikawa, Taeko. "From a Refugee Camp to the Minnesota State Senate: A Case Study of a Hmong American Woman's Challenge." *Hmong Studies Journal* 7 (2006): 1–23.

Zia, Helen. *Asian American Dreams: The Emergence of an American People*. New York: Farrar, Straus and Giroux, 2000.

Index

other and othering, 13, 17, 18, 23, 24, 75, 94. *See also* racialization

"overregulation," 69–70

Pa Houa, 108–110
paranormal experiences, 109, 110
parenting, hypo-, 94
Pathet Lao, 10, 11, 12
patriarchy, 8, 58, 73, 74, 136. *See also* heteropatriarchy
Paymar, Michael, 82, 86
Philippines: Ilongots, 159n55
phone banking, 118, 119, 120, 124–125, 127, 128–129
photography in activist campaigns, 130–137
plural marriage. *See* polygamy
polygamy, 22–23, 25, 59–60, 67, 72–74, 77–79, 81, 88; Geddes, 15; Hmong public opinion, 127; as hyperheterosexual, 56, 67, 72; Minnesota Amendment 1 and, 121, 126, 127; Mormons, 83; Sinsay, 133–134; UK immigrants, 169n63; Vang Pao, 21
pronouns, 148, 149
prostitution, 5, 46, 51, 53

qeej, 99, 132–134
queer invisibility, 90, 92–93, 95, 96, 106–108, 116, 146, 149
queer theory, 95, 96, 98, 106, 129, 136

racialization, 2–8, 13–14, 17–20, 24–31, 43–45, 50–55, 63; gangs and, 44, 47–49; *Gran Torino*, 44; Minnesota marriage bills, 59, 63, 65, 66, 77, 80, 86–88; in press, 45; queerness and, 91–92, 94, 96, 123, 129, 146, 149, 151; in sex crime

trials, 31, 34, 35, 38–41, 43; US secret war in Laos, 11–12; and victimhood, 27
rape, 34, 35, 53, 161n6, 162n24, 164n49. *See also* gang sexual violence
rebirth of souls, 98, 99–101, 103, 105, 133, 174n29
Reddy, Chandan, 129
rescue narratives, 42, 80–81, 82
reticence, 90, 92–93, 95–98, 102–106, 110, 114–115, 138
Robinson, Clayton M., Jr., 38
Roosevelt, Margot. *See* Hornblower, Margot
Rosaldo, Renato, 159n55

same-sex marriage, 117–145
"saving face," 95, 96–97, 98
Schein, Louisa, 43–44
Schleh, Jeanne, 32–33, 35, 38, 39
Schubert, Frank, 119
Schumacher, Robert, 35
sensationalism in media. *See* spectacularization and sensationalism: in media
sex crimes, 30, 33, 36, 49. *See also* gang sexual violence; rape
sexual division of labor, 15
sexual violence, gang. *See* gang sexual violence
shamans and shamanism, 97, 103–105, 108–114
Shimizu, Celine Parreñas, 5
Simpson, Audra, 23–24
Sinsay (Xeem Xais), 133–134
Siv Yis (twenty-first-century shaman), 112–114
Skoglund, Wesley, 77, 78, 79–80, 85, 86
slow death, 96, 97, 98, 115, 151
soul rebirth. *See* rebirth of souls